THE CONTRADICTIONS
OF MODERN MORAL PHILOSOPHY

The Contradictions of Modern Moral Philosophy is a highly original and radical critique of contemporary moral theory. Paul Johnston demonstrates that much recent moral philosophy is confused about the fundamental issue of whether there are correct moral judgements. He shows that the standard modern approaches to ethics cannot justify – or even make much sense of – traditional moral beliefs. Applied rigorously, these approaches suggest that we should reject ethics as a set of outdated and misguided claims.

Rather than facing up to this conclusion, most recent moral philosophy consists of attempts to find some way of preserving moral beliefs. This places a contradiction at the heart of moral philosophy. As a result it is often impossible to tell whether a contemporary philosopher ultimately rejects or endorses the idea of objective right and wrong.

On the basis of a Wittgensteinian approach Paul Johnston puts forward an alternative account of ethics that avoids this contradiction and recognises that the central issues of ethics cannot be resolved by conceptual analysis. He then uses this account to highlight the contradictions of important contemporary moral theorists such as Bernard Williams, Alasdair MacIntyre, Thomas Nagel and Charles Taylor.

Paul Johnston is the author of *Wittgenstein and Moral Philosophy* and *Wittgenstein: Rethinking the Inner*, both published by Routledge.

ROUTLEDGE STUDIES IN ETHICS AND MORAL THEORY

THE CONTRADICTIONS OF MODERN MORAL PHILOSOPHY

Ethics after Wittgenstein

Paul Johnston

London and New York

First published 1999
by Routledge
1 New Fetter Lane, London EC4P 4EE

Simultaneously published in the USA and Canada
by Routledge
29 West 35th Street, New York, NY 10001

Routledge is an imprint of the Taylor & Francis Group

Typeset in Times New Roman by
Exe Valley Dataset, Exeter, Devon
Printed and bound in Great Britain by
MPG Books Ltd, Bodmin

British Library Cataloguing in Publication Data
A catalogue record for this book is available
from the British Library

Library of Congress Cataloging in Publication Data
Johnston, Paul, 1962–
The contradictions of modern moral philosophy: ethics after
Wittgenstein / Paul Johnston.
    p.   cm. — (Routledge studies in ethics and moral theory: 1)
Includes bibliographical references and index.
ISBN 0-415-20848-3 (hardcover: alk. paper)
1. Ethics, Modern—20th century.   I. Title.   II. Series.
BJ319.J64   1999
170′.9′04—dc21   99-24074
                                                                        CIP

ISBN 0-415-20848-3

[16382]

FOR LENA

CONTENTS

'What are we quarreling about, for goodness sake? You're this sort of man and I'm that sort of a man, what about it? And, moreover, both of us are—'

'Scoundrels.'

'Yes, scoundrels, if you like. You know perfectly well that that's only words.'

'All my life I didn't want it to be only words. I went on living just because I didn't want it so. Now, too, I want it every day not to be words.'

'Well, everyone of us tries to find a place where it will be best for him. A fish—I mean, everyone seeks his own kind of comfort. That's all. That's been known for ages.'

(Dostoyevsky, *The Possessed*, p. 610)

PREFACE

This book is a critique of modern moral philosophy. It seeks to throw light on what is involved in believing in right and wrong and in so doing suggests that most contemporary accounts of ethics are deeply confused. Not only are the philosophers who put forward these accounts uncertain whether their role is to clarify or to contribute to moral debate, they are not even sure where they stand in relation to ethics itself. On the crucial question of whether there are correct ways of acting (and correct judgements on human action) modern philosophers want to have it both ways. They reject the claim to correctness that is the distinguishing feature of moral judgements, but nonetheless want to continue making judgements of this kind. This contradiction arises from a combination of conceptual confusion and genuine ambivalence. On the one hand, it reflects a failure to understand ethics and, on the other, real doubts about the validity of moral claims. The peculiar consequence of this is that it is often hard to tell whether modern moral philosophers do or do not believe in right and wrong.

In recent years dissatisfaction with the interminable debates about moral concepts (reinforced by a desire to show the relevance and practicality of philosophy) has encouraged some philosophers to turn away from these issues and concentrate instead on advancing substantive moral claims. But this strategy, too, has its drawbacks. One is that, until the confusions about the nature of moral concepts are cleared up, these will continue to obstruct and distort moral debate, and it seems odd to suggest that philosophy should ignore this. Another difficulty relates to the status of the views a philosopher might advance, for what basis can she claim for them qua philosopher? Is she claiming that conceptual analysis can establish and/or refute moral views? If so, she needs to justify this claim and if not, she needs to explain the basis of her contribution to the debate. As these comments suggest, there is no avoiding the task of clarifying moral concepts. Philosophy's record in this area may not be impressive, but it is a necessary and important philosophical task.

The way this book approaches this task is unfashionable in several ways. One is that it accepts Ludwig Wittgenstein's claims about the nature of philosophy. His emphasis on the search for clarity (as opposed to truth) involves a significant change in the aim of philosophy, and this is particularly evident in relation to ethics. The lofty ambition of resolving the great questions of life is replaced by the humbler, but achievable goal of conceptual clarification. This approach (with its much-misunderstood commitment to leaving everything where it is) may seem an abdication of responsibility compared with efforts by the great philosophers of the past to lay down the correct way of understanding the world. The changed goal, however, is based on a recognition that the attempt to wring truth out of concepts is misguided.

Most contemporary moral philosophers do not accept, or at least do not act in accordance with, these Wittgensteinian claims. Their own position on these issues is much less clear. As a result their work tends to amalgamate substantive claims and logical points and so leave it unclear when the philosopher is describing conceptual relations and when she is advancing her own substantive views. Furthermore, uncertainties about philosophy's status and the wish to be 'scientific' constrain and colour the views that are actually advanced. While the Wittgensteinian approach deliberately avoids trying to answer the great questions of life, much contemporary philosophy casts doubt on the meaning or importance of these questions, but then offers highly debatable answers to them. This book seeks to show up the confusions this involves and so clarify the real issues we face.

Another unfashionable aspect of this book is its rejection of the idea that all aspects of human activity must be explained in causal terms. This idea conflicts with the key concepts involved in human thought and action and in this way contributes to modern philosophy's problems in understanding ethics. Anyone who starts from the assumption that the individual's behaviour is causally determined by her dispositions is likely to have difficulty with the claim that there are values that everyone should recognise and act upon. Similarly, anyone who holds that an individual's beliefs about how people should act are the causal product of her upbringing will have problems giving a meaningful account of reflection on right and wrong.

Various people have assisted in the preparation of this book, but my main debt is to Stephen Mulhall who in part provoked the book and who certainly helped improve it. The weaknesses that remain are, of course, mine.

1

THE CONTRADICTIONS OF
TRADITIONAL ETHICS

Moral judgement has this in common with religious judgement
that it believes in realities that do not exist . . . [It] belongs, as
does religious judgement, to a level of ignorance at which even
the concept of the real, the distinction between the real and the
imaginary, is lacking: so that at such a level "truth" denotes
nothing but things which we today call "imaginings". To this
extent, moral judgement is never to be taken literally: as such it
never contains anything but nonsense.
(Nietzsche, *Twilight of the Idols*, p. 55)

In seeking to understand the world, one issue every individual faces is
whether she accepts the notion of objective right and wrong: does she believe
that judgements about human action simply express the preferences of a
particular individual or does she believe that there is a correct perspective on
human action that everyone should adopt? The traditional (but not
unanimous) answer to this question has been that there are indeed right and
wrong answers about how people should act. Recently, however, scepticism
about ethics has become much more extensive and today it is not clear
whether our society as a whole should be characterised as accepting or
rejecting the possibility of objective moral claims. One reason for this shift is
the success of science, which has called into question traditional moral views
and has prompted various kinds of relativism. It has also discouraged the
idea that there are fundamental differences between human action and the
behaviour of other animals or, indeed, causally determined processes in non-
living things. Other intellectual developments have also undermined moral
beliefs. The modern challenge to religion, for example, casts doubt on the
status of ethics—at least to some it has seemed that if God is dead,
everything is permitted. Progress in formulating psychological, social and
cultural explanations of how and why beliefs are formed poses a further
threat, since it suggests that our moral judgements should not be taken at
face value. Overall, there seems a real question as to whether, knowing what
we do, we can still believe in right and wrong.

This issue looks surprisingly different when considered from a less theoretical perspective. Measured against our actual practice the suggestion that ethical thinking has lost its hold in our society seems exaggerated. Paradoxically, the modern world seems characterised not only by scepticism about ethics but also by the clash of strongly held moral views. Take the controversy about abortion. This debate highlights the divisions that can arise in our society, but it also refutes the suggestion that modernity and moral certainty are antithetical. Indeed, it could be argued that in some ways people today are more ethical than their forebears insofar as certain aspects of human life that were previously not believed to raise moral issues are now seen as doing so. The rise of vegetarianism and of new concepts such as animal rights suggest that, far from withering away in our society, ethical notions are gaining new force and fresh applications. Despite theoretical misgivings about ethics, the modern world seems strongly attracted to ethical ways of thinking and on occasion seems willing to embrace moral codes even more demanding than those held in earlier times.

The ambivalence in modern attitudes to ethics is also apparent in contemporary moral philosophy. On the one hand, traditional claims to moral truth and to objectivity in ethics[1] are widely seen as incoherent or misguided and even those who do defend the claim to objectivity recognise that their interpretations of this idea would not necessarily be familiar or indeed acceptable to morality's traditional advocates. Very few philosophers, however, have argued that ethics should be rejected as such; instead most contemporary moral philosophy consists of attempts to explain why, despite everything, ethical thinking is justified and necessary. Although the break with the traditional claim to objectivity is not always emphasised, the implied reform of our practices is usually seen as a positive development and philosophers have variously welcomed the chance to make ethics fully rational or celebrated the overthrow of objectivity as a liberation, the opportunity to recognise ethics as a human creation. More recently, however, there have been some voices of disquiet. Alasdair MacIntyre has suggested that we live in the aftermath of a conceptual cataclysm and that the language of morals is in a state of grave disorder (*After Virtue*, p. 2). Bernard Williams has gone further and argued that ethics can never be everything it claims to be (*Ethics and the Limits of Philosophy*, p. 199). It seems, therefore, that while some contemporary philosophers continue the enterprise of justifying ethics, others are already elaborating views that suggest that these projects can never fully succeed.

The definition of ethics is itself a matter of controversy and some philosophers have suggested that it would be best to start with as broad and open a definition as possible. For example, we could use the word 'ethics' to describe any set of principles according to which an individual leads her life regardless of the content of those principles. This may seem a sensible suggestion, but there are good reasons for not accepting it. The first is that this sort of purely formal definition is misleading and can even be offensive. For example, few would be ready to talk of 'Stalin's ethics' even though his actions were in accordance with certain long-term 'principles', e.g. that an action was good if it was conducive to Stalin's obtaining or maintaining power. A more important argument against this kind of definition is that it directs attention away from the fundamental problem of moral philosophy, viz. the obscure claim that there are standards of conduct that everyone should recognise as correct. What is puzzling about ethics is not the fact that most people have long-term goals in life, but the claim that there is a correct perspective from which human action should be judged. This idea embodies a concept of objectivity that does not seem to make sense. The related claim that moral judgements are true also seems problematic. Although in every-day life we apply the notion of truth to empirical and to moral judgements, this seems unjustifiable in view of their different natures. In the case of empirical judgements, the notion that one set of claims is correct and all others wrong seems easy to understand; with moral judgements, however, this is not so. Once we are no longer talking about how things are but about how people ought to act, what could it mean to claim that one set of judgements is uniquely privileged?

For these reasons the most appropriate starting point for our discussion is not a definition of ethics but the fundamental logical point that any judgement about human actions will inevitably be from one perspective among the countless number that are logically possible. While we can assess actions against a wide variety of criteria and may conclude that such-and-such an action is better in the sense that it is in the interests of society as a whole or better from the perspective of a particular individual or group of individuals, it would seem to make no sense to claim that a certain way of acting was better as such. The problem with ethics is that it is based on precisely this claim. The moralist asserts that actions can be right or wrong in absolute terms and seeks a privilege for her point of view that she seems unable to justify. She claims her judgements correspond to a standard that should be recognised by everyone, but she cannot explain what this is supposed to mean. How can there be an independent standard of human action? And what basis is there for claiming that there are principles of conduct that apply to everyone?

Insofar as the moralist offers any answers to these questions, her statements merely replace one puzzle with another, and yet the source of confusion seems to be a logical error. In denying that the criteria she applies are on a par with other possible criteria, she seems to be making a claim which from a logical point of view is simply wrong. Since assessing actions involves adopting a particular perspective and since various perspectives are logically possible, it seems clear that no set of judgements can claim an absolute privilege. Nonetheless, that is what the moralist claims for her beliefs. Furthermore, rather than treating her as deranged, many of us join

3

her in making such claims. We, too, endorse or condemn certain types of action and reject any attempt to make these judgements coherent by relating them to a particular goal, perspective or set of desires. We, too, want to say that such-and-such an action is simply wrong.

The above remarks help to explain why modern philosophy finds ethics so problematic. The idea of a correct point of view from which actions can be judged seems a contradiction in terms. Self-evidently there are many different possible points of view and, although we can assess the merits of these points of view (adopt as it were meta-points of view), the move to a higher level does nothing to eliminate plurality and so leaves the notion of a correct point of view no clearer. The problem would not be avoided by treating 'correct' as meaning 'correct from society's point of view', for however we defined society's point of view it would still only be one point of view among others and there would be no reason why everyone should take it into account. In itself society's point of view is no more correct than Jane Smith's point of view or the point of view of the majority of left-handed fifteen-year-olds. There are also problems with the suggestion that 'correct' means 'correct from the universe's point of view'. This notion seems just as obscure as the original claim, and it, too, seems contradictory, for what these words seem to be trying to express is the idea of a point of view that is somehow not just a point of view. In fact, the logical difficulties remain even if we invoke the concept of God, for even God's point of view would still be a point of view. The claim that certain standards had been endorsed by the most powerful being in the universe would give us good reason for conforming to them, but it would not make them 'correct'. The problem is that in this context it is just not clear what being correct is supposed to mean.

The incoherence involved in trying to make absolute judgements of value is highlighted in a lecture on ethics which Wittgenstein gave in 1929. He argues that the attempt to make non-relative judgements is inherently flawed and that therefore all ethical statements are an abuse of language. 'The *absolute good*, if is a describable state of affairs, would be one which everybody independent of his taste and inclinations, would *necessarily* bring about or feel guilty for not bringing about. And I want to say that such a state of affairs is a chimera. No state of affairs has, in itself, what I would like to call the coercive power of an absolute judge' (*Philosophical Occasions 1912–1951,* p. 40). Wittgenstein argues that to be coherent a value judgement must either be the judgement of a particular person or be relative to a particular goal. However, he notes that the whole thrust of ethics is to deny this. The result is nonsense, for ethical statements 'run against the boundaries of language' and this endeavour is 'perfectly, absolutely hopeless' (ibid., p. 44). Nonetheless, he is reluctant to condemn ethics and suggests that its nonsense does at some level mean something. By running up against the boundaries of language it hints that there is something more, points towards the higher but fails to recognise that this cannot be put into words. Today the mysticism of this conclusion with its specific background in the *Tractatus Logico-Philosophicus* seems merely eccentric. Less contentious is Wittgenstein's admission that ethics 'is a document of a tendency in the human mind which I personally cannot help but respecting deeply and I would not for my life ridicule it' (*PO,* p. 44). Even if we share that sentiment, however, we cannot ignore the fact that moral judgements are nonsensical; taking refuge in mysticism, as Wittgenstein does, seems a poor alternative to facing up to the contradictions of ethics.

The peculiarities that Wittgenstein noted also come out in other ways, for the moralist contrasts her judgements with expressions of preference and typically would deny that in condemning, for example, lying she is simply expressing a preference for truth-telling (or a distaste for lying). Furthermore, she seeks to give substance to this distinction by rejecting the idea that one way of improving the situation would be for her to change the way she reacts, whereas if all that was at stake was a preference, this would at least be an option. These denials, however, seem beside the point. After all, the fact that she acts as if her judgements were independent of her does nothing to change their logical status. Another strange facet of the moralist's position is her apparent rejection of the truism that an individual's actions (and her judgements of actions) reflect her wants. This comes out if we suggest that her claim 'You ought to do N' means 'I want you to do N', for typically she will disagree and argue that what she wants is irrelevant. Suppose she is being offered something already promised to another. She may say she wants what is being offered but add that it ought to be given to the other person. If we conclude that this shows that her desire that the promise be fulfilled is stronger than her desire for the object in question, she will reject this as a misleading description of the situation. Her claim is that the existence of a promise overrides any desires she may have. A sudden increase in her desire for the object (or even in her need for it) would not affect her position on who should receive it. The moralist's claim is that in certain cases the individual's action can, and should, be based on what is right in contrast to what she happens to want.

One response to these puzzles is to see ethics as an anthropological curiosity and to treat it as a strange fact that many (or most) human beings are inclined to commit themselves to principles which cut across their own desires and sometimes involve the sacrifice even of their own lives. The moralist, however, is likely to take issue even with this 'neutral' observation. She denies that it is a matter of her (or other people) being inclined or disposed to observe certain principles. Her claim is that it is the correctness of the principles that leads her to adopt them, not the fact that she happens to be disposed in a particular way. Furthermore, she is ready to accept the corollary of this, that if she was committed to a different principle (had different dispositions, etc.) she would be wrong. One despairing response to this might be to classify the moralist as someone who has a disposition to believe that her judgements are not simply the expression of particular dispositions. Again, however, the moralist will treat this analysis as a misleading irrelevance. While unable to deny that what she says reflects a particular viewpoint, she claims that her judgements themselves are true and that the viewpoint itself is right quite apart from the fact that she holds it. But this just seems incoherent. It is as if the moralist believes she can pull herself up by her own bootstraps. She puts forward certain views and insists that they be treated not as her personal opinion but as objective truth. Having embraced a particular position, she congratulates herself on it being the correct position and wants us to take her self-endorsement as independent confirmation.

Another way of underlining these points is to consider the question of how we are supposed to determine what is right and wrong. Vague references to intuition do nothing to answer this question and even if there were objective moral values, it is not clear how we would access them, for there seems to be no way of distinguishing between something being right and it merely seeming right to us. This difficulty helps explain why there are conflicting views about what is right. If we accept the notion of objective standards, it seems inevitable that each individual will proclaim her own views as the unique and universal truth. Employing the metaphor of perception does nothing to improve the situation, for the moralist can offer no way of distinguishing between perception and mis-perception. The metaphor is also called into question by the wide variation in moral beliefs. If we started to have similar disagreements about taste, we would reclassify it as a subjective experience rather than a perception, a move many consider long overdue with respect to ethics.

The above points underline the strangeness of moral claims, a strangeness disguised by our everyday familiarity with them. From a logical point of view, the idea that there is a correct perspective from which human action should be judged seems misguided. It seems clear that something can only be judged as right or as good relative to a particular set of criteria or in relation to a particular goal or purpose. The ethical claim that certain actions are correct[2] and ought to be recognised as such by everyone whatever their aims and preferences is perplexing. The temptation is to ask 'How did we even start to think this way? Where on earth did this idea come from?' Whatever the answers to these questions may be, there seems no justification in continuing to make these strange claims.

These doubts about the coherence of ethics can only be increased by the position the moralist takes on human action, for she claims not only that everyone ought to act in accordance with the standards she advocates but that the existence of these standards in itself furnishes a sufficient motive for acting in accordance with them. This seems to cut across any sensible approach to practical reason. Rather than specific causes explaining why the individual acted as she did, this approach suggests that the causal account can be magically interrupted at any point by the intervention of the moral law. As well as being misguided, this seems somewhat hypocritical, for, although the moralist claims that 'ought implies can' (that an action can only be incumbent on an individual if that action is within her power), she shows no interest in an assessment of the individual's dispositions and seems to hold that the mere 'fact' that the individual ought to act in a certain way can (and should) be a sufficient motive to action. From a scientific perspective, this raises two obvious questions: first, why should ethical motivation be so different from any other? Second, how is it that this type of motivation escapes the causal laws that govern everything else in the universe? The belief that human beings are set apart from the rest of the world (from the rest of 'Creation') may have seemed plausible in the past, but it is generally seen as outdated today. If ethics rests on such views, this is yet another reason for concluding that ethics needs either radical reform or complete abolition.

This conclusion (and fear of it) has dominated modern moral philosophy. Faced with the contradictions of ethics, philosophers have tried to make sense of traditional ethics and, when this has failed, have concluded that the only way to coherence is through a greater or lesser degree of reform.[3] Most of the reform proposals have concentrated on the way ethical claims are defended and only to a much lesser extent has it been recognised that any reform will have implications for the content of ethics—putting in new foundations is bound to cause disruption to the house itself. If the details of reform are controversial, however, there is a large measure of agreement on the wider picture. It seems clear that the central task of moral philosophy must be to eliminate the incoherence that plagues our moral concepts, and if we cannot do this, then we should abandon this type of concept altogether.

Before choosing the path of reform it is natural to consider ways in which ethical concepts might be made coherent. As we have seen, the problems arise from the claim that there are actions that are not just correct from a certain perspective, but correct full stop. The two most obvious ways of trying to make this claim intelligible involves either trying to relate moral claims to the interests of the individual or exploring the idea of a connection with the needs of society. In both cases, the aim is to bring ethics back down to earth, to transform it from a set of metaphysical standards that inexorably demand respect into a body of principles which can be explained and for which reasonable support can be offered. The simplest solution would be if we could show that acting morally was always (or generally) in the individual's interest. This would immediately remove any element of paradox and would clarify the meaning and the force of ethical judgements. The claim that someone acted wrongly would be a variation of the claim that she acted foolishly, and it would be supported by a general explanation of why unethical action was foolish.

Unfortunately, this approach runs straight into problems, for the point of the concept of rationality is to avoid controversy about ends by focusing on means. Recognising that we disagree about the former, we use the concept of rationality when we want to argue that someone's actions were misguided in relation to her own avowed aims or in relation to an uncontroversial notion of what her interests are. If an individual's aim is to travel from Moscow to Paris as quickly as possible, other things being equal, she will be acting foolishly if she chooses to go by coach rather than by plane. Similarly, if someone chooses to pay above the minimum price for a product without any gain to herself even in terms of convenience, she will usually be said to be acting irrationally. To apply this approach to ethics, however, is paradoxical, for this is fundamentally about ends—what is at stake is the issue of what the individual's aims should be. Furthermore, the one thing that is clear about moral action is that it is often not in the individual's interests in any straight-forward or uncontroversial sense.

These points may seem to clash with the fact that many philosophers (from Plato onwards) have argued that the immoral individual unwittingly acts against her own good. However, the point about such positions is that they are based on substantive and highly controversial notions of what an individual's interests are. The puzzling notion that there are correct ways for people to act is not eliminated but is present in the claim that a particular (and controversial) definition of the individual's interests should be recognised by everyone as correct. In other words, this sort of approach does not show that acting morally promotes interests we all uncontroversially have; rather it makes the tautological claim that insofar as the individual ought to act morally, acting morally is in her 'true' interests even if she herself denies this. In itself, there is nothing wrong with this approach; its use of the notion of interests, however, is extremely misleading, for we usually use this concept where the definition of interests is uncontroversial. Although it may be in the criminal's 'true' interests to be caught and punished, this outcome is not in her interests on any normal definition. Similarly, it would be odd to claim that the only person who consistently pursued her own interests was the moral individual, whereas selfish people, for example, regularly allowed their interests to suffer. Putting aside the issue of confusion, even if we accepted the notion of 'true' interests, this would leave the fundamental problem untouched. Take the claim that our 'true' interests lie in helping others. This embodies a particular moral view on how people ought to act; it does nothing, however, to clarify or to justify the strange idea that there are correct ways of acting.

A different way of trying to link ethics to the individual's advantage involves arguing that acting morally is in her interests insofar as the dictates of ethics curb the human tendency to sacrifice long-term gain to momentary pleasure. On this approach, ethics is a catalogue of maxims that have been shown to help people maximise their happiness in the long-term. The problem with this approach is that it avoids the real issue. Treating ethics as the name of a set of strategies that can help the individual maximise her satisfaction implicitly abandons the claim that there are ways of acting that are incumbent on everyone. Now all that is at issue is the individual's satisfaction, and since people have different preferences, it seems clear that different strategies will be appropriate for different people. Some people may maximise their happiness by acting in ways that have traditionally been called 'moral', others will not. The important point is that the idea of a correct way of acting has been dropped. If all actions are simply the expression of different preferences, there is no basis for trying to make qualitative distinctions between them. If an individual sometimes (or always) prefers momentary pleasure to long-term satisfaction, that is her choice and there is nothing further to be said. The idea that defines ethics has been rejected in favour of a recognition that different individuals will have reason to act in different ways. Some may opt for 'safe' pleasures and others will not, but however the individual acts, there will no longer be any question of her action being objectively correct.

This last argument might be cast in a different form by invoking recent work on the Prisoner's Dilemma,[4] for this seems to show that co-operation may be the best long-term strategy for the individual (or at least an element in the best strategy). However, for the reasons just discussed, game theory is irrelevant to the task of clarifying ethical concepts. One way of bringing this out is to note that the moral response to the Prisoner's Dilemma is that the individual should confess if she committed the crime and not confess if she did not. The point is that, while ethics is concerned with the correct way of acting, game theory is concerned with exploring issues about what it would be rational for the individual to do in pursuit of her self-interest. Although game theory may show that in certain circumstances the ruthless pursuit of short-term self-interest may be counter-productive, this does not throw any light on the idea that certain ways of acting are incumbent on everyone. In the case of the Prisoner's Dilemma the best strategy for an individual to adopt will depend both on her aims and on her preferences (and her abilities). For an individual who is good at deception or who enjoys it, lying may often be a good way of maximising her satisfaction, while a poor deceiver or someone who feels bad about deceiving others may find that honesty is the best policy. Thus consideration of the Prisoner's Dilemma (even in its reiterated form) does not justify moral behaviour and, more fundamentally, it avoids rather than clarifies the distinctive ethical claim that there are correct ways of acting which should be recognised as such by everyone.

A final way of trying to relate ethics to the individual's interests is to argue that society can only flourish if its members hold ethical views and that, since a flourishing or at least well-ordered society is in the interests of everyone, this gives the individual grounds for holding ethical views. Unfortunately, this argument is fallacious. Even if it were true that society was impossible unless its members held moral views, this would not mean that it was in the interests of each individual that she hold moral views; rather, it would show that it is in her interests that everyone else (or at least most people) hold moral views. Against this, it will be said that the individual cannot expect other people to hold moral views if she does not do so herself. In logical and practical terms, however, the two issues are unrelated. The individual may follow a rigorous moral code and have the misfortune to live in a cut-throat society or she may reject all constraints on her desires and discover that others do not. Even where her stance on ethics does have an impact on the position of others, this would only mean that it was in her interests that others believe she holds moral views. In short, it is unlikely that most people would be sufficiently compensated for the costs of acting morally by the effect their moral actions had in promoting morality generally. Even in the unlikely event that one individual's example did have a significant impact, this would only be an argument for being seen to be moral and it would not apply on occasions where the individual was confident that the true nature of her action would be undetected. This response may seem to miss the point of the earlier objection, for the key idea behind it is that the individual has no right to expect other people to follow moral principles if she has no intention of doing so herself. This claim, however, reintroduces the very concepts we have been trying to eliminate. The basis of this approach turns out to be the moral claim that, if the individual wants other people to follow certain principles, it would be morally wrong of her not to follow them herself.

In view of these problems it may seem more promising to explain moral claims in terms of some link with society's interests. Ethics seems largely concerned with social interaction and it seems clear that the aim and the effect of ethics is to improve the quality of that interaction. The difficulty, however, is making a link back to the individual without invoking the ethical concepts that are supposedly being explained. For example, if ethical principles are presented as a form of social contract, a useful set of rules for social interaction, the key question is what supports the adoption of these rules. If it is claimed that adopting them is in the interests of all and so in the interests of each, we are back with the fallacious argument we have just discussed. If, however, it is claimed that the idea of a contract presupposes good faith on the part of those making it, a moral concept is invoked to explain moral concepts and the whole enterprise is undermined. The point is that the attempt to justify ethics in pragmatic terms must be pragmatic throughout. It cannot appeal to any conception of how it is correct to act. This implies that if ethics is simply a social contract, the contract must be policed. If we want to defend truth-telling not as an objective duty but as a useful social institution, we must seek to organise society in such a way that telling the truth is literally the best policy. Insofar as we fail to do this, the individual will have no reason to tell the truth when she does not want to do so. Although it is possible that a better outcome for everyone would be obtained if everyone simultaneously made an irrevocable commitment to moral perfection, this is not an option. The costs of policing may in a sense be wasteful, but we cannot wish them away by a collective pretence that obeying the rules is always and necessarily in the individual's interests.

A somewhat different approach is to argue that 'You ought to do X' simply means 'X is in the general interest' or 'X is for the best from society's point of view'. This substitution seems attractive because the appeal to society seems an appropriate terminus for argument: if something is in society's interests, what more could be said in its favour? This position might then be supported by the claim that societies with ethical values have been 'objectively endorsed' by their evolutionary success, since societies with no or with weak ethics tend to be short-lived. This last suggestion may or may not be true, but like earlier claims it raises the question of why an invocation of the good of society (or even of the species) should matter to the individual. If this is not a disguised appeal to traditional moral beliefs, it is hard to see why it is relevant. One response would be to argue that these considerations simply do matter to people, but this suggestion alters both the scope and force of ethical considerations. Once we drop the strange idea that there is a correct perspective on how we should act, we also lose the idea that the dictates of morality apply to all and have an overriding force. We are back to individuals acting on their preferences, and therefore some will have reason to act one way and others another. If acting morally simply means acting in a way which is in society's interest, only individuals who happen to want to further the general interest will have a reason to act in this way. This account therefore ceases to be distinctively ethical. Furthermore, insofar as it makes sense, it is largely parasitic on the moral concepts that have implicitly been rejected, for where the individual does have a desire to further the general interest, the basis for this 'desire' will usually be a belief that she ought to further the general interest. In other words, this perspective (the general/social/impersonal) gets its prestige from the very ethical concepts we are seeking to avoid. The claim that 'You ought to do X' means 'Do X because it is in the general interest' gets its force from the fact that 'You should act in the way that is best for everyone not just for yourself' is a crude but not totally inaccurate summary of the moral codes most of us support.

Against this, it might be argued that even in a world without moral beliefs we would still develop ties of affection to those around us and so acquire a tendency to take their interests into account. However, this kind of argument is of limited value: rather than justifying moral judgements such as 'You should not steal', it supports the trite principle 'You should not steal where you will find the pain this causes to those around you so distressing that it outweighs the pleasure you get from the theft'. In fact, this approach does not really move away from the principle (or non-principle) 'Do as you are inclined do'. Where the individual has what would traditionally be called moral scruples, reference to the contingent degree to which she desires the good of those around her is unlikely to be relevant; if someone is on the point of stealing money from a friend, *ex hypothesi* her desire for the money outweighs her desire that her friend does not to suffer the distress of being stolen from.

More complicated versions of this approach run into the same problem. For example, it might be argued that people have preferences about the sort of person they want to be and that this is the basis of the ethical constraints of their action. The reason the individual acts morally is to avoid being (or becoming) the sort of person she condemns. This seems an interesting suggestion, but only because its implications are masked in ambiguity. Insofar as this approach genuinely avoids the notion of correctness, it turns every moral dilemma into a kind of gamble, for the individual has to assess the costs of potential future self-disapproval against the benefits of acting immorally. Furthermore, the basis of her disapproval is fragile: she does not believe that acting immorally is objectively wrong, but simply takes into her calculations the fact that she will feel bad about herself if she acts in a certain way. If this is how she understands her 'scruples', it seems likely that she will gradually lose them.

The fundamental flaw in this approach as an account of ethics is that it rejects the notion of correctness. This approach does not involve the individual acting on the basis of a claim that certain actions are objectively correct; rather, action is based on a certain type of complex preference. Someone who adopts this approach has no basis for distinguishing her actions (and her views) from those of someone she condemns. Immoral actions (and views) are simply the expression of different preferences. Furthermore, there is no scope for the suggestion that one set of preferences is better than any other. Although we may have preferences about what preferences we and others have, these have no objective significance. The preferences we prefer in ourselves and in other people are not superior to the others, it is just that we happen to prefer them.

Giving up the attempt to justify ethics in terms either of the individual's interests or society's, some philosophers have taken a linguistic approach to clarifying ethics. One idea is to start from the truism that human action is characterised by its intelligibility. On this view, an individual's actions can only be seen as voluntary if she can offer an account of why she committed them, and if this account is an account for others, it must take into consideration their concerns. To put it in a slightly different way, the individual's account will only be a real explanation or justification if it involves a reference to the justificatory concepts current in that society and built into its language-games. This argument is plausible but rests on a confusion:

explaining an action is not the same as offering a justification for it and, while it is true that the individual must be able to explain her actions if we are to see them as intentional, there is no logical compulsion on her to justify them. If an individual only ever explained her actions in terms of her own interests, this would be unedifying but perfectly intelligible.

As it happens, most people do try to justify their actions in the face of criticism. People are generally concerned about what others think of them and therefore try to present their action in such a way that other people will agree that they were justified in acting as they did. The point, however, is that although they have to be able to explain (or give reasons for) their actions, they do not have to try (or be able) to convince others that their actions were justified. It would be quite intelligible for an individual to make no attempt to justify her actions in terms which others find acceptable. She may advance reasons which those around her find obnoxious or, rejecting the vocabulary of right and wrong, she may simply explain that she did what she wanted to do. We may criticise her for this but not on grounds of linguistic incompetence. Although the attempt to make moral thinking logically compulsory has a strange fascination, it cannot possibly succeed, for there is nothing unintelligible about accounts of actions that are self-centred or which invoke reasons that are generally or almost universally condemned as unacceptable.[5]

The weakness of the linguistic approach can be illustrated by considering what is usually considered its best case—promising. The argument here is that anyone who denies that breaking a promise requires some sort of justification is not just morally wrong but linguistically incompetent, for doing this shows a failure to understand the concept of a promise. Furthermore, the range of justifications is not up to the individual; our concept, and the practice, of promising, defines a set of possibilities from which she must choose—on pain of demonstrating that she does not understand the concept. One strange feature of this approach is that linguistic incompetence goes proxy for moral error as if what was really wrong with immoral action was that it implied linguistic incompetence. The flaw in the argument, however, is that it confuses understanding the concept of a promise with having a moral commitment to promise-keeping. The individual may recognise that certain words create an expectation in others but she need not see this as posing any kind of constraint on her action. As far as she is concerned, a promise may be a mere form of words, a trap for the foolish.

Against this, it might be argued the obligation exists even if the person who made the promise does not recognise this. But this is a substantive claim. Tautologically, anyone who believes that keeping promises is the correct thing to do will claim that a promise-breaker is failing to recognise a constraint which she ought to recognise. It is important, however, to separate the question of whether the individual understands the rules of the institution of promising from the question of what she believes to be the correct thing for her to do after she has made a promise. The individual can understand that she is supposed to do what she promises without being committed to the moral claim that keeping promises is the correct thing to do. Indeed, if she rejects ethics, she will not accept the whole idea of there being a correct thing to do and therefore could not possibly accept that if she makes a promise, the correct thing for her to do is to keep it. None of this, however, means that she does not understand the institution of promising.[6]

A slightly different linguistic argument involves claiming that moral judgements are distinguished from expressions of preference by having prescriptive implications for everyone, and that for this distinction to stand up, these prescriptions must be universal in form. This would seem to impose certain formal limits on what can count as a moral position and so show that anyone who wants to go in for prescription must respect these limits. The argument might then be taken further on the grounds that the universality of the judgement's form has implications for its content, so that, if the prescription is to apply to all, the concerns of all must be taken into account. One problem with this approach is that it leaves unexplained why anyone should want to make this sort of prescriptive judgement at all. The assumption seems to be that people simply have this peculiar urge and that it is the philosopher's job to explain to them how it can be satisfied without any logical impropriety. This leads on to a more fundamental point, for, even if we placed formal limits on what we would be prepared to describe as a moral position, this would be a purely verbal move and would not resolve the real philosophical issues which relate to the distinctive moral claim that acting on certain universal prescriptions is incumbent on everyone. If it turns out that all ethics is about is the fact that some people have an inexplicable penchant for making judgements of a certain form, then all we could do is wish these people well. Traditional morality would be replaced by an idiosyncratic language-game. *Ex hypothesi* we would all have agreed that a moral claim such as 'Everyone should love their neighbour' does not mean that this is objectively what everyone should do; rather it means 'I prescribe that everyone love their neighbour, even though I recognise that other people have no particular reason to pay any attention to my words'.

The above review suggests there is little hope for ethics and it may seem that there is no alternative but to accept that ethical considerations only give a reason for acting to those who are already disposed to favour the Good. Unfortunately, even this modest approach does not rescue traditional ethics, for it still involves the unexplained idea that there is an objective distinction between the Good and the Bad. Unless this distinction can be explained, any conflict between the moral and the immoral can only be seen as a clash of two tribes, one of which is prone to making incoherent claims about its objective superiority. This approach also has an internal problem, for it implies that the immoral have no reason to be moral. From a traditional perspective, this suggests that they do not deserve to be condemned. If the question of whether an individual favours the Good is treated as a contingent factual matter, it seems reasonable for the immoral to reject any criticism of themselves on the grounds that it is not their fault that they happen to be disposed in a particular way.

Faced with the failure of this last project, the temptation is to retreat even further and treat ethics simply as the name either of a type of consideration or of a type of perspective on human action. On this approach 'You ought to do X' should be taken to mean 'From a moral point of view, you ought to do X' or 'In terms of moral considerations, you ought to do X'. If we then ask what makes something a moral consideration or what defines the moral point of view, the answer is social convention or tradition. This is a radical step, for implicitly it rejects the idea of a viewpoint that is in itself correct. It implies that moral considerations are not overriding and that there is no reason why every individual should take them into account. Once this is recognised, however, it becomes very unclear why we want to define a viewpoint of this kind. This brings out the basic flaw in this approach, for the reason we group these considerations together (and what makes them relevant) is the survival of the idea that everyone ought to take them into account. In other words, we are back to the claim that there is a correct point of view. If we want no truck with this idea, surely it is better to abandon ethics altogether, rather than pretending that it can live on as the label of a viewpoint we have all come to recognise as incoherent?

This brief survey of possible approaches to ethics makes disheartening reading, for it suggests that the claims of traditional ethics simply cannot be made coherent. One contemporary philosopher who has made a determined effort to think through the implications of this conclusion is Bernard Williams. In his book, *Ethics and the Limits of Philosophy* he, too, surveys the various philosophical efforts to give ethics a coherent foundation and concludes that such projects will never succeed. Emphasising the importance of this conclusion, he argues that recognition of this failure is a turning point in the history of philosophy, for it involves the discipline coming to terms with the collapse of its greatest hopes. He is also sensitive to the conclusion's social consequences, for accepting it implies radical changes in the way we understand ourselves and the social world in which we live.

In particular, Williams urges us to reject a strand of ethical thinking which he calls 'morality' and which he considers confused and inhuman. We should dismiss, for example, the idea that moral considerations are overriding or that the moral law applies to everyone, even those who explicitly reject it. More generally, he argues that the failure of the justificatory project shows that ethical thought as such involves an illusion, for making a moral judgement involves denying the inescapable truth that the ultimate supports of ethical values are people's dispositions (*ELP*, p. 51). The heart of his book

15

is an attempt to grapple with the gap this creates between the view from out-side (ethics is a matter of dispositions) and the view from the inside (ethics is a matter of truth). Philosophically and culturally he suggests that a solution to this conflict will in part involve a return to the Greeks, that is to say, a return to pre-Christian thinking where the emphasis is on the role of ethics in promoting human flourishing rather than on the idea of a unique, morally correct view of the world.

Williams' starting point is the Socratic question 'How should one live?' which he takes to be a practical rather than an ethical question. It does not mean 'What life morally ought I to lead?'; rather *should* is simply *should* and, in itself, is no different in this very general question from what it is in any casual question, 'What should I do now?' (*ELP*, p. 5). He argues that moral philosophy is the search for an answer to this question which will apply to everyone. Success would give ethics an objective basis, but he is convinced this is impossible. He rejects arguments in terms of rationality in the style of Kant or, more recently, Alan Gewirth on the grounds that they rest on misconceptions about practical reason; and he discounts arguments in terms of well-being on the grounds either that they are based on untenable metaphysics (Aristotle) or, if couched in terms of psychology, that they yield no determinate conclusion. This creates the central problem around which Williams' book turns, for once we reject the idea of an absolute understand-ing of human nature,

> a potential gap opens between the agent's perspective and the outside view. We understand—and, most important, the agent can come to understand—that the agent's perspective is only one of many that are equally compatible with human nature, all open to various conflicts within themselves and with other cultural aims. With that gap opened, the claim I expressed by saying that agents' dispositions are the 'ultimate supports' of ethical value takes on a more skeptical tone. It no longer sounds enough.
>
> (*ELP*, p. 52).

The hint of threat is intentional: in Williams' view, we moderns face an irresolvable dilemma—although reflection shows our ethical beliefs to be irremediably flawed, they are so deeply part of us that we cannot simply dispense with them.

The background to this dilemma is a rejection of the traditional moral claims we discussed earlier. In part this rejection is distinct from the failure of the justificatory project, for even if the search for an objective grounding for ethics had succeeded, Williams holds that this would not have justified the naive claims the advocates of ethics often make. In particular, he believes that the notion of ethical truth is misguided, for at the reflective level ethical beliefs are not 'world-guiding' (*ELP*, p. 152). We must therefore recognise that values are not 'in the world' but are 'in some sense imposed or projected onto our surroundings' (*ELP*, p. 111). Although it never seems this way from the inside, the real basis for moral beliefs is people's dispositions (*ELP*, p. 52).

Williams believes that in itself recognition of this point is not a bad thing; indeed, 'it can be seen as a liberation, and a radical form of freedom may be found in the fact that we cannot be forced by the world to accept one set of values rather than another' (*ELP*, p. 128). It is obvious, however, that a clearer recognition of the nature of ethical claims will have implications for their scope and content. We will need to restructure our ethical practices in the light of a reflective and non-mythical understanding of them and 'the practices of blame, and more generally the style of people's negative ethical reactions to others, will change' (*ELP*, p. 194). Some traditional ideas will not survive. For example, the notion that the moral law applies to everyone will give way to a recognition that if it applies, this is because we apply it (*ELP*, p. 192). Thus Williams urges a double break with tradition—not only does our basic understanding of ethics need to change, but this entails at least some alterations in the content and scope of ethical claims.

Despite this, Williams does not urge us to abandon ethics altogether. On the contrary, he believes that society is only possible if a large number of people embody ethical considerations in their lives. This raises the obvious question of why individuals should hang onto their moral beliefs if they are not objectively justified. In response to this, his first move is to reject the suggestion that ethical scepticism is the natural state (*ELP*, p. 26). He claims that for most of us commitment to some sort of ethical belief is the status quo, so that what we need is a reason to jettison these beliefs rather than a reason to adopt them. According to him, failure to recognise this point is the central flaw in earlier foundational projects, for they sought a justification of ethics that would necessarily apply to everyone, whereas what is really needed is that more modest thing, a justification for us. 'The aim is not to control the enemies of the community or its shirkers but, by giving reason to people already disposed to hear it, to help in continually creating a community held together by that same disposition' (*ELP*, p. 27). The idea behind this claim is that some of our dispositions are so much a part of our identity that we must debate from these dispositions rather than to them. According to Williams, while reflection can, and often should, lead us to modify our ethical beliefs, it cannot and does not need to justify why we have such beliefs in the first place.

Williams stresses that our dispositions are the underlying basis of the beliefs we have, but he is keen to balance his conservatism with criticism. On the one hand, he welcomes the fact that our ethical beliefs reflect the social world in which we have grown up, since he believes that it is shared ethical conceptions that give social life its richness. (Without them, the world would be a Hobbesian war of all against all.) On the other hand, he emphasises that these beliefs need to be subject to critical examination. This can create problems, for he believes that reflection shows our beliefs cannot be all they claim to be, and this recognition can be personally and socially disquieting. In his view, however, what matters is that we can come to be satisfied with the dispositions we have. In other words, we should recognise that the key concept in ethics is neither truth nor decision, but confidence (*ELP*, p. 170). The ideal would be a society whose members were able to combine a capacity for reflection with a practical confidence in the dispositions they had come to acquire. Unfortunately for the philosopher, achievement of this goal is a matter of social practice rather than philosophical theory-building.

> How truthfulness to an existing self or society is to be combined with reflection, self-understanding, and criticism is a question that philosophy, itself, cannot answer. It is the kind of question that has to be answered through reflective living. The answer has to be discovered, or established, as the result of a process, personal and social, which essentially cannot formulate the answer in advance, except in an non-specific way. Philosophy can play a part in the process, as it plays a part in identifying the question, but it cannot be a substitute for it. This is why it is a misunderstanding to ask, in the way ethical theorists often ask, 'what alternative' one has to their formulations. They mean, what formulation does one have as an alternative to their formulations, either of the answer or some determinate heuristic process that would yield the answer; and there is none. There might turn out to be an answer to the real question, and this would indeed be an alternative to their formulations; but it would not be an answer produced in the way that their demand requires an answer, as a piece of philosophy. To suppose that, if their formulations are rejected, we are left with *nothing* is to take a strange view of what in social and personal life counts as something.
>
> (*ELP*, pp. 200–1)

In the end, philosophy has to admit defeat. There is no determinate theoretical answer to the Socratic question 'How should one live?'; instead we as individuals, and as a society, must seek in our lives together to find not the correct answer to this question but an answer with which we can be satisfied.

Williams' conclusion is typically modern; indeed, he himself sees his book as an attempt to resolve the distinctively modern dilemma created by the clash between reflection and traditional moral beliefs. His approach can also be seen as modern in other ways, for insofar as it is involves a rejection of objective ethics, it reflects a world in which the force of moral claims has already weakened. According to Williams, this should largely be seen as a loss of illusions. Although we may feel nostalgia for a time when the world was 'magical', i.e. believed to be value-laden (*ELP*, p. 165), and although one of our society's major problems is that too few ethical ideas have survived (*ELP*, p. 117), in general the change should be seen as a transition from ignorance or error to truth. It is worth noting, however, how far Williams—and by extension modern society—has moved. The claim that moral concerns are not overriding but just one type of consideration among others involves a major change in attitude to ethics; indeed, it amounts to an outright rejection of traditional moral views.

This point can be illustrated by considering an example from Williams' own work, for in an earlier book[7] he suggests that the painter Gauguin was right to abandon his wife and family, since the result of this decision was the production of works of great art and no one today could wish that he had chosen otherwise. Here, it is characteristic that art appears as the last refuge of absolute value. Somewhat strangely, belief in art seems to survive belief in right and wrong, as if it were easier to accept that there can be no objective judgements about human actions than that there are no objective distinctions in art. Leaving this point to one side, what is more significant is that from a traditional point of view Williams' comments are the paradigm of an immoral argument, for they suggest that the ends can justify the means. From this perspective, the difference between the position of contemporary moral philosophers and that of Dostoyevsky's Raskolnikov is merely one of degree. If Gauguin had needed to murder someone (or a group of people?) to finance his trip to Tahiti, then presumably this too would have been justified by what he achieved when he got there.

The distance between Williams' position and traditional ethics is obvious in his attack on the set of ideas he calls 'morality', but it also affects his accounts of the pre-modern philosophers he refers to. For example, he claims that 'Socrates sought a rational design of life which would reduce the power of fortune and would be to the greatest possible extent luck-free' (*ELP*, p. 5). This suggests that ethics is the refuge of the cautious and of those dismayed by the unpredictability of life; and yet this seems an odd suggestion insofar as adopting a moral stand led to Socrates' death. It would seem his attempts to reduce his exposure to misfortune were singularly inept. In the case of Aristotle, Williams argues that the only feature of his ethics which can survive the debunking of his metaphysics is the attempt to ground ethics in psychology, and yet he seems unworried that this turns the quest for human flourishing into a drive for normalcy, an exultation of happiness in some minimal, scientifically-defined sense. By contrast, Williams sees Spinoza as failing to realise that a proper scientific description of the world will be devoid of ethical terms and so cannot be the appropriate perspective for ethical thought.

If it were, we should be strictly committed to thinking about ethical life not only from that perspective, but using only the concepts available within it. That is certainly impossible. Those concepts are, roughly, those of the concepts of physics, and it is an unsolved problem how much even of psychological vocabulary could possess that absolute character.

(*ELP,* p. 111)

The point of citing Williams' interpretation of these philosophers is not to defend their positions against his, but to illustrate the problems he has in understanding them. In each case the weakness of Williams' interpretation reflects a real difficulty in making sense of traditional claims: it is almost as if he literally cannot understand what they are talking about.

Once we recognise the extent of Williams' differences with traditional ethics, the change in his tone from grim-faced optimism to near-despair assumes a different significance. In fact, the conflict in modern society between a theoretical rejection of moral concepts and a practical commitment to them is played out in Williams himself and the merit of his work is the attempt to confront the problems this creates. If we were as self-aware as he, we, too, might hesitate before trying to teach our children the difference between right and wrong, for objectively the difference seems to be illusory. The only reason Williams can see for continuing to teach our children the difference is that:

> we ourselves (most of us) are identified with some ethical consider-ations and have a conception of human well-being that gives a place to such considerations. We wish, consequently, to bring up our children to share some of these ethical, as of other cultural, concep-tions, and we see the process as good not just for us but for our children, both because it is part of our conception of their well-being and also because, even by more limited concepts of happiness or contentment, we have little reason to believe they will be happier if excluded from the ethical institutions of society. Even if we know that there are some people who are happier, by the minimal criteria, outside those institutions, we also know that they rarely became so by being educated as outlaws. As a result of all that, we have much reason for, and little reason against, bringing up our children within the ethical world we inhabit, and if we succeed they themselves will see the world from the same perspective.

(*ELP,* p. 48)

This is hardly a ringing endorsement of moral education. It seems we should pass on our values because this suits us and because it is not absolutely certain that our children would be better off without them. Interestingly, on a social level even this argument does not apply; since ethical values cannot be objectively grounded, we should stand back from trying to affect the future. 'We should not try to seal determinate values into future society' (*ELP*, p. 173).

The above remarks illustrate the extent to which Williams has moved away from traditional moral claims, and given the apparent incoherence of the latter, that movement may seem understandable, indeed, praiseworthy. The question that remains, however, is whether anything distinctively ethical can be salvaged from the incoherencies of the past. Without the claim to correctness can ethical considerations retain a place in our deliberations? Williams' overt answer is yes; the tone of his book, however, indicates the real possibility of a negative answer. His official position rests on denying that our ethical commitments need some further basis. Although we cannot justify our ethical beliefs (or the dispositions underlying them) 'all the way down', he believes that this is not necessary, since our deliberations must start from where and who we are. In his view there is no need to justify our disposition to hold moral beliefs, all that is necessary is that our knowledge and reflection in general do not undermine those beliefs. Unless our beliefs can be explained (e.g. as arising from personal insecurity or from a group's need for an external enemy) or can be shown to have negative consequences (e.g. they are psychologically or socially destructive), we have no reason to lose our confidence in them.

This position seems very reasonable: while it recognises that our moral beliefs are not objectively justified, it allows scope for reflection and so rebuts the suggestion that we are clinging to our beliefs in the face of the truth. Unfortunately, and as Williams is aware, it is hard to hold the different elements of this position together. In particular, there is a permanent tension between the internal and the external view. The individual who believes that murder is wrong and condemns those who claim otherwise must recognise that objectively speaking the only difference between her and them is that she happens to have one set of dispositions and they another. Williams suggests there is no reason to dwell on this way of looking at things, but doing so seems unavoidable, for how can we continue to make moral judgements if we accept that ultimately those judgements reflect how we are disposed rather than objective truths about what it is we claim to be judging?

Putting this question to one side for the moment, let us explore Williams' position by considering his account of how reflection might lead an individual to change her moral view. Suppose someone came to the conclusion that her disposition to believe that homosexuality was wrong was a product of her own insecurities and she consequently sought to become less homophobic. This seems to be a good example of how knowledge can undermine a moral belief. Unfortunately this example is less straightforward than it seems. The first problem for Williams is why the existence of an explanation should cause the individual to try to change the way she is disposed, for she must know that there will always be possible explanations of her disposition

21

whatever that disposition may be. Furthermore, if there is no truth of the matter, why should any of these explanations bother her? If she believes that objectively one position is as good as another, why should she disturb her prejudices?

This objection brings out a key point, for Williams' approach undermines the very possibility of reflection on moral issues. If moral beliefs are simply a product of the way the individual happens to be disposed, there is no scope for claiming that any judgement is right and in this way the very possibility of debate is eliminated. Once we accept that there is no truth of the matter about whether homosexuality is right or wrong, there is nothing for moral reflection to get a grip on. The only issue for the individual is which dispositions she would like to have and which she would prefer to avoid. Unlike moral reflection, this sort of assessment will not generate conclusions about how everyone should act. On the contrary, its results will depend on the individual and on the situation in which she finds herself. For example, in a homophobic society the individual may want to be disposed to condemn homosexuality; on the other hand, if she enjoys challenging the consensus, she may prefer to be disposed to condemn homophobia. As these examples suggest, this assessment process is very different from moral reflection. It may also seem a rather strange process. The important point, however, is that from Williams' point of view this is all there is to think about, for he believes that in themselves questions about the rightness or wrongness of homosexuality are misguided.[8]

This criticism of Williams may seem to clash with a genuine feature of moral argument, for the sort of explanations he alludes to do play a role in ethical debates. In real life, however, they get their force from the idea that the condemnation of others is unjustified if it reflects a weakness in us rather than the correct assessment of the moral status of the action being judged. This idea cannot be invoked by Williams, since it involves precisely the type of claim he urges us to abandon. In particular, it implies that condemnation is only justified if it relates to the merits of the issue in question and, therefore, that our reaction is not just a matter of dispositions but that there are circumstances in which condemnation may be correct. To mask this point Williams has to resort to ambiguity. He presents reflection as a process whereby the individual examines her dispositions and rejects those she is dissatisfied with; but this ignores the key issue of how the individual understands this dissatisfaction. If she treats this, too, as an expression of how she is disposed, her self-examination does not involve moral reflection at all. In our example, if the individual is dissatisfied with her disposition this simply indicates that she is in the uncomfortable position of reacting negatively to homosexuals and disliking the fact that she reacts negatively to them. Faced with this conflict between her dispositions she might try to wean herself from either reaction or she might try to minimise her discomfort by avoiding situations where her homophobic feelings were provoked.

Whatever she decides, her problem is purely practical. Unless she makes the kind of claim Williams rejects, there is no question of her reaction to homosexuality being right or wrong and it is therefore simply a matter of managing her dispositions in the way that suits her best overall.

To underline these points it is worth considering more closely the role psychological explanations do play in moral argument. The first point to note is that the possibility of explaining how an individual came to hold her view does not give her a reason for adopting the opposite view. If, for example, there was social pressure to believe that homosexuality was morally acceptable, this could explain why some people held this view but it would not show that it was wrong. In fact, any putative explanation is external to the moral debate. The only issue for moral reflection is whether a particular type of action is right or wrong. What confuses Williams is the fact that one way of trying to persuade someone to change her moral position is by trying to convince her that what she takes to be the perception of a truth is in fact a reaction with particular psychological causes. However, the individual can only accept the explanation as relevant if she admits that her position itself is wrong. Someone who believes that homosexuality is immoral will reject as irrelevant any claim that hostility to homosexuality is associated with insecurity. From her point of view, if this claim was true, all this would show was that there was a contingent co-relation between being insecure and holding the correct belief on homosexuality. Only if the individual wavers in her belief that homosexuality is wrong can she accept the explanation and see her position as a prejudice with particular psychological causes.

Williams' notion of confidence seeks to mirror this reflective process without invoking the concept of correctness. His idea seems to be that we expose our moral beliefs to attempts to explain them and if they survive this process, we can feel comfortable sticking with them. This sounds reasonable but only because it is ambiguous. In fact, even in this version the notion of correctness is vital, for unless we believe that moral beliefs can be correct, we cannot test them for their validity. If our moral beliefs can only ever be an expression of how we happen to be disposed, we cannot confront specific beliefs with the suggestion that we hold them not because they are correct but because some psychological process led us to embrace them. Conversely, if after the reflective process we are still 'confident' in our moral beliefs, this can only mean that we believe they are correct. The ambiguity in Williams' position lies in the way he tries to avoid this point by claiming that believing a view to be correct means being happy overall to hold it. This interpretation undercuts the whole idea that we are assessing our beliefs for their validity and takes us back to the earlier interpretation of his position; rather than reflecting on the rights and wrongs of an issue, we are back to arranging our dispositions in the way that suits us best.[9]

Let us consider another example. Suppose it was discovered that people with an absolute commitment to personal integrity had more psychological

23

problems than those who did not, e.g. they were more prone to depression. This is presumably the sort of argument Williams is thinking of when he invokes psychology as a possible source of objective justifications in ethics. Once again, however, there is a gap between the level on which this argument operates and moral reflection. If an individual believes that people should always honour their commitments, she cannot abandon this belief because the difficulty of living up to it might make her depressed. If she believes that this is the correct thing to do, she cannot accept the costs of acting in this way as a valid argument against it. The opposite assumption—that psychology can provide an objective input into reflection on how we should act— involves abandoning ethics entirely. On this approach, the issue for the individual is 'Which of my reactions is it in my interests to jettison and which not?' and that is certainly not a question that reflects a commitment to a moral approach.

Williams suggests that everyone must at least agree that they should seek to jettison reactions that psychology can show to have adverse consequences, but this is misguided. Anyone who takes a moral position is committed to rejecting this idea and instead to holding that our views on human action should reflect the merits of the issue, not an assessment of the consequences of holding those views. To the claim that everyone must want to avoid psychological damage the moralist might reply, 'if trying to lead a morally good life drives you crazy, then go crazy'. Contrary to what Williams seems to assume, the moral notion of the correct way of acting is not part of a search for the lowest common denominator of human motivation, the bare minimum of what everyone can be assumed to strive for. In fact, his approach is of little use even in relation to people who do reject ethics, since the definition of adverse consequences (and the issue of what priority they should be given) reintroduces all the controversies that the reference to the 'objective' findings of psychology was supposed to eliminate. If, for example, it could be shown that trying to be a top sportsperson increased the risk of suicide, this would not necessarily stop people from seeking sporting success. In short, the findings of psychology have no part to play in moral reflection and only play a marginal role in the non-moral individual's assessment of which dispositions she would be glad to have.[10]

These arguments show how far Williams' position is from anything that resembles traditional ethics, and he himself sometimes seems to recognise this point. For example, he argues that ethics should be seen not as a search for truth (or correctness) but as a search for a way to live together socially. This kind of statement, however, disguises the real issue, for Williams rejects the claim to correctness and therefore in a significant sense rejects ethics itself. At best his approach might encourage us to agree on certain principles and seek to force each other to stick to them; in other words, there would be a real social contract and it would have to be policed. Insofar as we agreed that murderers, liars, etc. were a bad thing, we might set up systems to deter them (and ourselves) from acting in this way. But this would not amount to regaining our belief in moral values. If we ever felt inclined to murder or lie, the question for us (and for anyone) would be whether acting in this way was worth the risk of whatever social penalties were attached to these actions.

Williams seeks to use his emphasis on dispositions to give this position a twist, for he implies that the best way of policing the contract might be to cause everyone to be disposed not to break it. Society would condition everyone to believe that acting in certain ways was wrong, and as a member of society we would be happy for ourselves to believe this because everyone's believing so was in our interests. The fact that everyone includes each of us as an individual is the price we would have to pay for living in the sort of society we want to live in. There are two points to make about this idea. First, it too does not amount to a return to ethics. This sort of programming would be like giving the individual a behaviour-altering drug at birth: she would act in certain ways not because she believed that acting in those ways was correct, but because it had been made impossible for her to do otherwise. Second, it is not very plausible. This suggestion relies on the individual not being able to change her programming. She is allowed to think 'it is good that we are all programmed in a way that makes social life possible', but she cannot reflect that it would be better if everyone but she was so programmed. Or rather she can think this but only if she is so thoroughly programmed that she will not respond to it. What saves the morally good but reflective individual is the assumption that she cannot change, that becoming an amoralist is not a real option for her. From Williams' point of view, the only barrier to despair is the hope that in practical terms we will not be able to take the message of reflection fully on board.

The final way in which Williams tries to defend ethical dispositions is to argue that they are so much a part of us that there can be no question of our jettisoning them. This is a desperate and rather implausible form of defence. It seems hard to believe that these inconvenient (and error-based) dispositions are so deeply rooted that we cannot fine-tune them over time and if we can, we seem to have every reason for defining ourselves in weaker and weaker ethical terms. Against this, Williams argues that being true to ourselves is a key aspect of human well-being. This seems a strange suggestion, for the individual is supposed to recognise the mistaken nature of her beliefs and yet persist in acting according to them in order to remain true to herself. This, too, seems implausible and it is hard to imagine an individual acting on this argument in real life. If someone wishes to steal, it seems unlikely that she will refrain out of loyalty to a non-reflective self that holds the admittedly confused idea that stealing is objectively wrong. This is not to deny the importance of integrity; like all moral concepts, however, this concept involves the claim that there are correct ways of acting. If a company director with working-class roots resigns over job cuts, this is because she believes it would be wrong for her to act against her former fellows, not because the emotional costs created by her ties to them outweigh her potential gains from the deed. She acts in a certain way because she believes that doing otherwise would be wrong, not because she cannot help but act that way.

Williams' account of this kind of situation is rather different, for he emphasises the idea that some of the individual's dispositions are so fundamental that she would find changing them difficult or impossible. Even if this claim was true, however, it would have quite different implications. On this approach, moral scruples appear not as claims about how it is correct to act but as internal shackles which the individual cannot change. The implication would be that, although the individual knows that it is meaningless to say that objectively she must act in a certain way, she still has to take into account the fact that she is unalterably disposed to feel bad unless she acts in a certain way. Here the internal and the external view do come together, but not because the individual remains committed to the idea that certain actions are wrong. She does not hold moral beliefs; rather, she has dispositions which she recognises are not in themselves justifiable but which she has to take into account. This is what Williams' defence of moral reactions amounts to. What has happened is that the individual's moral beliefs have been replaced by an internalised version of the external view; since the disposition is hers and is deep-seated, it is something she has to take into account when reflecting. Ethics is rejected, but 'moral' habits persist. Although the external view undermines the notion of conscience, it may not instantly or totally eliminate pangs of conscience; moral beliefs are rejected, but to a certain extent the individual may continue to act as if she still held them.

The failure of Williams' book underlines the impossibility of constructing a moral position that avoids the claim to correctness. His attempts to develop a coherent non-objectivist ethics fail, while his occasional lapse into objectivist judgements only serves to emphasise just how difficult it is to abandon the type of claim he believes is misguided. Despite this, and given that there are features of traditional morality that many people find objectionable, we may conclude that what is wrong with Williams is that he tries to hold onto ethics. One difficulty with this conclusion, however, is that having rejected ethics we cannot claim that past moralities were wrong or unjust, for this itself involves making objectivist claims. This reflects a wider dilemma, for although people today may be less ready to make judgements about how others should lead their private lives, they find it harder to abandon objectivist ethical claims in relation to other matters, e.g. in relation to murder or torture or when it comes to questions about how society should be organised or whether animals have rights. Unfortunately, rejecting moral beliefs entirely seems almost as problematic as trying to hang onto them.

In the face of these problems we may want simply to brush the difficulties aside—after all, if we feel compelled to make moral judgements, why shouldn't we make them, despite knowing their flaws? The point, however, is that moral judgements involve a claim that we have now recognised to be mistaken. We cannot therefore continue to make this kind of judgement. The only sense in which we can continue as before is if we decide to indulge our dispositions and continue to react negatively to people whose actions we used (misguidedly) to claim were objectively wrong. There is nothing inconsistent or confused about this position, but it is unlikely to be stable, for once we reject ethics, our dispositions may change. For example, we may continue to dislike lying, but if we see our reaction as having no objective basis (or as a hangover of our misguided objectivist beliefs), we may be more ready to override it when doing so is to our advantage. Over time, therefore, our moral scruples are likely to diminish. Of course, there is no reason for us to be unhappy at this prospect, for *ex hypothesi* the destination will not seem so bad when we arrive and, who knows, maybe we will only lose a few scruples and not the really big ones. Even if we do stay largely where we are, however, we will have undergone a revolution in our understanding of ourselves and of our reactions. We might use the same moral terms, but they would have lost their distinctive meaning. Although we might describe murder as 'evil', we would recognise that this does not involve claiming that it is objectively wrong, but simply reflects the fact that at the moment we personally happen to be disposed to condemn it.

2

BELIEVING IN
RIGHT AND WRONG

Here we come up against a remarkable and characteristic phenomenon in philosophical investigation: the difficulty—I might say—is not that of finding the solution but rather that of recognising as the solution something that looks as if it were only a preliminary to it. 'We have already said everything.— Not anything that follows from this, no, *this* itself is the solution!'
 . . . The difficulty here is: to stop.

(Wittgenstein, *Zettel,* para. 315)

The arguments of Chapter 1 suggest that the contradictions of ethics are insurmountable. It seems that traditional ethical concepts are incoherent and that this incoherence cannot be eliminated. This conclusion is difficult to accept and seems to leave us caught between the philosophical inadequacy of ethical concepts and the almost indispensable role they play in our lives. Although we may reject ethics as incoherent, most of us will find abandoning it difficult and will, like Williams, run the constant risk of lapsing into objectivist judgements. Before taking this step, therefore, it is worth reconsidering the problem. The contradictions we have discussed arise from a recognition that judgements about how we should act are different in kind from judgements about how things are. This seems to imply that in relation to the former there is no room for the notion of correctness. In logical terms, different assessments of an action seem to be on the same level. If one person says that it is right to act in a certain way and another denies this, there is no obvious way of settling the matter. No truth about the world can resolve the issue and there seems to be nothing independent for either party to appeal to. The inescapable conclusion seems to be that all judgements on human actions are expressive of a particular point of view and that, since there is no way of independently arbitrating between the innumerable points of view that are logically possible, none of them can claim to be objectively correct.

The claims of someone who believes in right and wrong fly in the face of these apparent truisms. Such a person denies that her judgements on human action are just an expression of her preferences (or of how she happens to be disposed). Instead she claims they are correct and reflect standards everyone should recognise. One way in which she may emphasise the status she claims for her moral judgements is by asserting that they would be correct even if everyone (including herself) believed the opposite. These paraphrases all reflect the same idea, viz. that there are correct and incorrect judgements on human action. The crucial point, however, is that the moralist is not claiming a logical privilege for her views. She accepts that from a logical point of view there is no basis for distinguishing between different judgements on human action. Nonetheless she believes that there are differences everyone should recognise. Her position is that rival judgements about human action do not simply express different points of view or different preferences (or even preferences for preferences) but that there is a set of judgements which ought to be made by everyone. This is what believing in right and wrong amounts to. What is distinctive about ethical positions is that they involve claiming that there are right and wrong answers in relation to human action.[1]

But what does this claim mean? How can a judgement on human action be correct? This may seem to be the central issue but, as we shall see, it is not. The point is that there is no scope or need for further explanations. The moralist believes that understanding the world correctly involves recognising certain judgements of human action as correct; in her view there are judgements everyone should make regardless of their dispositions or preferences. She believes that anyone who denies this fails to understand the world as it should be understood. If we press her and ask why the world should be understood in this way, our question is meaningless. She can say how she believes everyone should understand the world, but the reason she thinks everyone should accept this view is because she believes it is correct. Here, what needs to be recognised is that reasons come to an end, and this is true whatever position we take. The difference between the moralist and the anti-moralist is not that the former believes reality or rationality somehow compels us to act in certain ways, but that she believes there are correct judgements on human action (judgements everyone should make), whereas the latter does not believe this. Both advance rival views of how the world should be understood; only one of those involves claiming that judgements of human action can be correct; but the explanations of both eventually come to an end. At that point all either can say is 'This is the view that I believe is correct'.

Even if this is accepted, it may be argued that the moralist's position involves a circularity; indeed, in Chapter 1 we noted the self-congratulatory way in which the moralist seems to think she can both make a judgement and give it an independent stamp of approval.[2] The point, however, is that in defending her position as correct, the moralist is not merely demonstrating her commitment to a particular view, but is making a substantive claim about the type of judgement involved. She is claiming that judging human action is not a matter of expressing a personal preference, but that there are correct judgements, i.e. judgements which everyone should make. This is important because in the case of judgements about how we should act, and in contrast with judgements about how things are, the individual does not have to accept this idea. On the contrary, it is perfectly coherent to claim that there are simply rival points of view and that none has any special validity. For those who believe that this latter position is correct, the only issues in relation to judgements on human action are the practical ones of who favours which point of view and which point of view prevails.

These points are important, for understanding ethics involves recognising that belief in ethics and rejection of it are both logically possible. Just as it would be wrong to see someone who believes in right and wrong as claiming that a special type of entity exists that magically compels everyone to act in certain ways, so too it would be a mistake to see someone who rejects ethics as making the absurd claim that she is indifferent about how people act. Consider the case of someone who denies there are correct views on human action but dislikes violence. Such a person can certainly try to ensure that others react similarly and that sanctions are applied against those who commit violence. The status of her judgement, however, will be different from that of the moralist, for she will accept that she advances her view not because it is correct but because it reflects the way she happens to be disposed. By emphasising the aspects of violence which she dislikes, she may try to elicit a similar reaction in others, but in all of this she would simply be seeking to minimise the occurrence of something she dislikes. By contrast, the moralist claims that violence is wrong and that this should be recognised by everyone, regardless of their personal preferences or of how they happen to be disposed. Since she believes that there are right answers to questions of how people should act, she cannot avoid the apparent arrogance of claiming that her views should be universal. Believing that everyone ought to act in a certain way, she has no choice but to maintain that someone who claims otherwise is wrong.[3] Here, it is not a matter of the individual twisting the argument to endorse her own position but of her believing that reflection should lead everyone to recognise as correct (and act in accordance with) certain standards.

When this sort of claim is discussed in philosophy, the temptation is to keep asking what the claim means even when all possible explanations have already been given. The moralist believes that there is a perspective on human action which is correct, i.e. which should be adopted by everyone. In other words, she believes that anyone who understands the world as it should be understood will recognise that there are correct and incorrect ways of acting. Once she has made this clear, what more can she say about correctness? Of course, if we are interested in her specific moral views, there may be much to say, and different individuals will offer different accounts of why they believe in right and wrong and what this belief involves. They may claim that understanding the world correctly involves recognising God's existence or the existence of a natural order in the world or that it involves a respect for life or a recognition that every human being is deserving of respect. Whatever the nature of their particular views, however, there is no scope (or need) to supplement them with a general explanation of what correctness means. Questions such as 'How can a value judgement be correct?' or 'How can an action be right?' look like legitimate demands for information but actually express a rejection of the ethical approach itself. The real issue for each of us is whether we believe there are judgements on human action that should be accepted by everyone or instead hold that all such judgements are on a par and simply reflect the preferences or dispositions of a particular group or individual. This is not a question, however, that can be answered by analysing concepts.

These points are hard to accept. Rather than providing our moral claims with foundations, they may seem to highlight their precarious state. We may believe that everyone should recognise that lying is wrong, but if someone denies this, our claim suddenly seems very flimsy, for all we can say is that this person is wrong and is failing to recognise something that ought to be recognised by everyone. Furthermore, if this person ignores our claim, this will not necessarily have any adverse consequences for her except, of course, that she will fail to act in the way that we believe everyone ought to act. What, in particular, makes this situation seem unsatisfactory is the contrast with disagreements in relation to empirical claims, for in that context, if we are right, the other person will in principle sooner or later find this out. If we tell someone that a certain liquid is poisonous and she drinks it anyway, the correctness of our claim will prove itself in a very real way. If we tell her that it would wrong to drink the liquid, it seems that only words stand in the way of her drinking it, and she may well drink the liquid and thereafter neither express nor experience any regret at so doing. These sort of concerns drive us to seek a stronger account of ethics. We want to be able to demonstrate that our moral judgements are not mere words and that they are more than simply an expression of our preferences. Until we can achieve this, the status of our moral claims seems dubious.

But this approach is misguided. It seeks to assimilate moral judgements to empirical judgements, and it is based on a desire for reasons that are logically impossible to reject. Both these errors reflect a failure to recognise the distinctive nature of moral claims. In particular, it is wrong to argue that unless moral judgements can be given logically unshakeable foundations, they must be treated as mere expressions of preference. On the contrary, in making a moral judgement we are specifically not expressing a preference, but are claiming that everyone capable of reflecting on the issue or situation should reach this particular conclusion. We are claiming that recognising its

31

correctness is part of understanding life and the world correctly. Error in this context, however, is quite unlike error in relation to empirical claims, and for that reason there can be no automatic assumption that the individual will regret acting immorally and come to see her previous views as incorrect. People can fail to recognise what the moralist believes are the most important things in life and still be happy, but this does not affect the moralist's claim that they are acting in ways that they (and everyone else) should recognise as wrong. If we conclude from this that the moralist's claim is 'mere words', this amounts to rejecting the idea of right and wrong. It implies that in our opinion the correct way of understanding the world involves recognising that there are no correct judgements on human action.

As these comments suggest, many of our difficulties in understanding ethics arise from a failure to recognise that reasons come to an end. This is a general philosophical problem, but it creates particular difficulties here because substantive disagreement confronts us in a way it does not elsewhere. When Wittgenstein imagines a people who do not accept induction or who reject our concept of an object, the exercise is philosophically useful, but unreal. Ethics, however, confronts us with an area where people's deepest views are in conflict—not just because we disagree about the correct ways for people to act, but because we also disagree about whether or not there are correct ways for people to act. There is no way of resolving these disputes, but this does not mean they are empty. Each individual will reach conclusions about how the world should be understood, but there are no agreed methods for moving from the 'evidence' to the conclusions. If someone believes there is an inherent order in the world and then rejects this belief as a mistake, she cannot justify her new view by reference either to a logical proof or to a piece of unequivocal empirical evidence. Similarly, if she believes that human life is the chance product of evolution and then comes to dismiss this view as superficial, her reasons for doing so may be hard to specify. Experience (and her reflection upon it) will have led her to change her mind, but there is no guarantee that she will be able to put this into words or that what convinced her will convince everyone. On the basis of her thoughts and experiences, she advances a particular view and whether or not she accepts the idea of objective ethical standards, she cannot eliminate the possibility that other people will reject the view she believes to be correct.

One response to these points is to ask how the individual herself knows her position is right if she cannot prove it. This question is usually pressed in relation to the moralist rather than the anti-moralist, for if there are correct judgements on human action, there seems a real issue as to how we can determine what they were. The traditional response is to refer to intuition, but, as critics of this response have pointed out, to claim that the individual knows by intuition says little more than that she knows because she knows.

However, against the background of the points we have been making, it should be clear that the initial question makes no sense. If the individual believes that judging human action is not just a matter of expressing a personal preference but that there are views everyone should hold, all she can do when faced with a moral issue is make a judgement as to what she believes to be the correct view. She says what she thinks is right, but the question 'How do you know that your judgement is right?' makes no sense, for there is no scope for specifying a way or method. An individual can outline her moral views, but this process cannot eliminate the need for us to take a stance. If instead we keep asking for further reasons, this may simply be one way of expressing our rejection of the view she is advancing. This point can be illustrated in relation to general moral principles, for the question 'How do you know that hurting people is wrong?' makes no sense. There is no 'how' to specify and, if the question means 'Why is hurting people wrong?', it is not so much a question as a refusal to accept the claim that everyone should recognise that hurting people is wrong. Such questions may make moral claims look unsupported, but only because they seek justifications where none are necessary or possible.

The above points should not be seen as some sort of special pleading in defence in ethics, for the same issues arise in relation to any claim about how the world should be understood. The claim that values are *not* objective is as substantive and unprovable as the claim that certain values should be recognised by everyone. The point is that while some people claim that understanding the world correctly involves recognising that there are correct ways of acting, others deny this. To say that judgements about how people should act (or claims with implications about how people should act) cannot be part of the correct way of understanding the world is simply one way of affirming the latter view. It is not an independent assessment of the dispute, but the position of one of the parties to it. Those who deny that there are correct ways of acting can explain why they hold this view, but their reasons, too, come to an end. They, too cannot eliminate the logical possibility of disagreement. Thus the moralist and her opponent are in the same situation. Each claims that her way of understanding the world is correct,[4] but neither can prove her claim.

It might be objected that this approach seems to make having a world-view logically compulsory, but this misses the point. It is debatable as to whether it is humanly possible to avoid answering all the great questions in human life (such as whether God exists, whether actions can be right and wrong and whether life has a meaning), but even if it were, there is no particular merit in trying to do so. It could not be seen as a matter of not giving hostages to Fortune; rather it would be like trying to pass an exam by refusing to answer any of the questions.[5] Different people's understandings of the world may have different degrees of elaboration and of sophistication, but the key distinction as far as understanding ethics is concerned is between those who hold that there are actions which should be recognised by everyone as right and wrong and those who reject this claim.

This approach with its invocation of the Wittgensteinian notion of bedrock will seem suspicious to many; some will see it as a glib response to real philosophical issues, while others will see it as a form of irrationalism. The first charge can only be met by giving an account of the implications of this approach and by using it to confront other contemporary views and that is precisely what this book as a whole seeks to do. The second charge, however, involves misunderstanding the notion of bedrock, for the impossibility of proof does not mean that there is nothing really at stake or that those who adopt different positions do so at random. On the contrary, the individual's views in this area will usually be among her most fundamental convictions, and they might be said to reflect all she has thought and experienced in trying to understand the world. It may be difficult or impossible for her to crystallise the whole of her experience into a few words, but it would be strange to claim that the belief is therefore irrational. If a lifetime of experience is not an adequate basis for belief, what would be? Here, what we need to get away from is the demand for proof and the belief that without proof there is only arbitrariness.

A different objection is that the notion of bedrock insulates the ethical view from criticism; if the practice (or language-game) cannot be refuted from the outside, any claims the practice makes would seem to be self-endorsing and unchallengeable. This does seem to imply a form of irrationalism, for either the individual is outside the practice and cannot criticise it or she is inside it and *ex hypothesi* will not want to. This objection is based on a misunderstanding of the notion of a practice. Furthermore, it confuses logically unanswerable criticism and criticism *tout court*, and while the former does not exist, there is no barrier to the latter. Neither the person who defends ethics nor someone who attacks it are immune from criticism, but any criticism is necessarily part of the substantive controversy. If someone criticises ethics as an elaborate piece of human self-deception, it is no defence for the moralist to say that it is logically possible to hold her view. If she wants to participate in the debate, she must try to explain why she holds her view and why she believes the rival account is wrong. It will not, however, be a matter of proving her position or refuting that of her opponent, but of trying to convince the other person of the correctness of a particular view. And, of course, there is always the possibility that neither party will convince the other. The debate will come to an end and, although each party should recognise that the other's view is logically possible, each may continue to maintain that the other is wrong.

The underlying source of difficulty here is our commitment to an idea of rationality that is incoherent. We want the chain of reasons and explanations to go on indefinitely or if not, to end in a super-reason which somehow justifies itself and so rules out the possibility of anyone rejecting it. When the force of this incoherent demand is turned on ethics and is not met, there is a temptation to see this as showing that ethics is incoherent or unfounded. The incoherence, however, is in the demand itself and on this impossible test rejecting ethics fails just as much as affirming it. When the anti-moralist concludes that ethical claims are a delusion, she is making exactly the same logical move as the moralist. Neither position is adopted arbitrarily, but neither has some sort of magical self-justifying property which compels assent on pain of making a logical error. If we ask whether both positions are reasonable, the answer depends on what the word 'reasonable' is taken to mean. On the one hand, it is clear that after much thought some human beings have reached one conclusion and some, the other. For this reason few people would want to say that either position was frivolous or stupid. On the other hand, it would make no sense to suggest that both positions were reasonable in the sense of being justified, for this would be to endorse both positions simultaneously. In this sense, to ask which position is reasonable is to stop describing the two positions and start assessing them.

This comment brings us back to a fundamental point, for in relation to the questions raised by ethics there is no avoiding the need to take a substantive stance. To demand an independent position from which the validity of one or other position is unequivocally clear is simply another way of demanding that logical or conceptual argument resolve the issue for us. The demand for an independent view is the demand for a super-reason, the fantasy of a way of understanding the world which justifies itself by logic alone. When this demand cannot be met (which by its nature it cannot), the temptation is to conclude that there are simply different ways of understanding the world and that none of them is right or wrong. What is not recognised, however, is that this apparent truism is itself a substantive view: it rules out the moral idea that there is a correct way of assessing human action. But the impossibility of grounding the moral approach in a super-reason does not show that the equally unprovable opposite approach is correct.

Against this background we can see that our initial dismissal of the notion of correctness in ethics rested on a flawed understanding of the logic of moral judgements. Modern philosophers have properly emphasised that empirical and moral judgements are different in type, the first describing how the world is, the second relating to how we should act. Quite rightly, they argue that since 'Grass is green' and 'Murder is wrong' are different types of propositions, they cannot be true in the same sense. From this, however, there is a tendency to conclude that moral judgements cannot be true or correct in any sense. In this way the distinguishing feature of moral judgements (the claim to correctness) is treated as bogus. This is mistaken; what needs to be recognised is that the claim to correctness does not have the same meaning here as it does in relation to empirical judgements. The point

35

is that while the notion of independent standards against which our judge-ments can be checked is inherent in the idea of empirical judgements that describe the way things are, this is not the case in relation to judgements on human action. Here, it is quite coherent to claim that all the individual can do is express a particular point of view and that as such all points of view are on a par. What is distinctive about ethical positions, however, is their rejection of this idea. The moralist claims that there are correct judgements on human action. She claims that there are judgements everyone should make or, to put it the other way round, she denies that all judgements on human action are simply the expression of a particular individual's pre-ferences or dispositions. This is the fundamental issue on which the two parties disagree, but there is no scope for an independent resolution of it.

The above remarks show how our reluctance to accept that reasons come to an end stands in the way of our understanding ethics. For modern philosophers, however, there is a further problem, for certain cultural trends favour an approach which by implication rules out ethical claims. Ironically, this itself provides a further illustration of the possibility of conflict at bedrock. These trends reflect the tremendous success of science and lead to the general assumption that all phenomena including human behaviour can be explained in causal terms. The work of Freud, on the one hand, and that of neurologists etc., on the other, have encouraged the idea that the causal approach should be extended to the analysis of human behaviour, so that a human being is effectively treated as a complex machine.

It is not clear how this approach can be harmonised with intentionality or indeed with the rationality implicit in the notion of thought itself; what is clear, however, is that it is at odds with ethical thinking. If we hold that the individual's beliefs on human action are simply the causal product of her background, it makes no sense to suggest that there are beliefs everyone ought to have. Similarly, it would be strange to urge everyone to seek to act in accordance with a particular set of standards if we believed that the individual's behaviour was in fact causally determined by her dispositions. In short, seeing human action entirely in causal terms makes understanding ethics impossible, for the latter is premised on the idea that people are capable of recognising right and wrong (as opposed to causally acquiring certain views) and that in principle everyone can and should act on this recognition.

We shall consider the causal approach further in Chapter 6, but for the moment it is sufficient to note that it is one type of substantive view that rejects the distinctive moral claim that there are correct and incorrect ways of acting. Whatever its merits or demerits, this view is a party to the substantive conflict rather than a neutral observer of it. The tendency of modern philosophers to reject ethics[6] can therefore be seen partly as reflecting a misunderstanding of ethical claims and partly as expressing the genuine conviction that such views are out of date and unacceptable. It is part of the confusion, however, that substantive views are mixed up with logical or conceptual analysis, so that a type of claim modern philosophers reject is presented as no claim at all, i.e. as incoherent.

To put the above argument in context it is important to note that the issue of bedrock does not only arise in relation to ethics. On the contrary, the basic point applies generally. The logical possibility of rejection cannot be eliminated in relation to any substantive claim—if someone rejects all the reasons we can give in support of a particular claim, all we can do is reaffirm our belief in the claim's correctness and note that we consider the other person's approach to be wrong or misguided. Wittgenstein discusses this sort of issue in *On Certainty* but he focuses on claims that we share. He does this because his aim is to explore the idea that reasons come to an end even in relation to claims we all hold to be certain. Our stress on bedrock in relation to ethics, however, should not be taken to imply that the only area where real as opposed to potential clashes at bedrock occur is in relation to judgements on human action. There are a whole range of general claims where people disagree and where this disagreement does not necessarily reflect a lack of evidence but arises from different beliefs about the right way of understanding the world.

An obvious example of this kind of disagreement, and one we shall discuss in more detail shortly, is religious belief; there are, however, many others. The variety of claims that are grouped together under the heading of the paranormal are examples of cases where what some people believe to be reasonable explanations are treated by others as obvious non-starters. Similarly, there is no agreement in our society on the question of whether there is life after death and there is no means of reaching agreement. The reasons people give for their beliefs on this issue, like any other reasons, come to an end. Not only do people disagree but they do not even agree on what 'evidence' might resolve the issue. Each party thinks the other party's approach to the issue is wrong, but there is no way of securing agreement on what the right approach is. In particular, there is nothing the two parties agree on that can be invoked as a means of resolving the argument.

To illustrate these points consider the case of a belief which we would all now reject, viz. the alchemist's belief that all metals are essentially the same substance and that it must therefore be possible to transform lead into gold. This is not a claim we can now take seriously. It belongs to a framework which we all reject and which is at odds with our whole approach to the investigation of the world. What the alchemists regarded as a possibility (the transmutation of lead into gold) is for us an absurdity. This does not mean, however, that belief in alchemy is no longer logically possible. Someone could reject the scientific approach we believe is correct and advocate a very different approach. We might claim that this alternative approach mixes empirical claims and misguided metaphysical principles, but then our approach, too, rests on certain non-empirical ideas, e.g. that every event has a cause and that causes operate in certain kinds of ways. The clash between our approach and that of the alchemist does not mean there could not be discussion, but any agreement would be contingent. In principle, there is no guarantee that we could convince someone that our approach (and the knowledge it generates) is correct.

To make these points, however, is not to suggest that alchemy may in fact be correct. We believe that our scientific theories are right. This is our assessment of the truth of the matter. If we explained what we know to an alchemist (gave her our reasons for rejecting her claim), she may or may not accept that we are right. The logical possibility of disagreement is not, however, a reason for us to hesitate. We can maintain that we are right despite it being logically possible to say that we are wrong. Furthermore, we do distinguish between issues we consider genuinely debatable and those we do not. We may accept that our current state of knowledge leaves open the question of whether the universe will expand indefinitely, but the question of alchemy we consider resolved. What for the alchemists is an insight is for us an indication of a primitive or misguided understanding of the world.

This brief discussion underlines the general importance of the notion of bedrock, for if a claim is substantive, it must be logically possible both to affirm and to deny it. Although we can offer reasons for the claims we make, it is always possible to reject these. These logical possibilities, however, are not a basis for doubt nor do they call into question our claims to knowledge. Our knowledge claims are claims we make, but we make them because we are satisfied they are correct. If we came across a people who believed it was prudent to light fires before dawn to encourage the sun to rise, we would see them as foolish and as having a primitive and misguided understanding of the world. We might try to prevent them lighting fires and when the sun rises anyway explain to them that their views have been refuted. If, however, they continued to believe the fires were necessary and held that other special factors must have intervened to allow the sun to rise in this particular case, we may either continue trying to persuade them or simply treat them as hopelessly benighted. In disputes about ethics the situation is essentially the same. If two groups of people (or two individuals) disagree on the fundamental question as to whether there are objective values (or on specific questions about what those values are), they may try to persuade each other, but if neither succeeds, they will continue to see each other's actions as misguided and each other's way of understanding the world as wrong.

The case of religious belief may seem to conflict with some aspects of this account, for while it underlines the possibility of disagreement at bedrock, it may seem to call into question any distinction between claims about the world and claims about how people should act. Acquiring a belief in God is not a two-stage process whereby the individual first raises the question of whether a certain being exists and then ponders her attitude to that being. In fact, coming to believe in God's existence simultaneously involves embracing particular moral views about the duties we owe this being. The points we have been making, however, do not involve claiming that questions about what exists and questions about how we should act must be treated separately. On the contrary, an individual's understanding of the world will bring together both types of claim. Just as a religious understanding of the world involves beliefs about the world and about how people should act, acceptance of a rather different type of understanding of the world may combine the belief that consciousness is a chance product of evolution with the belief that there are no correct judgements about how people should act. (It is worth noting, however, that it would be possible to hold that the world was created and yet deny that there were correct ways of acting,[7] or hold that consciousness was a chance product of evolution but that all conscious beings should recognise certain actions as wrong.)

These different views illustrate the scope for disagreement at bedrock, but they also indicate why it might be difficult for the individual to formulate specific reasons as to why she believes what she does. As Wittgenstein notes in relation to religious belief,

> Life can educate one to a belief in God. And *experiences* too are what bring this about; but I don't mean visions and other forms of sense experience which show us the 'existence of this being', but, e.g., sufferings of various sorts. These neither show us God in the way a sense impression shows us an object, not do they give rise to *conjectures* about him. Experiences, thoughts,—life can force this concept on us.
>
> (*Culture and Value,* p. 86)

It would be misguided, however, to argue that if suffering, for example, leads people to believe in God, this belief must be an illusion, a product of their needs rather than something that reflects reality. The individual does not select this belief as the most comforting, trick herself into forgetting the selection process and then start holding it. Rather, her experiences convince her that this is the right way to understood the world. If she should later change her mind and takes a different view, this would not show that adopting a view was an arbitrary process or that all views were equal. It would simply underline the obvious points that reaching a conclusion on such fundamental issues is a difficult matter and that any conclusion is permanently open to revision.

These points can be illustrated by considering the idea of a miracle, for, as Wittgenstein argued in his lecture on ethics, even the most extraordinary event is not in itself miraculous. If one of his listeners had suddenly grown a lion's head and roared, this would not necessarily have to be seen as a miracle.

Whenever we should have recovered from our surprise, what I would suggest would be to fetch a doctor and have the case scientifically investigated and if it were not for hurting him I would have him vivisected. And where would the miracle have got to? For it is clear that when we look at it in this way everything miraculous has disappeared; unless what we mean by this term is merely that a fact has not yet been explained by science which again means that we have hitherto failed to group this fact with others in a scientific system. This shows that it is absurd to say 'Science has proved that there are no miracles'. The truth is that the scientific way of looking at a fact is not the way to look at it as a miracle. For imagine whatever fact you may, it is not in itself miraculous in the absolute sense of that term.

(*Philosophical Occasions 1912–1951*, p. 43)

The point is that invoking the notion of a miracle involves accepting a certain way of understanding the world. Someone who claims that a miracle has occurred is underlining the special impression a particular event made on her—the fact that it impressed her as a sign from God.

So how should we assess this claim? The nature of the issue at stake rules out the idea that it can be resolved by a straightforward appeal to the evidence, for any evidence has to be interpreted. The person who spoke of a miracle knows that other explanations are possible, or, if none are immediately apparent, that they may one day emerge, but despite this she is convinced that the event had a quite different significance. This reaction may seem foolish to some, but it would be wrong to claim that it is confused or irrational. It would also be misguided to argue that, since the individual's belief could be mistaken, it stands in need of further support. At some stage the individual must decide whether or not she believes that God exists and has intervened in the world in this particular case. She cannot as it were insist that every divine communication is backed up by another confirming its validity and so on ad infinitum.[8] Reasons come to an end, both for those who accept the miracle and those who deny it. The same applies in relation to acceptance or rejection of the possibility of miracles in general, for the belief that every event has a (physical) cause is part of a certain way of understanding the world and is as open to challenge as the religious believer's claim that God exists.[9]

This treatment of religious belief contrasts with that of many contemporary philosophers who seem to think religion can be dismissed without much argument. Bernard Williams, for example, rejects out of hand the idea that we should see the correct judgements on human action as a set of laws or commands sanctioned by the promised punishments or rewards of God. Although he agrees that this account would give us a reason to act morally, he claims that we 'know that it could not be true—*could* not be true, since if we understand anything about the world at all, we understand that it is not run like that' (*Ethics and the Limits of Philosophy,* p. 32). This is an interesting claim, for even if we agree with it, the question arises as to how we know that it is true. In fact, Williams is making precisely the sort of bedrock appeal that we have been discussing; he is so sure that this way of understanding the world is incorrect that he cannot begin to list the reasons against it. In his opinion it is just obviously wrong. If someone persists in maintaining this view, all he can say is that she has an understanding of the world which he believes is crude and misguided. The nature of the issue makes such confrontations inevitable. We cannot prove that it is wrong to view the world in these terms or that our view is correct, but this does not mean that we should conclude either that adopting one view rather than the other is an arbitrary matter or that 'objectively' there is nothing at stake between them.

At this stage it may seem that we have exposed the weak point in our argument, for if we can reject a moral view as wrong because it is crude, this might seem to indicate that adjudicating between moral views is simply a matter of assessing our reactions. In fact, this is the point Williams makes against religious belief. Noting that many Christians would reject the notion of God as schoolmaster-in-chief as crude, he claims that this admission is fatal to religion in general.

> If ethical understanding is going to develop, and if religion is going to understand its own development in relation to that, it seems inevitable that it must come to understand itself as a human construction; if it does, it must in the end collapse.
>
> (ibid., p. 33)

The same point would apply to ethics with the same negative consequences. The argument, however, is flawed. Describing a way of understanding the world as crude or superficial is one way of expressing our rejection of it, but this does not imply that there is no correct way of understanding the world. Williams, for example, clearly sees the God-as-schoolmaster conception as a product of fear rather than as a potentially correct account of reality. He rejects this approach because he believes it has the wrong basis or, to put it another way, because he is convinced by another account of the world which includes an explanation of how this conception might arise. However, a religious believer might see this conception as a crude version of the truth. In her view this conception is wrong not because it uses the concept God in its account of the world but because it is crude in moral terms. Indeed, she might even see it as irreligious insofar as God's power rather than his Goodness is seen as the reason everyone has to obey Him. *Pace* Williams, therefore, the fact that we use such words as crude or superficial in rejecting

41

ways of understanding the world does not mean that we believe *all* conceptions of the world are mere human constructions. If we reject the God-as-schoolmaster conception as wrong, it is because we (like Williams) believe that a different way of understanding the world is correct.

This criticism of Williams brings out the way in which his position rests on a double standard, for, while religious and ethical conceptions of the world are seen as human constructions in a derogatory sense, the picture of the world as a purposeless interaction of causes is taken to be simply true. This is confused. There is nothing to stop Williams advancing any particular set of substantive claims, but it is misguided to suggest that other views can be rejected on conceptual or philosophical grounds. Similarly, it would be wrong to claim that empirical investigation can resolve these issues. Williams suggests that what we have found out about the world rules out religious (and, it would seem, moral) views, but it makes no sense to treat the question of God's existence (or the question of whether there are correct ways of acting) as akin to an empirical issue such as whether black swans exist. Religious belief (and belief in right and wrong) raises issues which go beyond the shared framework of beliefs which govern our day-to-day claims about the world and no discoveries within that framework can resolve the issue one way or another.

The scope for disagreement here relates to claims both about what exists and about how we should act. In principle, there is no series of events or discoveries that could force everyone to recognise that God existed, but even if something occurred that did convince everyone of the existence of a phenomenally powerful being, there would still be a question as to whether it was God in a religious sense, i.e. an infinitely good being everyone ought to worship. In such a situation, some might claim that it was our duty to worship this being. Others might claim that it was our duty not to worship it.[10] While others might persist in claiming that there is no correct response and that any claims about how people should act simply express the preferences or the dispositions of the person who makes them.[11]

Williams' approach to religious belief ignores these points and illegitimately rules out views that are logically possible. He tries to use the large degree of agreement in our society on the framework for investigating reality to establish a particular way of understanding the world which excludes both a belief in God and a belief in right and wrong. It is not the case, however, that everyone agrees with the conception of the world that Williams assumes is correct. Furthermore, even those who largely agree with his account of the world may not accept his claim that all judgements about human action are essentially the expression of individual preferences/dispositions. This is a further substantive claim and no empirical evidence nor any philosophical analysis could establish its correctness. If Williams sees religion (ethics) as a crutch for those who cannot accept that God does not exist (that values are not objective), his opponents may see his position as a crutch for someone who cannot accept the reality of God's existence (the burden of duties and responsibilities that are incumbent on everyone).

The example of religious belief underlines the possibility of disagreement at bedrock. Answers to questions about how we should understand the world and how we should live cannot be resolved by logic or by an appeal to agreed 'facts'. Rather, the individual puts forward the view she believes to be correct based on what she has thought and experienced. Where individuals disagree, there is no independent way of resolving the disagreement. It may happen that one persuades the other or it may not. This conclusion may seem deeply unsatisfactory in a work of philosophy, but on one level it is entirely unsurprising. Indeed, with the end of metaphysics most philosophers have recognised that the question of how we should make sense of the world cannot be definitively answered by some philosophical theory. It is ironic, therefore, that many then proceed to treat the claim that the world has no objective meaning, and the claim that there are no correct ways of acting, as philosophically or scientifically proven. By contrast, our account makes clear that taking up any position on these matters involves a substantive move which others can always challenge. On these questions the philosopher speaks not as an expert, but as a human being, and for that reason her opinion has no greater or lesser call on public attention than anyone else's.

Philosophy's 'failure' is not so much a defeat as the waking from an impossible dream, for insofar as these questions do have answers these cannot be given in a way that is beyond dispute. The naiveté of the opposing suggestion is in some ways comic:

> I read '. . . philosophers are no nearer to the meaning of 'Reality' than Plato got, . . .'. What a strange situation. How extraordinary that Plato could have got even as far as he did! Or that we could not get any further! Was it because Plato was so *extremely* clever?
>
> (*Culture and Value,* p. 13)

What philosophy can do is clarify the logical structure of our concepts and identify the real issues which face us. It can neither prove nor disprove the idea that there is a right and wrong, but it can work to untangle the many confusions thrown up when, rather than just employing this idea, we seek to reflect on what it means.

To underline the points we have made, it is worth considering the very different view put forward by Alasdair MacIntyre in *After Virtue* and other writings. In his opinion 'the most striking feature of contemporary moral utterance is that so much of it is used to express disagreements; and the most striking feature of the debates in which these disagreements are exposed is their interminable character' (*AV,* p. 6). He notes that these arguments invoke incommensurable concepts, pitting talk of rights against claims of justice or the notion of liberty against that of equality, and he argues that they are interminable because in our society there is no recognised way of deciding between such claims. Despite this, the claims made purport to be objective. As he points out, our moral judgements presuppose 'the existence of *impersonal* criteria—the existence, independently of the preferences and attitudes of the speaker and hearer, of standards of justice or generosity or duty' (*AV*, p. 9).

In MacIntyre's view this presupposition is not justified. Since in our society there are no rational ways of resolving moral arguments, the appeal to independent standards must be seen as spurious. The distinction between moral judgements and preferences collapses, and it is therefore not surprising that the doctrine of emotivism which denies that distinction flourishes. Although he believes that the language of moral judgements is indelibly objectivist, MacIntyre claims that the way in which we use that language is emotivist. His explanation of this gap is the loss of the shared rational criteria which once justified the notion of objectivity. In default of these criteria our moral language and our moral practices are radically flawed. People who make moral judgements believe they are appealing to independent impersonal criteria, but all they are in fact doing is expressing their feelings to others in a manipulative way (*AV*, p. 13).

This argument involves several confusions. At its heart is the claim that the absence of rational ways of resolving moral argument fatally undermines the claim to objectivity which is implicit in our moral concepts. As we have tried to show, this is not the case. The widespread existence of disagreement about how people should act does not undermine the claim that there are correct ways of acting. By treating disagreement as a sign of conceptual catastrophe, MacIntyre conflates the logical possibility of disagreement with the contemporary problem of social fragmentation. This confusion is sustained by a misguided rationalism, for he runs together the notions of objective criteria and of rational criteria, insisting that, unless we can prove the validity of moral claims, the idea that only one position is correct will be shown to be misguided. This does not follow. Someone who claims that there are correct ways of acting (or claims that a specific type of action is wrong) cannot prove this claim, but this does not show that her claim is incorrect. As we have seen, neither those who claim that there are ways everyone should act nor those who claim that all judgements on human action are essentially the expression of preferences can prove their positions, but this does not mean that their disagreement is not real. On the contrary, each side has a substantive position and can try to persuade the other that it is correct.

Thus what MacIntyre calls interminability is not the result of some feature of moral discourse specific to our society; rather, the logical possibility of disagreement is a necessary feature of any substantive claim. Even in a homogenous society the reasons that can be given in support of the claim that there are correct ways of acting (and in support of particular moral judgements) come to an end. It is a mistake, therefore, to suggest that our moral claims are incoherent because they cannot fulfil the nonsensical condition of its being logically impossible to reject them. In elaborating his own position MacIntyre makes a further mistake, for he identifies rational criteria with socially agreed criteria, so that resolving the clash between incommensurable concepts is no longer seen as irrational if there are socially-agreed ways of doing so. From a logical point of view, however, social agreement is irrelevant.[12] The logical status of a particular view is not changed by the number of people who hold it, or their percentage size in society. If the absence of logically unchallengeable criteria did undermine the idea of objectivity in ethics, this would be true regardless of whether a society was homogeneous and never experienced moral disagreement or was fragmented as ours is and regularly had to cope with it.

MacIntyre, however, believes that if moral claims cannot be proved, they must be arbitrary. He argues that 'if we possess no unassailable criteria, no set of compelling reasons by means of which we may convince our opponents, it follows that in the process of making up our own minds we can have made no appeal to such criteria or such reasons. If I have no good reasons to invoke against you, it must seem that I lack any good reasons' (AV, p. 8). This is misguided, for it makes incoherent demands of what is to count as a good reason. The idea of unassailable criteria makes no sense and it is not one the moralist is committed to. The claim that pornography is degrading to women offers what many believe is a good reason for restricting or prohibiting its sale, but it is not a reason which everyone is logically compelled to accept. The arguments for it do not go on for ever nor do they end in some magical super-reason no one can reject. The anti-pornography campaigner does not hold that rejecting this claim is logically impossible; rather she holds that rejecting it is wrong and that failure to accept it is a failure to treat women as they ought to be treated. This example shows what is wrong with MacIntyre's argument, for he takes the existence of moral disagreement to indicate that our judgements on human action are mere expressions of preference. This is precisely what the moralist denies. In doing this, however, she does not have to claim that reason or reality forces us to accept certain reasons. Rather, she makes the contestable but coherent claim that there are certain reasons everyone ought to accept.

MacIntyre's rationalism prevents him from recognising these points. He believes that the claim to correctness is an aspiration to rationality (AV, p. 9) and holds that the appeal to independent standards is only sustainable if rejecting moral claims can be shown to be incompatible with rationality. This skews the argument against the moralist, for MacIntyre insists she prove that the standards she appeals to are indeed independent and when she cannot do this, concludes that her claims are merely manipulative. This illustrates how much he shares both with the emotivists who criticised moral claims and with the philosophers he sees as trying to give morality rational foundations.

45

As he rightly notes, the latter project 'had to fail'; the reason for this, however, was not some distant conceptual catastrophe, but the incoherence of the project itself. The point is that any chain of reasons must come to an end and at that stage a claim is made which must be accepted or rejected. Since this substantive move is a logical necessity, it makes no sense to see its occurrence as a flaw or failure. The individual cannot prove that her moral judgements are not merely a manipulative attempt to impose her preferences on others, but this does not undermine her claim that there are standards everyone should recognise. In relation to any specific moral judgement all she can do is try to convince the other person that the judgement she makes is one that everyone should make and that it should not be treated merely as a reaction she happens to have. What she cannot do is fulfil the impossible task of providing the claim that her view is correct (and ought to be held by everyone) with some support which it is logically impossible to reject.

The extent to which MacIntyre agrees with the emotivists who explicitly rejected ethics can be illustrated by considering his criticism of G.E. Moore's intuitionism. Moore claims that 'good' is the name of a simple, indefinable property which the individual detects in states of affairs, and he holds that propositions which declare something to be good are 'incapable of proof or disproof and indeed [that] no evidence or reasoning may be adduced in their favour or disfavour' (*AV*, p. 14). According to MacIntyre this doctrine is plainly false, and when it is welcomed by Keynes as the beginning of a renaissance, MacIntyre describes this as great silliness. He then claims that when the Bloomsbury group actually discussed ethics, what was going on was manipulation rather than the appeal to independent standards. As Keynes himself recognised, victory went to whoever could speak with the greatest appearance of clear undoubting conviction; the weapons of battle were Moore's gasps of incredulity and head-shaking, Strachey's grim silences and Lowes Dickinson's shrugs.

MacIntyre takes all of this as evidence for his thesis that the rise of emotivism reflects the emptiness of intuitionism, and he may be right to accuse intuitionism of philosophical naiveté and the Bloomsbury group of self-indulgent posturing. His overall analysis, however, is confused. What he and the emotivists find offensive about intuitionism is the idea that moral judgements cannot be given a foundation, and yet as we have seen, this is one way of expressing an important and valid point. Someone who believes that hurting people is wrong may try to convince other people that this claim is correct but she cannot prove it. Furthermore, if her attempts at persuasion fail, she does not have to retract her claim that this principle ought to be accepted by everyone. The claim that goodness is a non-natural property may be a poor way of making this point, but it seems plausible to suggest that the idea that a moral judgement involves a substantive claim which cannot be further justified was at least part of what Moore was trying to get at. Certainly it enables us to understand better why people such as Keynes welcomed intuitionism as a release, for it is right to emphasise that ethics is not a matter of rationality or of metaphysics but of the individual making the correct judgement.

In contrast to Moore, the emotivists claimed that the impossibility of proof undermines the idea that the individual is making a judgement as opposed to merely expressing a preference, and for all his opposition to emotivism MacIntyre endorses this part of their argument. His summary of the position is illuminating:

> what emotivism asserts is in central part that there are and can be *no* valid rational justification for any claims that objective and impersonal moral standards exist and hence that there are no such standards. Its claim is of the same order as the claim that it is true of all cultures whatsoever that they lack witches. Purported witches there may be, but real witches there cannot have been, for there are none. So emotivism holds that purported rational justifications there may be, but real rational justifications there cannot have been, for there are none.
>
> (*AV*, p. 18)

The error here lies in the misguided notion of rational justification, but this is an error that MacIntyre shares with the emotivists. Both want the moralist to prove that there are correct ways of acting, and in the absence of such proof they claim that moral discourse can only be manipulation. What they fail to recognise is that the claim that there are no correct ways of acting is an unprovable as the claim that there are.

MacIntyre's failure to understand the logic of moral claims is illustrated by his reference in the above quotation to witches, for this suggests that the existence of moral standards can be compared to the existence of a type of being or thing. Later, this doubt is reinforced when with characteristic vigour he dismisses the notion of human rights: 'the truth is plain: there are no such rights, and belief in them is one with belief in witches and unicorns' (*AV*, p. 67). The point, however, is that the claim that people have rights is not similar to the assertion that a certain kind of thing exists; rather, it is the way certain people express their view on how human beings should be treated. MacIntyre supports his attack on the notion of human rights by arguing that no one has offered rationally compelling arguments for their existence, and he takes it as a tacit admission of defeat that their defenders have claimed that it is a self-evident truth that human beings possess them. His reference to logically compelling arguments, however, is confused, while his opponent's talk of self-evident truths is a reflection of the fact that reasons come to an end. If someone rejects the idea that people have a right not to be tortured, there may be little we can say to her to convince her that this claim is correct.[13] No amount of explanation or justification can abolish the substantive move contained in taking up a particular moral position; the fact, however, that it will always be logically possible for someone to challenge that move shows neither that it is irrational nor that it is arbitrary. Unless we abandon such rationalist assumptions, understanding moral claims is impossible.

Against the background of these points it is ironic that MacIntyre sees himself as a defender of ethics. Although he believes that most contemporary moral claims are conceptually confused, he does not think that such claims as necessarily misguided. On the contrary, he believes that moral theory and practice can 'embody genuine objective and impersonal standards which provide rational justification for particular policies, actions and judgements and which themselves are in turn susceptible of rational justification' (*AV*, p. 18). His purpose, therefore, is constructive. His books are an attempt to repair our concepts after the conceptual catastrophe he believes has occurred; their aim is to lay the ground for a rational form of moral discourse.

At the heart of MacIntyre's positive account are the virtues, but he explains these in terms of three other concepts—that of a quest, a practice and a tradition. The virtues are what enable an individual to advance in her quest for the Good, a practice to flourish and a tradition to prosper. Furthermore, these three elements tie in closely with each other. MacIntyre argues that the individual's quest for the Good will necessarily involve participation in practices which he defines as complex forms of social activity with internal goods whose pursuit systematically extends human powers to achieve excellence and human conceptions of the ends and goods involved (*AV*, p. 175). Similarly, he holds that this participation must take place within the context of an ongoing tradition which structures the individual's choice between practices and shapes her understanding of the Good in a way no specific practice could. The virtues are those excellencies which are necessary for success in these three related contexts, and MacIntyre believes that we therefore all have reason to acquire them. Furthermore, at any one time and within a specific tradition, a particular understanding of the virtues will provide rational criteria according to which moral issues can be judged.

The motor for this account is MacIntyre's wish to eliminate (or at least reduce) the scope for disagreement about judgements on human action. His first task, therefore, is to show that everyone has a reason to be moral. To this end he argues that every individual must strive to give her life narrative unity and that this requires cultivation of the virtues. He also claims that enjoyment of the internal goods of at least some practices is crucial to every human life and that the cultivation of the virtues is necessary for this too. These claims seek to rule out conflict on the question of whether people should act morally; they do not, however, tackle the issue of disagreement between rival moral views. MacIntyre seeks to deal with this problem by using the third element in his account—the notion of a tradition. He argues that coherent moral judgements are only possible within a living tradition and he seems to accept that various traditions may coexist within a society; indeed, to some extent he welcomes healthy competition between them.

One striking aspect of this account is that its first two elements point in a slightly different direction from the third, for while the former parallel traditional attempts to deduce ethics from rationality, the latter hints at the possibility of multiple 'valid' moralities and suggests that the real aim is finding a social solution to the problem of disagreement. Implicitly abandoning the attempt to prove that certain ways of acting are correct, this part of MacIntyre's account has the more limited objective of finding an alternative to 'subjective' ways of judging human action. Not surprisingly, what this leads to are socially agreed ways of judging. However, the motivation for this move is misguided, while the move itself simply avoids the real issue which is the claim that there are correct ways of acting. Furthermore, MacIntyre's confusions about objectivity and rationality leave his argument full of tensions. As a liberal he is keen to maximise the individual's freedom, but he also wants to eliminate disagreement and is therefore tempted to place constraints on what individuals can and cannot believe. On the one hand, he argues that the individual is free to search for the Good as she pleases. On the other hand, he claims that the parameters of her quest are given by the traditions within which she finds herself. While his project involves moving away from the idea of one correct morality and hints at the idea of various traditions, his commitment to rationality leads him to favour the idea that ultimately one tradition must be right.

To underline these points it is necessary to consider MacIntyre's argument in detail and the best place to start is with his claim that human lives are essentially narratives. This claim forms part of his attempt to show that ethics cannot be rejected. Discounting empiricist and existentialist conceptions of the self, MacIntyre claims that 'the self inhabits a character whose unity is given as the unity of a character' (*AV*, p. 202). If we ask about the success or failure of someone's life, it must be in these terms, and this therefore provides a basis for objective judgements about what is good for a particular individual. 'What is better or worse for X depends on the character of the intelligible narrative which provides X's character with its unity' (*AV*, p. 209).

This approach may seem reasonable, but its apparent reasonableness conceals a mass of ambiguities. The notion of narrative unity is presented first as a necessary feature of human life, then as a task the individual must strive to complete. MacIntyre bases the claim that our lives are narratives on various uncontroversial points about human action; later, however, he treats the claim not as a description of certain features of human life but as a disguised injunction to give priority to unifying one's life in a particular way. Eliminating this ambiguity creates problems whichever way it is done. On the one hand, if narrative unity is treated as an inescapable feature of intentional action, the search for it cannot guide the individual in her choices: all it excludes are actions which we cannot see as intentional in the normal sense, e.g. the actions of the mad. On the other hand, if the notion of unity is given some content, it is not clear why the individual has to want a unified life and it is certainly not clear why she has to make the search for this unity her top priority.

The relation of this approach to ethics is also unclear. Consider the situation of a bad person on her deathbed who has a last chance to do good. MacIntyre's argument could be called upon to justify any number of possibilities, but none of them are distinctively ethical. On the one hand, if all that is at stake is the possibility of ascribing an intention to the agent, any action she chooses will form part of a possible narrative. On the other hand, if the notion of narrative unity is treated as contentful, different actions will follow depending on the particular content we favour. It could be argued that acting badly would be most consistent with other choices she has previously made. Alternatively, it might be argued that a deathbed change of heart would tie in with earlier doubts and offer a more interestingly unified narrative. These different goals—that of a consistent life or of one that forms an interesting narrative—seem neither unavoidable nor particularly edifying. If anything, the criteria seem more aesthetic than ethical, and the underlying suggestion seems to be that how the individual acts is up to her with no question of any choice being objectively right or wrong.

Against this, MacIntyre might argue that the individual in our example should act in the way she believes to be right, and he might explain this by arguing that by definition only this action would give unity to her life in terms of her current understanding of the search for the Good. This does restore the ethical element to MacIntyre's account but at the cost of undermining his emphasis on narrative unity. The claim that the individual should try to give unity to her search for the Good turns out to mean that she should do what she thinks is right. This brings us straight back to the notion of correctness which MacIntyre tries to avoid.

MacIntyre supplements his argument in terms of narrative unity with an argument based on the notion of a practice. What attracts him to this notion is the fact that participation in a practice is dependent on the individual's acceptance of rules and criteria she herself does not determine. The other aspect of a practice that interests him is the notion of internal goods, that is to say, the pleasures that are specific to that practice. It is these goods that lead the individual to participate in the practice and justify her acceptance of its rules. These goods hold out the possibility of justifying virtuous action, for MacIntyre believes that the virtues are necessary for practices to flourish and that therefore everyone who wants the internal goods which practices provide has a reason for cultivating the virtues. Furthermore, he argues if practices are to flourish, the virtues must be cultivated for their own sake. Boldness in desperation is not true courage and reluctantly submitting to the just demands of a more powerful opponent is not true justice. In this way the internal goods of a practice seem to provide a rational justification of virtuous action; magically the notion of a practice seems to show that the individual's pursuit of her own good requires virtuous and, on occasion, heroic action. Since the notion of practice is deliberately drawn as widely as possible, it seems likely that all normal human beings will be participants in some practice or other. In that case, MacIntyre will have shown that we all have reason to cultivate the virtues even if the exact conception of those virtues may vary in relation to different practices and between different traditions.

The magnitude of this proof might itself give pause for thought and it would surely be surprising if rejection of the virtues turned out to be rationally impossible. The argument, however, is flawed. One way to bring this out is to note that in principle an individual might decide she was only interested in external goods such as money, fame or power, so the argument would not apply to her at all. In itself this is not a fundamental point, but it brings out the sense in which MacIntyre's argument is ultimately an appeal to desire. Internal goods are still goods and, although pursuit of them may require the suppression of other desires, pursuing them is still a matter of the individual seeking to maximise her satisfaction. What is being put forward, therefore, is no longer an account of how it is correct to act but an account of how people with certain types of desire will want to act. Ironically, the attempt to prove that we should all be ethical produces an account which is not ethical and which need not apply to everyone. To avoid making substantive claims about what is correct, MacIntyre has to base his argument on preferences and, although he chooses something he thinks everyone happens to want, this strategy affects the status of his argument.

Thus, even if MacIntyre's argument worked, it would not show that acting virtuously was the correct thing to do, but that it was good policy for those individuals who happen to value internal goods. Someone who happened not to want internal goods would have no reason to act morally.[14] This criticism can be extended, for even those who do want internal goods do not always have to make them their top priority. To take MacIntyre's favoured example, for most chess players part of the pleasure of chess is winning and there may therefore be occasions on which a player is prepared to use underhand means to succeed; she would like to play a good game and win, but she may prefer cheating to losing. In short, the internal good of participating in a good game of chess only gives a player a reason to resist the temptation to cheat when the pleasure she gets from being on the losing side of a good game outweighs the pain of losing it. If moral considerations are excluded, this may be true, but it is not an account of why everyone has a reason to be virtuous.

51

This point can be underlined by exploring MacIntyre's treatment of the virtues themselves, for his stress on internal goods (and more generally his attempt to justify ethics) conflicts with the distinguishing feature of moral action which is that the individual acts in a certain way because she believes that way is right and not for some other reason. Someone who acts justly because doing so will maximise her enjoyment of an internal good is not cultivating the virtues for their own sake. She is not acting justly because she believes this is the correct way of acting which should be recognised as such by everyone. In fact, what MacIntyre describes in connection with practices are not virtues but certain types of ability useful in achieving any goal. We may say that a chess player requires courage to follow through her plan, that carrying out the right plan requires patience and that she must justly recognise the merits of her opponent's moves. In none of these cases, however, are the 'virtues' exercised for their own sake. These statements simply amount to saying that chess-playing requires self-belief, self-discipline and a capacity for dispassionate analysis. These are abilities the chess player must cultivate but they are not virtues.[15]

In relation to the institutions that support a practice, there may seem to be a stronger argument in favour of truly virtuous action. It is not in the interests of the chess-playing practice that its governing bodies should be corrupt, and anyone who wants the game to flourish will want its administrators (and others) to act justly, be courageous, etc. More generally, it is plausible to suggest that any communal enterprise will be weakened by a lack of virtuous conduct on the part of those involved in it. MacIntyre therefore seems right to claim that if we want a practice to prosper, we must want the virtues to flourish in it. This version of the argument, however, is marred by a now-familiar flaw, for wanting the participants in our practices to be virtuous is not the same as wanting to be virtuous ourselves. The chess player may want chess administrators to be ready to make sacrifices for the good of the game, but this does not give her a reason to make genuine sacrifices herself. It remains the case that she will only have a reason to act justly where the internal goods she thereby gains are greater than the costs to her of the just action.

MacIntyre tries to avoid this problem by identifying the internal goods of a practice with the good of the practice itself, but this shift is not justified. Enjoying playing chess does not create a commitment to the good of the chess-playing practice as such. Any commitment is proportionate to the internal good the practices provides to that individual. This will rarely justify the sort of action taken by the genuinely virtuous, for the costs of such action will usually be greater than their benefits in increasing (or preserving) the individual's enjoyment of the internal goods of the practice. MacIntyre, however, assumes that, if an individual enjoys chess-playing, she must place the interests of the chess-playing practice above any other (selfish) considerations. This introduces action that is indeed virtuous, i.e. based on moral rather than prudential considerations, but this is at odds with the rest of the argument. We may all agree that the individual should act virtuously, even if those around her do not, but this is not because doing so will necessarily bring her internal or external goods, rather it is because we believe that this is the correct way to act. The point is that when it is a question of the virtues in a moral sense (i.e. the virtues exercised for their own sake), there is no alternative to substantive claims about this being the correct thing to do. Otherwise being honest or courageous, etc., simply means being able to tell the truth or be brave when this will best promote goals we happen to have.

The third strand in MacIntyre's argument seeks to use the concept of a tradition as a source of standards independent of the individual. As we suggested earlier, however, the motivation for this move is confused. On the one hand, standards do not become rational by being shared, and, on the other, there is nothing wrong with one individual advancing standards which she claims ought to be recognised by everyone but which are currently only accepted by her. The fact that she cannot prove that these standards should be accepted by everyone does not show that this claim is wrong, and if it did, this would undermine contingently shared standards just as much as those put forward by the lone individual.

What leads MacIntyre to ignore these points is his fear of disagreement; his use of the notion of a tradition, however, conceals rather than eliminates this problem. To imagine a society firmly united in a monolithic tradition is to imagine a society where disagreement happens not to exist, but this does not mean the moral standards of that society are less substantive than any other. The possibility of disagreement is not removed but simply hypo-thesised away. Even in such a society the possibility of disagreement remains not just in relation to the tradition as a whole but in relation to every claim within the tradition. There is scope for disagreement at the most general level (e.g. whether everyone ought always to act in a way that does not harm others) but also at every other level (e.g. whether telling 'white' lies harms others) right down to the most concrete (e.g. whether Jane was right to tell Jack that she was late because her car broke down). None of these possible disagreements can be resolved by an appeal to the evidence or by logical proof, and an appeal to the weight of historic opinion within some tradition as well as itself being controversial is beside the point. It makes no sense to say to the individual 'You cannot believe that everyone should act in this way because the tradition you belong to holds (or even all traditions in your society hold) that everyone should act in a different way'.

Against this, MacIntyre might argue that we are applying the notion of a tradition in too monolithic a way. In part this response illustrates the ambiguity of his approach, for at times he wants to use the notion of a tradition to abolish disagreement and at others to allow it in domesticated forms. At the start of *After Virtue*, any disagreement that cannot be resolved is condemned as irrational; later 'interminable' disagreements are allowed either as part of healthy debate within a tradition or as a debate between traditions. Some recognition that views differ is, of course, unavoidable, but this rather undermines the rest of the account. Suddenly it seems that disagreement is no longer a problem, for the notion of a tradition serves as an infinitely flexible way of invoking the past and so restoring to the individual the possibility of making claims about how it is correct to act. The cacophony of arbitrary claims is transformed into a dialogue of competing traditions, and this presentational switch is made more attractive by the vague suggestion that it may be possible to set limits to disagreement. The rationalist in MacIntyre consoles himself with the thought that one tradition must eventually emerge supreme; in the meantime it may be possible to silence the advocates of certain views with the spuriously factual claim that they are not part of a genuine tradition at all and therefore have no right to be heard.

A different facet of MacIntyre's conception of a tradition is his emphasis on the individual as the bearer of a particular social identity. He claims that every person is born into a set of social roles and that what is good for her has to be what is good for someone who inhabits those roles (*AV*, p. 205). Once again, the importance of this claim is that it seems to furnish impersonal standards, this time via the social conception of how someone in that role should act. Like his concept of a tradition in general, however, this idea has two contradictory functions, for it is intended both to constrain the individual and to give her complete freedom. MacIntyre recognises that the individual can reject the social conception of her role, noting that 'rebellion against my identity is always one possible way of expressing it' (ibid.). This admission reveals the emptiness of the argument; it is like limiting an individual's freedom by telling her she may move as far from a specific spot as she like as she long as she remains at some determinate distance from it. The advantage of the argument from MacIntyre's point of view is that the reference to society helps dispel his worries about the apparent subjectivity of any claim the individual might make. It seems that the individual's social role gives her a set of impersonal standards and that this impersonality is transferred to any standards by which she chooses to live her life as long as some connections of similarity or dissimilarity can be made between the two sets of standards. As before, MacIntyre's argument turns out to be an unsuccessful and unnecessary attempt to hide the issue of bedrock. The reference to society as a source of objectivity is empty and ultimately he is forced to recognise that the individual is not logically constrained by whatever social consensus may exist.

To underline these points it is interesting to contrast MacIntyre's position with that of Aristotle, whom he claims to follow. The central Aristotlean notion that Man has a *telos*, an essential nature to be realised, is rejected by MacIntyre as metaphysical biology, a confused attempt to do science conceptually. A better way of understanding this notion, however, is to see it as the expression of a substantive moral vision: on this account the good life as described by Aristotle is our *telos* not because we have an in-built biological impulse which causes us to seek it, but because it is the proper life for human beings. A person who exercises the virtues shows us the correct way to live and those who do not live this way do not deviate from some inherent biological norm but fail morally. To modern tastes, however, Aristotle's attempt to offer a definitive description of the good life may appear both naive and authoritarian. As a liberal, MacIntyre abandons the notion of *the* good life. Instead he suggests that there are many different types of good life and that it is up to the individual to define the good life for herself in her own personal quest for the Good.

The particular form of liberalism MacIntyre adopts creates fundamental differences between his account and Aristotle's; in particular, it has the consequence that the former is often not an ethical account at all. In place of the good life as the type of life a human being ought to live, MacIntyre sometimes suggests that the good life is whatever life the individual finds good, and this is clearly not an ethical view. At other times he suggests that the good life for human beings is a life spent searching for the Good. This may seem commendable insofar as it leaves it up to the individual to decide what her particular search will involve, but it also seems to imply that it is better to search than to find. Having rejected or ignored the notion of correctness, MacIntyre ends up endorsing whatever the individual does, provided she keeps travelling and never believes she has arrived. Here, fear of authoritarianism turns open-mindedness into the only absolute value. A less paradoxical liberal position would be based on the idea of autonomy and advance the moral claim that every individual has a right to decide the values according to which she will lead her life. It is important, however, to distinguish the claim that every individual has a right to decide for herself from the claim that whatever decision she makes will be right. Liberalism and subjectivism are not the same. The non-confused liberal respects the individual's right to choose but she does not claim that whatever the individual does will be right.

Another consequence of MacIntyre's liberalism is the fragmentation of the Good; in place of Aristotle's good life for Man, he offers the good life of the portrait painter, the chess player, the married person, etc. This move involves a dangerous ambiguity, for recognition of a plurality of goods can easily become an endorsement of a variety of pleasures. Instead of claiming that there are correct ways for human beings to act, we simply recognise that people get pleasure in different ways, e.g. by seeking different internal goods in different practices. For Aristotle, and for an ethical thinker, the virtuous life is a good life because the person who lives it is living as she ought; insofar as she lives virtuously she has every reason to be happy with her life. By contrast, MacIntyre avoids the distinctive ethical component (the claim to correctness) and seems to suggest that what is good about the good life is simply that the individual gets satisfaction from it.

Consider the example of Gauguin. On MacIntyre's account, when he has to choose between his wife and his art, the question is not 'What is the right thing to do?', but 'Which internal goods do I value higher—those of art or those of marriage?'. If creating great art means more to him than creating a great marriage, he will opt for Tahiti and show that for him that is where his Good lies. Here, the idea of acting in ways that are correct certainly seems to have been replaced by a process in which each individual assesses what will give her most satisfaction. It seems that nothing is Good but the individual's choosing makes it so. The suggestion that tradition will structure this choice does not change the situation, particularly since being guided by tradition includes rejecting it. In Gauguin's case, there may have been certain assessments of his situation which would have been more socially acceptable than others, but if he had stayed with his wife and invoked Aquinas, his decision would have been no more and no less rational than if he had left for Tahiti with an at-the-time barely comprehensible plea that his first duty was to his own artistic genius.

Looking at MacIntyre's position as a whole, it is clear that he is confused about the nature of moral claims. Having rejected traditional ethics on the basis of a misguided rationalism, he puts forward a series of expedients designed to eliminate the possibility of disagreement by linking moral claims to social agreement. The motivation for this is misguided, and the project itself is incoherent. Lack of clarity about the notion of correctness also means that MacIntyre is torn in different directions. For example, he is caught between his desire for proof and his liberalism with the result that he oscillates between forcing moral commitments onto the individual and offering her unmitigated freedom to seek her pleasure as she chooses. On the one hand, the individual must see her life as a narrative unified by the search for the Good, she must want to cultivate the virtues (since she wants internal goods) and she must place herself in relation to a tradition. On the other hand, any intentional action she chooses can be presented as part of the search for some good, the virtues turn out to be a set of capacities useful for achieving any ends and the individual's relation to her tradition can be anything from willing acceptance to total rejection. Similar confusions are apparent in MacIntyre's attempt to advance genuinely rational standards of moral action and debate. His identification of rationality and social acceptability leaves him caught between his emphasis on established social standards and his commitment to personal freedom. The more he rejects conventionalism, the clearer it becomes that what underlies any moral judgement is a claim to correctness, the offering of reasons for which comes to an end. Although MacIntyre seeks to hide the possibility of disagreement at bedrock, he cannot eliminate it, and while he fails to discuss the notion of correctness, he keeps being forced back to it insofar as he wants to keep his account distinctively ethical.

3

REASON AND MORAL
ARGUMENT

> Why do you demand explanations? If they are given you, you
> will once more be facing a terminus. They cannot get you any
> further than you are at present.
>
> (Wittgenstein, *Zettel*, para. 315)

In the previous chapter we tried to show how the moralist can combine a recognition that various views on how people should act are logically possible with the claim that only one view is correct. Compared with other philosophical accounts, this may seem a strange position, for, while many philosophers have claimed that the possibility of rational disagreement undermines the idea of objectivity in ethics, we have argued that the existence of disagreement is irrelevant to the issue of whether or not there are standards of conduct that should be recognised by everyone. On our account, what distinguishes ethical positions is the claim that the correct way of understanding the world involves recognising that there are correct ways of acting. This claim means what it says. It is not a claim that a certain type of entity exists; nor does it relate to what all rational beings qua rational beings must believe. The moralist does not hold that someone who rejects this claim is making a factual or a logical mistake, but rather that she is failing to accept something that should be accepted by everyone capable of thinking about the human situation.

As with any other substantive claim, the reasons that can be offered for the claim to correctness come to end: ultimately the individual must either accept or reject the idea that there are correct ways of acting. This is not to say that the individual can choose the position she prefers. On the contrary, ethical views are defined by their rejection of this idea, and our aim has been to clarify what this involves. As we saw in the case of MacIntyre, it is those who fail to recognise the nature of the claim to correctness in ethics who end up implying that judgements of human action are a matter of social or individual preference. In fact, this is an alternative way of raising the fundamental issue, for instead of asking 'Does the correct way of understanding the world involve recognising certain ways of acting as correct?', we could ask 'Are all judgements on human action simply the expression of different preferences or are there judgements that should be made by everyone?'. As this way of putting it illustrates, what is distinctive about ethics is not a claim about the kind of things that exist, but a claim about how we should understand the world and our relation to it.

One difficulty we face in making these points is that we are fighting on two fronts, for understanding ethics involves rejecting both rationalism and subjectivism. In fact, these apparent opposites go together, for both fight under the banner 'either proof or arbitrariness'. By contrast, a correct understanding of the notion of bedrock involves recognising that this dichotomy is false. The claim that everyone should recognise certain actions as wrong cannot be proved, but this does not show that it is incorrect. The opposing claim (that all judgements of human action are objectively equal) has exactly the same status, for it too cannot be proved. The point is that the individual has to make a substantive claim which she holds to be correct but with which it is logically possible to disagree. The same point applies to specific moral judgements. The question in relation to racism, for example, is not whether it is logically possible to hold this view but whether it is the correct assessment of how to treat people of different races. Someone who goes wrong here does not advance a claim that all rational beings qua rational beings *must* reject. Rather she adopts a view that it is claimed everyone *should* reject.

Recognising that reasons come to an end has implications for our understanding of all aspects of moral claims. For example, it involves abandoning the idea that the reasons we give for our moral views form a structure in which specific judgements are based on a succession of increasingly general claims, each of which is better supported than the previous one. In fact, once we recognise that our chains of reasons do not end in a super-reason that is beyond question, the notion of a chain is no longer appropriate. Consider a simple example. Suppose someone says a certain act is wrong and when asked why, explains that it would theft. When asked why theft is wrong, she explains that it is unfair on the person who is stolen from, and when asked why this should matter to us, she explains that we should respect the rights and feelings of others. It would be misguided here to claim that the individual's position gets better support as the argument progresses; rather, it becomes clearer exactly what her position is. Her statements are on different levels of generality, but each is just as substantive as the next and it is the claims as a whole that define her moral position.

As this example illustrates, the notion of a chain of reasons is misleading. It is not clear what it means to talk of adding an extra link to the chain, but an extra link certainly does not make the chain any stronger. All an extra explanation does is offer further clarification. If the above individual added that we should respect the rights of others because we are all God's children, this would not show that her position was better grounded than we had believed; at most it might show that it was a different type of position from that we supposed. Two important points follow from this. First, the content of an individual's principles is not separable from their application: we find out what she means by respecting the right of others, when she tells us what she believes is right in particular cases. Second, from a logical point of view it is irrelevant how many stages there are in the individual's argument or indeed how systematically she presents it. The fact that Kantian ethics involves a whole system of reasons does not prove anything against the claims of someone who takes a different view and holds, for example, that there are situations where it is right to tell a lie and that a failure to recognise this reflects an oversimplified and inhuman understanding of the world. The lengthiness (and the intellectual complexity) of the justifications offered for a particular view does not provide independent evidence that the view is correct.

One way of underlining these points about reasons is to consider a position that contradicts everything we have been saying, viz. the view that the ethical notion of correctness only makes sense if it is backed up by the claim that God exists. This view has some plausibility. The historical importance of religious conceptions makes it natural for us to view them as the model for objectivist accounts, and it is true that many secular moral ideas can be traced back to a religious origin. It is wrong, however, to claim that the notion of God gives a foundation to ethical claims in a way that other ideas do not. Invoking God involves exactly the same kind of substantive move as any other ethical position, and insofar as there is a temptation to see it as the only possible objectivist view, this is only because in this case the demand for further reasons is so obviously misplaced. The claim 'everyone should act in this way because God commands it' has a more obvious finality than the claim 'everyone should act in this way because it is the only way of showing a proper respect for other people'; nonetheless, it has exactly the same logical status. By justifying her moral judgement in terms of a belief in God, the individual does not give it a surer basis; rather, she explains what kind of moral position hers is. As with any other account, a point is reached when rather than articulating her view the individual asserts it: eventually explanation gives way to the substantive claim 'This is the correct way of understanding the world'.

Having made this point, it may still seem that in comparison with a religious view the bare assertion that certain ways of acting are right (or wrong) is undeveloped; it seems an embryonic moral position that only qualifies as such because of its potential. If someone who advances it cannot currently offer a fuller account, this must surely be something she aspires to. This suggestion is natural, but again raises problems, for it suggests that there are independent standards of what a moral position should look like, and yet any such standards are inevitably substantive. If unelaborated talk of right and wrong is only coherent if seen as part of a yet-to-be-elaborated account, does reference to a natural order of things count as one such account or is that, too, only coherent as part of an as-yet-undescribed wider whole? Once again, there seems to be pressure towards claiming that the only 'full' account is the religious one. To put the issue in more general terms, it would seem that something can only qualify as a moral judgement if it is part of a system with a particular kind of foundation.

At this stage, however, it is worth recalling traditional arguments about whether the Good is good because God wills it or God wills it because it is good. This debate is a perfect illustration of how raising a question at bedrock hits a mental blind spot. The injunction 'You should act in this way because God commands it' seems final until someone asks 'But why does God command it?'. When we reply 'because it is the right thing to do', the reference to God suddenly loses its air of finality and it seems as if the individual's whole account has been irrelevant to the real task of explaining what it means for something to be the right thing to do. The difficulty here lies in recognising that the idea of something being the right thing to do does not need (and is not susceptible of) further explanation. From this perspective, the claim that the Good is good because God wills it might be said to be less misleading, since as Wittgenstein put it, 'it cuts off the path to any and every explanation "why" it is good, while the second conception [the claim that God wills the Good because it is good] is precisely the superficial, the rationalistic one, which proceeds as if what is good could be given some foundation' (*Wittgenstein and the Vienna Circle*, p. 115). If we recognise this point, we can see that there is no basis for insisting that religious accounts are the only accounts that properly explain the ethical claim to correctness. Different moral positions explain the notion of correctness in different ways, some elaborately and some less so, but there is no scope for using this as an independent measure of their correctness.

This argument may seem to open the floodgates to subjectivism, allowing everyone to parade their casual prejudices as deep-seated moral beliefs; if moral beliefs do not even have to be systematically organised, doesn't this mean they can be anything the individual likes? From one perspective, however, this possibility need not worry us. If we decided to use the word 'moral' (or 'ethical') simply to refer to the logic of a certain type of claim, this would indeed mean that any view put forward as being one everyone should hold would count as moral. On this approach, however, the statement that the beliefs are moral simply tells us what status is being claimed for them; it does not give them a special dignity. If we believe they are foolish or misguided, we can condemn them as much as we like. Having made this point, however, it is worth recognising that there may be reasons why we want to restrict the words 'moral' to those claims to correctness which, even if we disagree with them, pass a basic (and substantive) test of adequacy or reasonableness. If someone claims she has a moral duty to fulfil her every desire no matter how capricious, we may listen to her arguments, recognise that she is claiming that this is the correct thing for her to do, but deny that her position deserves to be called moral.

If we want to make this sort of distinction (and most people do), we can apply any test we like. We should recognise, however, that the test is substantive, not logical. We can refuse the label 'moral' to positions that do not have a certain form or a particular type of content, but doing so does not amount to making an independent logical point against our opponent's claim that her position is correct. This sort of substantive test may be important in various contexts. For example, many people only accept a right to conscientious objection when the individual concerned can show that her opposition to war is a serious and deeply held view. More generally, our views on what should be prohibited by the state will reflect substantive distinctions between different types of moral disagreement. For example, we may believe that there is a correct view about contraception and yet hold that the type of issue it raises is not such that those who hold incorrect views should be forced to act in accordance with the correct view. By contrast, we may seek to force those who hold that murder is permissible not to act on their view.

In the above examples the distinctions we make all have legal consequences. In other situations what may be at issue is whether (or to what extent) we can respect the moral views of another person. For example, some people today will only recognise as legitimate moral views those which relate their claims that something is right or wrong to the notion of human suffering interpreted in some fairly straightforward sense. These people do not take claims that something is against God's will or an infringement of the order of the universe as seriously as they do other moral claims. In their view the only reasonable positions are those which involve a clear reference to human good. There is nothing confused about this kind of position, which is in a sense a form of rationalism, but it is clearly a substantive position. Confusion only arises if it is claimed that what is wrong with the other positions is that the reasons that can be given for them come to an end. In that respect 'You should not do it because it is against God's law' and 'You should not do it because it will cause human suffering' are equally mystical. In either case, if someone rejects the injunction, we can only tell her that we believe she is wrong. In the end, even the rationalist can only say: 'You should not cause human suffering because you should not'.

The key point in all of this is to recognise the substantive nature of the distinctions we make. If someone cannot present her moral views in a system we judge to be coherent, there is nothing to stop us from rejecting her position and condemning it as incoherent. There are no grounds, however, for claiming that it is logic that rejects the position rather than us. Having claimed that a position is not only morally wrong but not worthy of respect, there is no further gain in trying to claim that it is not logically possible even to hold it. In fact, what is wrong with the positions we most disagree with is that they are coherent but in our opinion deeply misguided; to suggest that Nazism is logically confused does not add to the charges against the Nazi, all

61

it does is hold out to her a specious plea in mitigation.[1] The source of error here is the desire to treat our own views as to what is coherent or reasonable as an independent test of whether a particular position is possible. Convinced a position is wrong, we are tempted to argue that it is incoherent or logically impossible.[2] The anti-abortionist may, for example, claim that anyone who is against infanticide cannot coherently support abortion. Similarly, her opponent may claim that anyone who accepts freedom of conscience must accept a woman's right to choose on this crucial issue. However, there is no independent way of assessing these claims. Any assessment of the coherence of a particular view or argument involves a substantive judgement and it is therefore wrong to suggest that those who do not accept this assessment are either making a logical error or are conceptually confused.

One implication of our account is that there is no such thing as refuting a moral view. Moral arguments can never have the form of a proof. Even if most people agree that a particular position is 'indefensible', it is an illusion to think that any amount of logic can compel its adherents to accept that this is so. It might seem, therefore, that our account undermines moral argument, for it seems to allow anyone who is having difficulty justifying her position to escape simply by invoking bedrock. But this criticism misunderstands the points we have been making, for, while the invocation of bedrock may end a moral argument, it does not function as a trump card. If in the course of an argument someone says 'I just disagree', she is ending the argument, not invoking an infallible way of winning it. As a third party, we may see her rejection of further discussion as a sign of weakness or as a disguised way of admitting defeat; on the other hand, we may not. The key point is that in the face of the conflict there is no way of assessing the two views which does not amount to a substantive decision in favour of one of them. We may believe the person who 'won' the argument was right, i.e. agree that the view she advanced was correct. Or we may believe that, despite the difficulty she had in presenting her case, the 'loser' was right. Any judgement we make ends our supposed neutrality, and the possibility of our concluding that the positions of both individuals are wrong simply underlines this point.

So where does this leave moral argument? To answer this question, let us first consider what is involved in developing a moral view. In judging a particular situation (or a type of situation) the individual has to decide what aspects of it she believes should be treated as most important in terms of decisions about how to act. She has to decide what she thinks are the morally relevant issues and consider how her assessment of this situation relates to her assessment of others, i.e. what other cases are similar in moral terms and what cases are significantly different. These are the questions that are the subject of debate in a moral argument. One person may claim that someone else is ignoring morally important factors or is bringing together cases that need to be treated separately. Or she may claim that the other person has not thought through her position and she may confront her with apparent consequences of it to test whether she really is committed to the view she seems to be putting forward. Typically, of course, attempts to persuade someone of the correctness of a particular moral view will take the form of a discussion. But it is would be wrong to treat other forms of persuasion as necessarily inferior or as irrational attempts to influence. There are many ways in which we may try to make another person see a situation in a different light, and there is no basis for claiming that a treatise packed with logical connectives is the only appropriate (or the most effective) means of persuasion. Someone who thinks that helping the poor is wrong because they only have themselves to blame for their misfortunes might change her mind after working with (or even just meeting) people in poverty. Or to take a rather different example, someone's cynical view of life and human beings may be altered by listening to Beethoven just as much as by reading Kant. There are many ways someone may come to hold a particular view; what is important, however, is not how she got there but whether or not we agree with her that the view is correct.

The key point in all of this is that all moral arguments are matters of persuasion. There is no question of a knock-out blow, showing that such-and-such a view cannot be held. To explore this point, let us consider the charge of inconsistency. Suppose someone is against abortion but favours infanticide. Our first reaction may be to label this position incoherent. It would be wrong, however, to say that the two judgements were logically incompatible, for they do relate to different situations and their combination represents a logically possible view. In saying that this position is inconsistent, therefore, what we are saying is not just that the position is wrong but that we cannot understand how someone could claim that it is correct. We cannot see it as part of a coherent view. If we now discuss this position with someone who holds it, there are three possibilities. We may come to understand the basis on which these two judgements are put together. Or we may convince the other person that she should abandon one of the judgements. Or the discussion may achieve little and we will continue to claim that the other person's position is incoherent and she will continue to claim that we do not understand her (and in one sense this is not something we will want to deny!). In all of this, however, it is important to remember that our difficulty in understanding the position (our belief that it is not just wrong, but incoherent) does not constitute independent evidence that it is wrong.

Against this, it may be argued that some positions are, as it were, absolutely inconsistent and simply cannot be held. What if someone puts forward a view that is literally contradictory, for example, claiming both that murder is right and that it is wrong? This is not a logically possible view, but what is wrong with it is that it does not define a position at all. Faced with someone who appears to be making these claims, we do not know what judgement to assign to her. Thus ruling out this sort of claim cannot be seen as the first and easiest stage in a project of putting limits on the positions it is possible to hold. All it does is replace the previous situation where we do not understand why someone makes two judgements with a situation where we literally do not know what judgement the individual is making. The point is not that this particular view can be shown to be absolutely and demonstrably wrong; rather the only absolute thing here is our inability to understand what view is being advanced. We have no idea at all what the individual is claiming. Looking at this issue from the opposite direction, we can note that however repugnant a position may be, if we can understand what judgements it involves, we must accept that it could be held. Indeed, the very fact that we can understand a view sufficiently to disagree with it (think it wrong) shows that it must be logically possible to hold it.

If we now return to the issue of inconsistency, we can note that this charge reflects a substantive rather than purely logical assessment of a moral position. In claiming that someone is being inconsistent we are saying that she is keeping apart what we believe belongs together and putting together what we believe belongs apart. We can try to persuade her of this, but our views on what is inconsistent, on what is a morally relevant difference and what is not, will always be substantive. We may believe that two apparently similar cases raise different moral issues, but when we explain the difference, there is no independently given standard against which our explanation can be assessed. If someone else believes the two cases are essentially the same, she will claim we are making distinctions where none ought to be made, but that is a substantive claim; it is what holding a different view amounts to.

Having accepted these points, however, it may still be argued that one way of refuting someone else's moral position is to show that even by her own standards the position is incoherent. Although in this case, too, the standards that underlie the charge of inconsistency are substantive, the individual cannot reject them since it was she herself who first advanced them. This suggestion does indeed correspond to one of the ways we engage in moral argument, but it needs to be handled carefully, for in principle it is only the other person's agreement that shows we are indeed applying *her* standards.[3] If she believes that human life is sacred and that abortion is permissible, we may try to convince her that favouring abortion conflicts with what she claims to hold most important and we may succeed. She may agree that her initial position was inconsistent and that opposing abortion is indeed the correct moral stance. On the other hand, she may insist that permitting abortion is consistent with her belief in the sacredness of human life. In that case, it will have become clear that we had misunderstood the meaning of her claim that human life was sacred.

This example underlines the general point that even when someone 'wins' a moral argument, this does not involve showing that a certain position was logically impossible; rather, it involves persuading another person to change her substantive view. Sometimes spelling out the consequences of a position may be enough to do this; or, as in this case, it may be a matter of making someone re-examine her judgements and decide not whether they are logically compatible but whether they are in her opinion consistent and whether she does indeed believe they are both correct. The claim that her initial substantive position was inconsistent or confused rests on an interpretation of her moral views she holds and the claim is only con- clusively established when she agrees to it. The temptation, however, is to want to treat the individual's values or principles and their implications as something that can be studied independently of the person who holds them. We want to say to the individual 'This is what your principles imply whether you like or not', and yet it is by affirming or rejecting the implications that the individual shows what her principles really are.[4] Although we may persuade someone that her position is confused or, by pointing to its implications, persuade her that it is wrong, it is always a mistake to transform our conviction that she ought to agree with us into the claim that logically she must do so.

It is wrong, therefore, to think that there are occasions when an inde- pendent observer would have to endorse the claims of one side of a moral argument. In putting forward a moral argument the individual advances a way of understanding a particular issue which she believes is correct, but since this is a substantive claim, any third party is drawn into the debate the moment she ventures to comment on it. To say a reason is valid is to endorse it as correct, and to say a consideration is pertinent is to endorse the way of understanding the issue that it involves. All such claims are just as substantive (and disputable) as the original claim. Recognising this, however, does not involve claiming that reasons are valid because we endorse them. That would amount to rejecting the notion of a valid reason. It would imply that reasons are simply masks for our personal preferences and this is exactly what the moralist denies. It is this denial (and the claim that there is a correct view) that provides the scope for moral argument. It also means that every move within an argument has the same substantive character. The moralist believes that there are valid and invalid reasons, justified and misguided distinctions, and when she endorses a reason as valid or a distinction as justified, she is not claiming that it has some special logical status, but that it embodies the approach to this issue which should be adopted by everyone.

Defending a moral view involves trying to convince another person that a particular view is correct and that it takes into account all the factors that are morally relevant. The key point, however, is that this will involve persuasion not proof. Someone who disagrees with moral judgements we hold to be correct is misguided, not stupid; her error is moral, not logical.

We can call into question the distinctions she makes, confront her with the consequences of her view and explain why we think such a view callous or superficial, but we cannot force her to abandon it. We may have right on our side, but not logic. If, for example, the other person does not accept that keeping someone alive indefinitely as a vegetable is an insult to that person's human dignity, we may have to accept that she will never come to hold what we believe is the correct view on euthanasia. Similarly, if she holds that a foetus should be treated as a human being from the moment of conception, no amount of evidence that sentience starts in the second trimester can force her to revise her opinion.

Given that disagreement is always logically possible, it may seem surprising that fruitful moral argument and discussion actually takes place. The point, however, is that, even if we disagree, there are usually some points of contact between our views. Our attempts at persuasion may (and often do) fall on deaf ears, but on other occasions, even where we differ, there are points of agreement or similarities of approach. This is most obvious when two friends are discussing what would be the right thing to do in a particular situation. Although they may disagree about the likely effects of a particular action, they will often share a common framework, so that if such-and-such were to happen, they both agree it would be morally relevant. Similarly, they may both agree about the nature of the moral problem, e.g. that the difficulty lies in the clash between someone's commitment to her work and her commitment to her partner. In these cases, the discussion may not be so much an argument as the exploration within a common framework of what would be the right thing to do in this particular situation.

Even in the different type of case where we argue about which general principles are correct, it is the closeness of our moral ideals that provides scope for discussion as opposed to the bald expression of conflicting, but equally possible, points of view. Our concepts of what is relevant and important may differ to a greater or lesser extent, but rarely to the extent that all discussion is futile. We are all likely, for example, to agree that if acting in a certain way causes human suffering, this is a bad thing, even if some nonetheless believe we should act that way, while others disagree. No anti-abortionist is likely to be happy about the plight of unmarried teenage mothers, while every pro-abortionist is likely to agree that it is unfortunate that large numbers of foetuses are produced which people want to abort.

Thus, even in one of the debates which most sharply divides our society, each party can to some extent recognise the concerns of the other, even if ultimately they regard the conclusions drawn from them as misguided or worse. In the face of disagreement this may be little consolation and it is certainly no basis for the incoherent project of trying to isolate these common values and use them to force unanimity. What it does illustrate is why moral argument is not a dialogue of the deaf. We disagree and cannot prove our positions to each, but generally our substantive views are not so far apart as to make all attempts at persuasion futile. A consideration which one individual holds to be important may have some weight with another, and while there can never be any guarantee of success, it is possible that the former may persuade the latter to change her mind and give it the same weight as she does.

This account of moral argument is likely to be controversial and it is worth contrasting it with more conventional approaches to this topic. The best way of doing this is to consider some examples from the area of political philosophy, where the direct connection with public debate means that the issue of what constitutes a valid argument is unavoidable. Here, our under-standing of moral argument becomes explicit and so it seems appropriate to draw our examples from this field. We shall begin by considering John Rawls whose book *A Theory of Justice* has rightly been seen as one of the most impressive philosophical works of the last fifty years. In Rawls, the stress is on rationality and on organising our moral and political beliefs into a systematic form. By contrast, Ronald Dworkin's book *Life's Dominion* is an attempt to 'reason from the inside out'. Rather than starting with a philosophical theory, he focuses on the practical issue of whether the law should permit abortion and euthanasia. Despite their differences, however, we shall argue that both Rawls and Dworkin fall victim to the confusions of rationalism; although neither would explicitly reject the idea that reasons come to an end, both are led towards denying it implicitly. This is far from a coincidence, for the confusions here are deep-seated. Furthermore, the strength of our commitment to a particular view can blind our judgement; convinced that one position is morally correct, we are tempted to claim that no other is logically possible.

    John Rawls's rationalism is not something he seeks to hide, and the whole aim of his work is to demonstrate that the central issues of political theory can be given a clear and systematic answer. The modest title 'A Theory of Justice' suggests a recognition that other theories are possible, but it is not surprising that this modesty gets pushed aside as he puts forward the theory he believes is correct. The reference to theory, however, reflects a wider ambiguity, for Rawls often writes as if ethical issues were of the same kind, and as unproblematic, as factual matters. Far from recognising the possibility of disagreement, he writes as if it is just a matter of developing the right theories with which everyone will be necessarily agree.

> The capacity for feelings of pleasure and pain and the forms of life of which animals are capable clearly impose duties of compassion and humanity in their case. I shall not attempt to explain these considered beliefs. They are outside the scope of the theory of justice, and so it does not seem possible to extend the contract

doctrine so as to include them in a natural way. A correct conception of our relations to animals and to nature would seem to depend
upon a theory of the natural order and our place in it. One of the
tasks of metaphysics is to work out a view of the world which is
suited for this purpose; it should identify and systemize the truths
decisive for these questions. How far justice as fairness will have to
be revised to fit in with this larger theory it is impossible to say. But
it seems reasonable to hope that if it is sound as an account of
justice among persons, it cannot be too far wrong when these
broader relationships are taken into account.

(*TJ*, p. 512)

Although this passage could be read simply to mean that our beliefs about
justice must fit in with our wider moral views, its tone suggests that it is
possible to identify moral truths in a definitive and independent way—as if
agreement on the theory of the electron prepares the way for agreement on a
theory of the natural order. Similarly, there is no recognition that the
'correct conception of our relations to animals' might be the subject of
substantive disagreement. Rawls seems to think that one day theoreticians
like himself will complete their account of the correct ethical system which
will then be joyfully accepted by all rational people.

The above passage may seem untypical, and elsewhere Rawls does seem to
recognise both that reasons come to an end and to a lesser extent that
substantive disagreement is always a logical possibility. His book, however, is
haunted by fear of reaching a point where 'the means of rational discussion
have come to an end' (*TJ*, p. 41), and this links up with his belief that any
reasonable set of moral beliefs must take the form of a system with every
moral judgement following from a limited set of first principles. Rawls does
not recognise the substantive nature of this second idea and he does not
explore the basis of this requirement. In fact, some of the comments he
makes suggest that he is confused about the very nature of the enterprise he
is engaged in. In particular, his talk of moral theory suggests that what is
going on is some kind of scientific explanation, whereas in fact what he is
doing is making a case for a particular moral view. This confusion is
important, for Rawls's substantive beliefs about the appropriate form and
structure of moral positions are treated as the standard requirements of any
scientific theory and therefore as unquestionable. More generally, his talk of
theory masks the substantive nature of his claims and misleadingly suggests
that rational discussion will one day eliminate all disagreements.

One way Rawls fleshes out his would-be scientific approach is by suggesting that the task of moral philosophy should be seen 'as the attempt to
describe our moral capacity' (*TJ*, p. 46). As his other remarks show, he sees
this as the search for a scientific model which will account for our
judgements, and yet, as his own notion of reflective equilibrium illustrates, it

is not a matter of explaining the judgements we happen to make, but of being sure that they are the judgements we should be making. This is a fundamental point. It shows why Rawls is wrong to compare our sense of justice to our sense of grammaticalness, for if we came to see justice as a matter of convention, our sense of justice would collapse. As we saw in Chapter 1, the individual cannot treat her value judgements simply as claims she is inclined to make. On the contrary, making a moral judgement involves claiming that the judgement is correct. What distinguishes the view that slavery is unjust from a dispreference for slavery is the claim that anyone who does not hold this view is morally wrong. In thinking about ethics, therefore, what we are trying to do is to come up with a coherent account of how we think people should act, and that is quite different from trying to develop a theory that will accurately predict the judgements we (or some other set of people) happen currently to make.

Ironically, these points are underlined by Rawls' own work, for his book is not an explanatory model of the judgements he personally makes, but a sustained attempt to persuade us that a certain way of thinking about justice is the right way of doing so. The search for consistency and coherence follows from the idea that there is a correct view, and although these standards are substantive, the process of ethical reflection involves applying them to one's own position. One way of reflecting on whether our judgements are correct is to consider how they fit together; by trying to present them in a systematic form we can see better where any tensions occur and on that basis decide what we really believe is right. The attempt to summarise our judgements in a single principle may also be useful in giving others an insight into why we see our judgements as going together. If, however, we succeed in putting forward a systematic account of our judgements, it would be misleading to follow Rawls and suggest that the first principles are the hidden causes of our judgements; rather, they are an attempt to describe these judgements at the most general level. If an individual explains that the key moral value is respect for human beings, this gives us a general idea of what type of moral position hers is. To discover what this principle means in detail, however, we will have to find out what specific judgements she makes. The principle 'always act in such a way that human dignity is respected' does not generate judgements; rather, by our specific judgements we show what we mean by it.

The best way to illustrate what is wrong with Rawls' approach to moral argument is to consider his remarks on intuitionism. Offering a broader definition than is usual, he defines this as any position which involves a plurality of first principles but includes no explicit priority rule for deciding between them. When they clash 'we are simply to strike a balance by intuition, by what seems to us most nearly right' (*TJ,* p. 34). Here, we can already see signs of a tendency towards the rationalism we described earlier. Rawls' talk of 'striking a balance by intuition' sounds mystical or arbitrary, while the phrase 'most nearly right' seems to concede that intuitionism can only ever be a makeshift, a poor second-best. However, the notion of approximation is inappropriate. It trades on the fact that in hard cases we may not be particularly happy with any of the possible courses of action, but that simply underlines what being a hard case involves. When the intuitionist finally says what she thinks should be done, she tells us what she thinks is right, not nearly right. There is no reason her judgement should be any more tentative than Rawls', and even if it is, this would only reflect the difficulty of that particular case. Every course of action may have some undesirable consequences, but that does not mean that the intuitionist believes no action is right.

The above quotation is no chance slip by Rawls; rather, it reflects his general approach. Only a few pages later he claims that 'intuitionism holds that in our judgements of social justice we must eventually reach a plurality of first principles in regard to which we can only say that it seems to us more correct to balance them this way rather than that' (*TJ*, p. 39). This ignores the fact that the reasons that can be given for *any* moral system eventually come to an end. In this respect, Rawls' explanations are no different from those of the intuitionist. His quotation is also misleading in another way, for it suggests that intuitionism is concerned with what seems, rather than what is correct. But this is confused and unfair. Even if we have one first principle (or, like Rawls, have a priority rule), all we can say is that it seems to us correct to apply this principle rather than a different one. Putting forward a moral view necessarily involves taking up a substantive position, but it is wrong to link this with subjectivism. It seems to Rawls that his systematised views are the correct account of justice, while it seems to the intuitionist that her less systematised account is the one everyone should hold.

Rawls' next move is equally confusing, for having treated intuitionism as a form of implicit subjectivism, he suggests that it might after all be true. 'We cannot take for granted that there must be a complete derivation of our judgements of social justice from recognizably ethical principles' (*TJ*, p. 39). This suggests that our moral judgements might be derivable from principles which were not recognisably ethical at all, which would be strange indeed. What Rawls seems to be trying to say is that a priori we cannot be sure what kind of systematic account we may be able to elaborate. Once we accept this, however, the task we face takes on a rather different complexion, for why should we insist that our moral system has any particular form? We might gain a certain aesthetic pleasure from presenting all our moral judgements as flowing from one principle, but even if we could achieve this goal, the intellectual elegance of our position would be no proof of its correctness. Take the problem of resolving clashes between the principles of liberty and equality. Rawls claims that describing 'a useful and explicit solution to the priority problem' (*TJ*, p. 40) would constitute a refutation of intuitionism. This is misguided. The intuitionist does not deny that it is logically possible to formulate a priority rule; what she denies is that doing this is the correct thing to do. She may, for example, believe that any conflicts between equality and liberty can only be solved on a case-by-case basis. Here, Rawls is again misled by his belief that a theory can provide our judgements with a more secure foundation. In fact, insofar as a 'theory' has any use, it is simply to present our judgements in a way that makes clear why we think they are correct and why we think they go together.

As his attack on intuitionism illustrates, Rawls is caught between a recognition that reasons come to an end and a belief that reasonable moral argument must aspire towards proof and a Euclidean-type system. The tensions in Rawls' position are evident in the fact that, while he accepts that any moral (or political) judgement must have some basis in intuition (*TJ*, p. 41), he wants to limit that basis as much as possible. This is confused, for the idea of quantification is meaningless; it makes no sense to contrast a big substantive move with a little one. It would be rather like saying that Catholicism is superior to Protestantism on the grounds that from the belief that the pope is infallible everything else follows. Rawls hopes to reduce the role of intuition by 'posing more limited questions and substituting prudential for moral judgement' (*TJ*, p. 44), but even if his arguments about what would be chosen in the original position were unimpeachable, the substantive move would be accepting that these were the right terms in which to discuss the basic order of society. As the so-called communitarians have argued,[5] accepting this premise involves thinking about ourselves and society in a very specific way. Of course, Rawls can (and does) try to persuade us that this is the right way to think about these issues, but it makes no sense to suggest that one huge substantive leap is logically superior to the small but more numerous jumps favoured by the intuitionist.

One way of defending Rawls would be to emphasise the fact that he is writing a book of political theory. Since he wants his principles to be accepted by a society whose members have differing substantive beliefs, the effort to employ as few controversial assumptions as possible seems entirely appropriate. This defence brings to the fore an interesting tension in Rawls' position, for his theory has two faces. The first might be called its Humean face, for he sometimes seems to be putting forward his theory as a compromise proposal for a conflict-ridden society. From this perspective, the form of his argument seems to be: given that there is much we disagree on, can we find a way of standing back from these conflicting views and of at least agreeing on the basic conditions for our interaction? This interpretation ties in with Rawls' claim that a theory of justice should only rest on a thin theory of the Good and it explains why he calls his theory 'justice as fairness'. However, such an approach is just as substantive as any other (including those based on thick theories of the Good). What is distinctive about it is that it puts forward a particular method of determining the basic institutions of our society that Rawls hopes everyone can recognise as a fair compromise, despite their different views on what is right.

But Rawls does not always stress the idea of compromise. On the contrary, he often suggests that his theory tells us what justice really involves; for example, he claims that 'the moral facts are determined by the principles which would be adopted in the original position' (*TJ*, p. 45). This is the Kantian face of his theory and points to the fact that his argument, far from minimising controversial assumptions, contains a very specific conception of what is important in human life. From this perspective, the original position is not about a tool which we can use to negotiate a compromise; rather, it is an exploration of how separate incarnations of reason should relate to each other. On this interpretation, Rawls' suggestion that his position involves a thin theory of the Good is less convincing. Furthermore, since the parties in the original position qua rational beings are undifferentiated, there is no longer any place (or need) for the ideas of negotiation and compromise. It is no longer a matter of being fair to rival accounts of the Good, but of recognising our true essence as rational beings. Making this point does not undermine Rawls' account, but shows how misleadingly it is presented. Rather than standing back from substantive beliefs, he puts forward a particular view of our nature, emphasising the importance of dignity and self-respect and seeing our good as lying in the free exercise of choice within the constraint of respecting that same power in others.

These criticisms of Rawls show how his reluctance to recognise that reasons come to an end introduce confusions into his argument. In his concern to be rational he treats ethics as a cross between geometry and science, so that the aim is to come up with the most powerful theory that can be generated from the lowest number of uncontroversial premises. Ethics, however, is not about building a theory to explain either the world or our judgements of human action; rather, it is an attempt to put forward a coherent account of how it is correct to act. Once we recognise this, there is little reason to insist that all moral views be presentable in the form of a system with a limited number of premises. It also becomes clear that it is not appropriate to suggest that the lower the number of premises, the better the system. If Rawls' account provides a systematic way of adjudicating between liberty and equality, this does not constitute independent evidence that it is superior to the intuitionist's claim that depending on the situation either principle may be more important.

The attempt to avoid disagreement by building an account on uncontroversial premises is also misguided, for either the premises will not contain the controversial conclusions or they will be more controversial than they initially seem. Rawls' approach may disorient his opponents insofar as apparently unobjectionable claims generate conclusions about the just structure of society that they reject. Once they have recovered from their surprise, however, all they have to do is to specify why the original position is not the appropriate starting point for examining these issues. Rawls outlines a particular approach to certain fundamental issues and makes the case for it in a very clear and therefore convincing way. He is wrong, however, to suggest that a good moral argument forms a structure in which the premises are independent of the conclusions and can offer them support. On the contrary, what needs to be recognised is that all elements of a moral account are on the same level. A set of principles and their implications mutually define each other and, whatever the form in which we cast our account, its premises are as substantive and open to challenge as its conclusions.

Our discussion of Rawls is intended to show how lack of clarity about the nature of moral belief distorts his approach to moral argument. In particular, an excessive fear of the possibility of disagreement makes him reluctant to recognise the substantive nature of his own position, while his desire to produce a quasi-scientific theory holds him back from openly advancing a moral ideal. Although the body of his work is an attempt to persuade us that a particular approach is both right and reasonable, he is tempted to imply that it is the only approach that is rationally possible. The pressures which push Rawls in this direction are not unique to him, and if we consider the rather different case of Dworkin, we can see the same pressures at work. Like Rawls, Dworkin believes he has found a way of putting an end to an apparently interminable argument. His concern, however, is with two specific problems rather than with the question of the basic structure of society. In *Life's Dominion*, he puts forward an impressive argument in favour of the right to abortion and in certain circumstances the right to die, but, since most of the book deals with abortion rather than euthanasia, we shall restrict our discussion to the former. Our aim will not be to make substantive claims about the issue of abortion itself, but simply to follow Dworkin's argument and try to clarify which of his claims are logical or conceptual and which are substantive.

Dworkin begins his book by noting the intractability of the abortion debate and the intense passions it rouses. He claims, however, that the current debate is confused, since both pro- and anti-abortionists treat the central issue as whether the foetus is a person and so has a right to life. Dworkin thinks that this is wrong, and he believes that it is this mistake which makes disagreement inevitable and so rules out any possibility of compromise. In his opinion 'once the confusion has been identified, we will see that a responsible legal settlement of the controversy, one that will not insult or demean any group, one that everyone can accept with full self-respect, is indeed available' (*LD*, pp. 10–11).

The first stage of Dworkin's argument involves distinguishing between two possible bases for objections to abortion. The first holds that 'fetuses are creatures with interests of their own right from the start, including, pre-eminently, an interest in remaining alive, and that therefore they have the rights that all human beings have to protect these basic interests, including a right not to be killed' (*LD*, p. 11). This he calls the derivative objection to

73

abortion, since it is derived from a rights claim. The second objection holds that 'human life has an intrinsic, innate value; that human life is sacred just in itself, and that the sacred nature of a human life begins when its biological life begins, even before the creature whose life it is has movement or sensations or interests or rights of its own' (*LD,* p. 11). This he calls the detached objection to abortion, since it does not relate to any rights claims. According to Dworkin, the intractability of the contemporary abortion debate arises from a failure to make this distinction, for he believes that it is incoherent to use the first objection as an argument for an outright ban on abortion.

Dworkin supports this claim by arguing that no being can have interests (and therefore rights) before it is conscious. Furthermore, he claims that the fact that the foetus was on its way to acquiring interests does not show it had interests at the times of the abortion.

> If Frankenstein's monster were actually brought to life, and felt and acted like a real person, then it would have interests like any other such person, and it would plainly be against those interests, in retrospect, if Frankenstein's apparatus had been smashed before the monster was created. But it does not follow that the collection of body parts on the laboratory table had interests before the switch was thrown, even though those body parts did exist, as just body parts, at that time.[6]
>
> (*LD,* p. 19)

Similarly, it is in each individual's interests that her parents conceived her, but had they not done so, this would not have been against anyone's interest, since the person whose interests would have been harmed would never have come into existence. Thus in Dworkin's view the derivative objection to abortion is fallacious if applied to the foetus before it is conscious. He also believes it is not a view anyone really holds. Most of those who oppose abortion would allow it when the pregnant woman's health was in danger. This shows that they do not literally see abortion as murder, for 'very few people believe that it is morally justifiable for a third party, even a doctor, to kill one innocent person to save another' (*LD,* p. 32). The same goes for when abortion is allowed in cases of rape or incest. Thus the real abortion debate must focus on the detached objection: the derivative objection only applies to late abortions and most of those who advance it as a general objection only do so because they have misidentified the real basis of their anti-abortionism.

So far Dworkin's argument may seem unobjectionable and in a sense a proper assessment of it is only possible against the background of his argument as a whole. Already, however, we can note a certain bias in the presentation. Take the notions of interests and rights. These notions figures prominently in Dworkin's moral system, but it would be a mistake to assume that this must be true of every moral code. Dworkin clearly believes that the justification for prohibiting murder is that the government has a duty to give equal protection to every citizen's interests including her right to life. He does not simply condemn murder as wrong but argues that it is wrong because being murdered is not in the interests of the murdered person and she has a right to have her interests respected. This may seem a reasonable position, but we do not have to justify our condemnation of murder in these terms; indeed, to some the stress on interests will seem misguided. One way of illustrating this is to consider the Dworkinesque example of someone on Death Row who kills a fellow-inmate. Most people would see this as just as much murder as killing in other circumstances, even if the victim has in a sense lost her right to life. As this example suggests, the stress on rights and interests is not always equally appropriate, and one might rightly suspect that Dworkin's stress on the victim's perspective—the fact that there is someone who has a legitimate objection to the murderer's planned action—is designed to further his later argument in favour of the right to abortion. It would be quite possible to base the legal prohibition of murder directly on the belief that murder is wrong, but he does not do this, since if he did, the anti-abortionist would use a parallel argument to claim that abortion should be illegal.

Even if we accept the primacy Dworkin gives to the notions of interests and rights, his attack on the derivative objection is not the refutation it is intended to be. His claim that only conscious human beings have interests and rights makes it clear why he focuses on these concepts (and links them) in the way he does, but his actual arguments against a foetus having interests and rights are weak. They boil down to claiming that assigning a foetus interests and rights would be ridiculous, since rights claims would mushroom uncontrollably. No one would claim that we have a duty to spend all our time having sexual intercourse on the grounds that not doing so is against the interests of those who might be conceived. Similarly, we all would agree that it would be absurd to say that Frankenstein's monster had rights before the switch was thrown. For these reasons, Dworkin suggests that talk of interests and rights is only appropriate after consciousness has been attained.

This claim embodies a substantive position that many may consider reasonable; however, it is not the only possibility. The obvious alternative places to draw the line are birth and conception, but even these by no means exhaust the possibilities. In fact, what lies behind Dworkin's argument is the assumption that we should only start treating the foetus as a human being once it is conscious, and yet that is the very issue in question. The anti-abortionist claims that a foetus is a person in a way that the unconceived (and the monster's body parts) are not. Dworkin might reply by stressing the notion of interests and claiming that it makes no sense to assign interests to something that is not conscious. This, however, is an attempt to win the argument by definition. There is nothing confused about saying that every individual should be treated as a person from the moment of conception. If Dworkin wants to insist that by definition rights can only be assigned to those with interests and by definition only conscious beings can have interests, he has colonised the words 'interests' and 'rights', but he has not proved that the alternative view is confused or fallacious.

Similar points apply with respect to Dworkin's attempts to show that no one really regards abortion as murder. Here again the direction of his argument is all too clear. The dichotomy Dworkin is seeking to force upon the anti-abortionist is that either abortion is in every respect like murder or it is different and by implication wrong in some less fundamental sense. This move is crucial, for unless murder and abortion can be separated, there is no prospect of claiming that the latter is a matter of personal choice. There is no reason, however, why the anti-abortionist cannot recognise the differences between abortion and murder and still claim that in moral terms they are wrong in similar ways. She may deny that aborting a foetus to save the life of the mother is like killing an innocent party to save another person's life and still maintain that in other circumstances abortion is essentially the same as murder. The whole point of the slogan 'abortion is murder' is precisely to fight against the moves Dworkin is preparing; it is a declaration that tolerance is inappropriate in this area. In particular, it emphasises that, unlike contraception, abortion raises moral issues which cannot be subordinated to a belief that the state should allow the individual to make her own moral choices.

Dworkin may reply that such views get their full expression in his account of the detached objection and, if so, this is fair enough. Some of his comments, however, suggest that, even if he wants to be impartial, he does not fully understand the views he wishes to oppose. For example, he claims that 'the real argument about abortion is that it is irresponsible to waste human life without a justification of appropriate importance' (LD, p. 58). One suspects, however, that few anti-abortionists would recognise this as a fair summary of their view.

So far we have pointed to elements of Dworkin's argument which the anti-abortionist might consider biased against her; the decisive issues, however, arise in the later stages of the argument and these centre on the idea that human life is sacred. This idea is fundamental. It is crucial to Dworkin's impartiality that his account of this concept gives the anti-abortionist a fair chance to express her views, and it is vital to the interest of the book that he believes the pro-abortionist's position can and should also be explained in terms of it. So what does Dworkin mean by the idea that human life is sacred? To explain it, he distinguishes between goods that are intrinsically valuable, i.e. have value independently of what people happen to enjoy, want or need, and those that are instrumentally valuable, i.e. have value only insofar as they help people get want they want. He subdivides the first group into those goods we want as much as possible of, such as knowledge, and others which we do not want to maximise but which we value once they exist.

> The hallmark of the sacred as distinct from the incrementally valuable is that the sacred is intrinsically valuable because—and therefore only once—it exists. It is inviolable because of what it represents or embodies. It is not important that there be more people. But once a human life has begun, it is very important that it flourish and not be wasted.
>
> (*LD*, p. 74)

Dworkin illustrates this notion by pointing to the importance we place on preserving a great work of art even if we ourselves are unlikely ever to see it or do not much like it. Similarly, most of us believe that we should preserve endangered species independently of whether this will bring tangible benefits. We also treat the success of our own species as an intrinsic good, wanting humanity to flourish both materially and spiritually long after our own deaths. Against this background we can understand why for almost everyone abortion is more than just a surgical operation: most of us agree that 'the deliberate ending of a single human life is intrinsically bad—objectively a shame—in the same way as the destruction of great art or the loss of important knowledge' (*LD*, p. 81).

This account of the sacred is bravely unfashionable and can be seen as one way of expressing the ethical idea of objective right and wrong. Dworkin's attempts to offer further explanations of it are, however, less convincing; indeed, he seems to back away from his original idea. For example, he argues that what we value in the sacred is the process which brought it about: the destruction of a work of art demeans a creative process we consider important (*LD*, p. 78), while the loss of a species is a frustration of either God's or evolution's creative effort. In either case, what we regret is 'the special badness of great effort frustrated' (*LD*, p. 79). Ironically, these explanations undermine rather than clarify the idea of the sacred. Presumably the difference between the frustration of a great and of a small effort is that, if the former had succeeded, the benefits would have been correspondingly greater. This makes talk of a special badness sound merely sentimental; it is as if we are so attached to the fruits of the process that we confusedly value the process even when it does not produce those fruits. Dworkin's later stress on investment is misguided in the same way, for what matters with an investment is the return. The fact that an artist lavished years of effort on a painting gives it no value if the picture itself is bad. Presented in these terms, the idea of the sacred seems weak. It looks precisely like the sentimental or superstitious attachment which, as Dworkin notes, some people have accused it of being. If there are good reasons for terminating an investment, there is no point on dwelling on the fact that in other circumstances the investment might have been highly advantageous.

Dworkin's difficulties only increase when he applies the idea of the sacred to abortion. His stress on the evolutionary history which precedes the conception of a particular foetus and his reference to its potentialities seem equally irrelevant.

> The life of a single human organism commands respect and protection . . . because of the complex creative investment it represents and because of our wonder at the divine or evolutionary processes that produce new lives from old ones, at the processes of nation and community and language through which a human being will come to absorb and continue hundreds of generations of cultures and forms of life and value, and, finally, when mental life has begun and flourishes, at the process of internal personal creation and judgement by which a person will make and remake himself, a mysterious, inescapable process in which we each participate, and which is therefore the most powerful and inevitable source of empathy and communion we have with every other creature who faces the same frightening challenge. The horror we feel in the willful destruction of a human life reflects our shared inarticulate sense of the intrinsic importance of each of these dimensions of investment.
>
> (*LD*, p. 84)

In his effort to persuade, Dworkin pulls together a host of ideas, but the result is unconvincing. While the pro-abortionist may feel that these lofty generalisations are irrelevant, the anti-abortionist is likely to feel her views have not been adequately expressed. Dworkin's paean to the wonder of life may explain why some regret the ending even of a pregnancy all agree is undesirable, but that regret still seems sentimental. From a rational point of view, his general comments seem to leave the particular case quite untouched, for if there are good reasons why this particular foetus should not continue to birth, of what relevance is a meditation on the wonder of life? Dworkin's subsequent invocation of the notion of waste is equally puzzling, for how can we waste a possibility which we can always recreate and the fruits of which we have in superabundance already?

These puzzles reflect Dworkin's own lack of clarity about the notion of the sacred. If we return to his original idea of the intrinsically good as what is valuable independently of our desires and preferences, we can read the above passage in a different light, for one way of expressing the idea of the sacred would be to say that there are certain things with which humanity has no right to interfere (or where interference needs special justification). On this account, concern about abortion does not reflect regret at a failed investment or wasted opportunity, but wonder at the process of life; who, the anti-abortionist might ask, are we to intervene in this mystery? What right have we to play the role of God? This is one sort of reason that might be given for opposing abortion, but it would be wrong to suggest that anyone who opposes abortion must endorse it (or something very similar). The only definitive way of finding out why someone believes abortion is wrong is to ask that person.

The next stage of Dworkin's argument involves claiming that pro- and anti-abortionists share a belief in the sacredness of human life and that their only disagreement is over the relative weights to be attached to the natural investment in that life and to the human investment. The liberal believes that what the mother (and potentially the foetus) will be able to do with the gift of life is more important than the gift itself.

> We can best understand the full range of opinion about abortion, from the most conservative to the most liberal, by ranking each opinion along a range extending from one extreme position to another—from treating any frustration of the biological investment as worse than any possible frustration of the human investment, through more moderate and complex balances, to the opinion that frustrating a mere biological investment in human life barely matters and that frustrating a human investment is always worse.
>
> (*LD*, p. 91)

Dworkin (rightly) believes there is no independent way of assessing which of these views is correct. He concludes from this that they should be treated like religious views, with the government allowing the individual freedom of conscience. It would therefore be wrong for any government to make abortion illegal, for doing this would build a religious view into the fabric of the state. In Dworkin's opinion, the only objection to abortion which properly respects the distinction between Church and State is the derivative objection, and that only applies once the foetus is sentient. On the basis of current scientific knowledge, governments can therefore confidently allow abortion up to at least twenty-six weeks with future advances only likely to extend the permissible period.

At the end of this argument the anti-abortionist may well feel hard done by. Dworkin seems to be arguing that since religious views will always be a matter of controversy, we should adopt a fair compromise and put our religious views to one side. What may seem odd to the anti-abortionist, however, is that, while the compromise involves her abandoning her opposition to something she believes is tantamount to murder, it leaves her opponent with exactly the legal situation she wanted in the first place. Some compromise. The result shows why Dworkin is so concerned to drive a wedge between abortion and murder and why, in particular, he must insist that laws against murder do not rest on a religious view in his sense. If he accepted that the notion of interests and rights was just as contestable (just as 'religious') as that of the sacred, the apparently reasonable suggestion that such claims should be set aside would lose its plausibility. This leaves Dworkin's argument looking very weak. The way to see the strengths it has, despite its weaknesses, is to see it as emphasising the modern value of autonomy. Dworkin's key point is that 'people have the moral right—and the moral responsibility—to confront the most fundamental questions about the meaning and value of their own lives for themselves, answering to their own consciences and convictions' (*LD*, p. 168). Unfortunately, this is exactly what the anti-abortionist disagrees with. Although the latter may accept the value of autonomy in some cases, for example, she may hold that contraception is wrong but that people have the right to choose, she believes that abortion is a different kind of issue and one way she expresses this is by claiming that abortion is murder. In this case, she does not accept that freedom of choice is more important than preventing a wrong. She and Dworkin have reached a bedrock of disagreement; his hopes of a compromise which everyone could accept turn out to be illusory.

Dworkin's attempts to rule out the possibility of disagreement illustrate how a legitimate commitment to our own views can blind us to the possibility of anyone reasonably disagreeing with us. Although he wants his argument to have the force of a proof, at key points in it he is inevitably reduced to assertion. For example, he insists that abortion is a totally different moral issue from murder and that abortion and contraception must be treated on the same basis (*LD*, p. 159), and yet these claims simply reiterate the substantive position his opponent rejects. Similarly, in the conclusion of his argument he writes as if autonomy must always be the supreme value or at least always triumph over religious or quasi-religious beliefs. As we noted earlier, however, the prohibition of murder could be said to rest on just such beliefs. The case of racism illustrates the same point. Like most of us, Dworkin holds that there is no right to be racist and that governments not only can but should write into their laws the quasi-religious view that all human beings are equal. Even if this value became controversial, he would reject any compromise proposal that racism be treated as a matter of personal choice.[7] Dworkin might reply that what is wrong with racism is not that it is clashes with our quasi-religious beliefs but that it is against the interests and the rights of particular individuals. This distinction, however, is spurious. On the one hand, the notion of rights is as 'quasi-religious' as any other moral claim, and on the other, there is nothing to stop either of his opponents invoking it. The anti-abortionist can claim that a foetus has rights and the racist can claim that certain people do not have them. Dworkin takes a substantive stand against both these claims, but it is a confusion to think that his stand against the anti-abortionist is somehow less substantive than that against the racist.

One way in which Dworkin disguises the substantive nature of his claims is by separating a moral concept and its interpretation and treating the latter as a factual matter. For example, he claims that most of us share the concept of the sacred and simply differ in how we interpret it, and yet this is misleading for precisely insofar as the concept means different things to different people it is a different concept. For the anti-abortionist, respect for the sacred may involve a respect for God or for Nature, while for the pro-abortionist it is specifically a respect for the human. If Dworkin's aim was simply to draw an interesting parallel between these ideas, there could be no objection; however, having divorced the concept from its interpretation, he seems to suggest that the best interpretation can be independently determined. In this way a substantive view (what respect for the sacred 'really' involves) is presented as if it were not substantive at all. Indeed, Dworkin's whole argument has this form, since he believes he can explain to the anti-abortionist what her views do and do not entail.

A different example of the way in which Dworkin tries to treat substantive issues as factual is his position on the US Constitution. In defence of Roe v. Wade, the precedent-setting Supreme Court case which held a Texan anti-abortion law to be unconstitutional, Dworkin attacks so-called original intent constitutionalism, arguing that the fact that the authors of the US Constitution did not intend to establish a constitutional right to abortion is not a decisive argument for the claim that one does not exist. Rather peculiarly, he supports this by invoking his own form of original intent, for, noting the Constitution's abstract concepts, he claims that its authors wanted them to be applied in the light of the best contemporary interpretation of what they involved. They 'intended a great constitutional adventure: that the United States be governed according to the correct understanding of what genuine liberty requires and how government shows equal concern for all its citizens' (*LD*, p. 137–8). As an account of intentions this is comically implausible, since it involves ascribing a strange moral modesty to the authors of the Constitution. Certainly the language they used seems to reflect the conviction that they knew what genuine liberty required rather than the belief that this was an open question they must entrust to the wisdom of the future. A deeper worry, however, is the idea of 'the correct understanding of what genuine liberty requires'. Here, substantive issues are inappropriately assimilated to factual questions. Furthermore, it is assumed that knowledge increases with time, so that where we disagree with the moral views of the authors of the Constitution we are necessarily taken to be right. The point, of course, is that we believe we are correct, whereas if they were alive today, they might well disagree.

To support his argument Dworkin considers a specific example, viz. the situation when one person asks another to buy her a healthy lunch. Here, it is crucial that he takes a factual question, for in this case it makes perfect sense to suggest that the speaker would want the person carrying out her request to do so in the light of the best medical knowledge at the time. This example is therefore not a comparable case. The second example he considers is more appropriate and concerns the case of a mother who instructs her son to be fair in business but who believes that ruining competitors by selling below cost price is a legitimate business practice. How should the son carry out her intentions? Separating the mother's commitment to fairness from its implications, Dworkin claims that the only accurate description of her intention is that her son 'do what is in fact fair' (*LD*, p. 137) and the person who determines what the facts are is of course the son. The weakness of this argument becomes clear if we change the historical order. Suppose a man who believes that predatory pricing is wrong tells his daughter always to be fair in business, and after his death predatory pricing comes to be considered acceptable. Would the daughter be right to say her father had no intention of forbidding her from engaging in this practice? Would it make sense for her to tell her father's ghost that as a matter of fact this practice just was fair? The point is the father and the daughter disagree about what is the correct thing to do, not that the latter possesses a piece of factual information the former lacked.

The confusion in Dworkin's argument on the Constitution can be shown in a similar way. The vast majority of people now agree that it is the government's duty to show equal concern for all citizens regardless of skin colour. Dworkin holds that it is a matter of fact that this is the best interpretation of equal concern: in applying it we are carrying out the intentions of those who wrote the Constitution even if they would be horrified at our actions. Suppose, however, that at some time in the future everyone agreed that certain people did not qualify for full citizenship, would we have to accept that their interpretation was factually superior to ours? Clearly not. What is confused here is the idea that any interpretation can be superior on purely factual grounds. The interpretation is as substantive (and potentially controversial) as the abstract principle; indeed, the two cannot be separated. We show what our belief in equality means by our treatment of particular cases. If later generations come to believe that animals have rights, it would be nonsensical for them to claim that our rejection of this idea was a factual error, that we had somehow misunderstood our own principles. If their belief in equality includes animals and ours does not, their belief involves a different concept of equality from our own. Our clash with them, as with the racist, is a substantive one; even if we present our views in the same terms, it makes no sense to suggest that there is a correct interpretation of the concepts involved that can resolve the issue impartially and unchallengably.

Here, we can return to the issue of abortion, for Dworkin believes the anti-abortionist must accept that the Constitution affirms a right to procreative autonomy. He argues that recent US legal history points to the development of such a right and even claims that the existence of this right is something 'any competent interpretation of the Constitution must recognise' (*LD*, p. 168). This is an odd suggestion, since it implies that the authors of the Constitution were not competent interpreters of what they themselves wrote. Supported by the changes in moral views reflected in recent legal history, Dworkin is tempted to claim that anyone reading the Constitution must see it as endorsing choice on the matter of abortion. In effect, he is saying that this issue cannot be a matter of debate despite the fact that it actually is. In relation to the previous example, we may all agree that it would be a terrible perversion of the principle of equal concern to see it as compatible with slavery, but the failure to accept this is not a matter of competence in interpreting the phrase 'all citizens should be treated equally'. A defender of slavery could simply claim that slaves do not count as citizens and so do not fall within the provision of this clause. We may all reject this new interpretation as immoral, but repeating the tautology 'all citizens means all citizens' cannot force the defender of slavery to recognise that the people she calls slaves are properly part of this totality.

The substantive clash we would face with an advocate of slavery is of the same kind as that Dworkin faces in his argument with opponents of abortion. There is no scope here for resolving the argument by factual investigation or by logical analysis. It is also confused to suggest that reasonable people should be able to compromise when an essential part of the dispute is the anti-abortionist's belief that this is the sort of issue on which compromise is not possible. Dworkin believes that abortion is a less fundamental question than murder, that the issues it raises concern a contestable value which a state should not impose on people but urge them to consider responsibly for themselves. For the anti-abortionist, it is not this sort of issue at all (whereas contraception, for example, might be). Like Dworkin on racism, she believes that the issues raised by abortion are more important than freedom of choice; to urge her to compromise on the grounds that her views are controversial misses the point. The essence of her position is that, in this case, she could no more accept limiting the state's role to urging responsibility than she could in the case of murder.

Our criticisms of Dworkin should not be taken as an endorsement of the anti-abortionist's substantive views. On the contrary, our aim has simply been to clarify the way his argument works and to illustrate the strength of the temptation towards a misguided rationalism. It is never easy in philosophy to accept that reasons come to an end, but this is particularly so where our deepest convictions are concerned. Even if we accept in principle that moral argument cannot be proof, there is a tendency to claim implicitly that it can be. Having said this, however, it would be unfair not to recognise the merits of Dworkin's book. His concept of the sacred does bring out an important aspect of the abortion debate, and the claim that it is shared by both sides of the argument is an ingenious plea for mutual respect. If he convinces each side that its opponent is not just being irrational or callous, but is pursuing a particular moral ideal, he will surely have achieved part of his purpose. Furthermore, his argument may persuade some of those who are against abortion to accept nonetheless that it should be legal. Thus Dworkin's book may help the anti-abortionist who believes that as a matter of logical consistency she must hold that abortion should be illegal, for it shows why this is not so and why allowing people to make their own decisions on abortion is compatible with believing it to be wrong. This is the compromise Dworkin offers, but it is one only very few will be able to accept. His attempts to go further only illustrate how difficult it is to take seriously views we believe to be wrong. We end up so persuaded by our own arguments that we believe they are proofs. We claim that our views cannot be rejected, whereas what is more accurate (and more to the point) is that in our opinion they should not be.

4

MODESTY, DOUBT AND RELATIVISM

He began talking about teaching ethics. Impossible! He regards teaching ethics as telling someone what he should do. But how can anyone counsel another? Imagine someone advising another who was in love and about to marry, and pointing out to him all the things he cannot do if he marries. The idiot! How can one know how these things are in another man's life?

(Wittgenstein in conversation with O.K.Bouwsma, in *Wittgenstein Conversations 1949–1951,* p. 45)

We have argued that believing in right and wrong involves holding that there are judgements on human action that ought to be made by everyone. To many this idea will seem outmoded and extreme. The absolutism which it involves may seem either naive or arrogant: how, it might be asked, can one individual claim to know what it is correct for everyone to do? It may also appear dangerous, for it seems a small step from someone claiming that she knows how everyone ought to act to her imposing her views on others. There are various other factors that may make us suspicious of the absolute nature of moral judgements. Today, most of us are aware of numerous value systems different from our own and, having discounted their claims to correctness, it seems appropriate to be wary about making such claims ourselves. Furthermore, it is not only with other groups that we have conflicts about values; within our society some moral ideals are fairly widely held, but there is still much disagreement. Against this background, the idea of absolute claims may seem more implausible than in the past, for in putting forward her moral views the individual cannot even claim that her values are those of an entire society. If it would be arrogant and misguided for a society to claim that its values were correct, it seems presumption beyond belief for an individual to make this claim. Considerations such as these are part of what lies behind the modern desire for a less absolute conception of morality. Keen to respect the variety of ethical claims, we may be drawn towards a more modest account of ethics, one which sees it as having a personal and/or social basis.

The most direct way of doing this is simply to relativise moral judgements so that correct is taken to mean 'correct for me' or 'correct in my opinion'. It is not at all clear, however, how these two elements can be combined, for once we stress the idea of correctness, universality seems to follow automatically. What would it mean, for example, for someone to say that murder was wrong but restrict her judgement to herself? She would seem to be claiming that it was permissible for anyone else to commit murder but not for her. This would not only be an eccentric position, but ironically it would be just as absolute as any other. An alternative interpretation would be to see the individual's attempt to relativise her judgement as an explicit recognition that others might disagree. Again, however, this makes little sense. On the one hand, her opponents do not need her permission to disagree, and on the other hand, there is a sense in which she cannot even give it. She can affirm the right of other people to have a position, but she cannot endorse their alternative positions without abandoning her own. If she believes murder is wrong, she must reject the claims of those who say it is permissible. The 'arrogance' of claiming that the only correct view about murder is that it is wrong is not altered if the person who makes this claim lamely adds 'in my opinion'.

The only way in which adding the phrase 'in my opinion' could be significant would be if this amounted to an acceptance that all judgements on human action were mere opinions, i.e. that they were all on the same level and simply reflected how a person happened to be disposed. However, if the individual comes to hold this view, she abandons the claim that murder is wrong. She is no longer claiming that condemnation is the correct response to murder. Rather, she treats her rejection of murder as the expression of a preference. Murder is something she is against, but she admits that this is simply a fact about her. Adopting this position does amount to embracing relativism, and for that reason it involves rejecting ethics. Anyone who takes this position is committed to denying that there is a correct view on murder, a view which should be held by everyone regardless of their preferences or dispositions.

While logically possible, this straightforward relativism is unlikely to seem attractive in relation to actions such as murder, and so it may seem unfair to focus on this example. Perhaps the idea of non-absolute moral judgements makes more sense in relation to more specific judgements or in cases where the moral issues are more finely balanced. Before considering this suggestion, it is worth noting that it concedes the possibility, indeed the appropriateness, of absolute moral judgements in at least some cases. The argument now is whether in addition to absolute moral judgements there are also relative moral judgements. Let us consider a concrete example. Suppose the father of a recently married woman dies and her mother who hates the thought of living in an old people's home asks to move in with the young couple. This may create a dilemma for the daughter if, for example, she fears that taking her mother in will place a strain on her marriage. So what is the correct thing for her to do? Many of us today would probably withhold judgement: the woman faces a dilemma the seriousness of which we can appreciate, but for that very reason we may feel that we have no right to tell her what to do. How can we possibly judge such an issue? How can we intervene in such delicate areas as her marriage and her relationship with her mother? Adopting this position, however, does not mean we believe that the woman should do whatever suits her best. On the contrary, most of us would insist that she recognise the moral dimension of her situation. We believe that she should do what is right rather than what she happens to prefer, but many people today also believe that only she is in a position to determine what is right in her particular situation.

These views are typically modern, but it would be wrong to see them as justifying the idea of relative moral judgements. As we have already argued, this idea is confused, for ethics and relativism are alternatives: either we believe that there are correct ways of judging human action or we hold that all such judgements simply reflect the preferences or dispositions of those who make them. There are, however, various beliefs (other than the incoherent idea that moral judgements are relative) that may lie behind the sort of positions described above. We may not believe that the right way to act to in this context can be expressed in terms of relatively simple rules, and so we may deny that one of the options she faces is the correct one in every case. Another possibility is that our reluctance to judge reflects what has been called 'moral modesty'. As with the suggestion we discussed earlier, there are two ways this idea can be interpreted. The first (implausible) interpretation sees the individual's refusal to judge other people as reflecting the belief that it is possible for her to do wrong but that other people cannot do so. This would be an eccentric position and it is not clear that it deserves to be seen as a form of modesty. The individual would believe in right and wrong but hold that for everyone apart from herself everything was permitted. The second (and more plausible) interpretation of moral modesty sees the individual as accepting that the concepts right and wrong apply to everyone but believing that she has no right to judge others since she does not know the full background to their actions. This position involves the same kind of absolute moral judgements as any other, for the person adopting it holds that there are standards of behaviour which apply to everyone. The only difference is that she is not prepared to make judgements about how the actions of others measure up to those standards. She may, for example, believe that it is only in her own case that she can assess the motivation that lies behind an action and so judge its worth. The general point is that although the morally modest individual believes that one set of standards applies to everyone, she does not presume to know how the actions of others should be classified and judged.

Such modesty may appear attractive in a world where we are not always sure what moral judgements to make, but its attraction has limits. In logical terms there is nothing to stop someone adopting this position universally, but in extreme cases such modesty is likely to seem out of place. For example, in the case of murder most of us are unlikely to think that making a judgement is impossible. Neither a general worry about the difficulty of knowing what is right and wrong, nor a sense that we do not know what the murderer was going through is likely to hold us back from saying that her action was wrong. Even where what is at issue is more personal, e.g. in matters of sexual conduct, there are few people who would feel unable to make a judgement in any circumstances. Most of us are only likely to adopt a position of moral modesty in a limited number of cases; we are not likely to see every case as difficult or unclear. Where we do take this position, however, it will not involve abandoning the belief that there are correct ways of acting but suspending judgement about what is correct in a particular case.

Returning to our example, we can see that there are various reasons we might be reluctant to judge. The first is lack of knowledge. We do not know what the woman's relationship to her mother is nor what impact her mother's moving in is likely to have on her marriage. Furthermore, however much she told us about these issues, there are obvious reasons why we might hesitate to claim that we fully understood the situation. Where personal relationship are involved, we may feel that only those involved in them are competent to make judgements and decisions. A second reason may simply be the difficulty of the case. We may recognise that there are no easy options in this situation, but not feel able (or required) to make a judgement on which option, either generally or in this particular case, is the correct one. We may also recognise that imagining the dilemma is not the same as having to face it. This worry may connect up with the question of knowledge. For example, we may be underestimating the strain the new arrangements would put on the marriage. A final reason for our hesitating to judge is a recognition that, not having encountered the situation personally, we may simply not have thought about the issue deeply enough. The issue of what duty children owe their parents may never have confronted us or we may have made some self-deluding assumption that makes the decision straightforward. Any of these factors may lie behind the belief that no one else is in a position to tell the individual what would be the correct thing for her to do. It is worth noting, however, that there are counter-arguments, for it may be argued that a third party can sometimes assess the situation more clearly. If the real problem is the difficulty of doing what is right, a third party may be well placed to prevent the person concerned deceiving herself into believing that the easiest answer is correct. Although moral modesty has its attractions, there may be occasions where moral advice and encouragement are also appropriate.

Against this, it may be argued that the real basis of moral modesty is the recognition that all moral choices are unique, and this would seem to challenge the idea of universal standards. The argument would be that if the woman in our example decided that she ought to act in a certain way, this should not be seen as implying that anyone else in that situation should act like her, since by definition no one else could ever be in that particular situation. However, if we consider this claim carefully, we can see that it does not really conflict with anything we have said, for it would be possible to hold that all situations were unique and still make the distinctive moral claim that there are correct and incorrect judgements of those situations. Such a position would be based on a rejection of moral generalisations. The implication would be that every situation needs to be assessed on its own particular merits and that any general injunctions were just as likely to promote moral error as correct action. But this does not imply that all assessments are equal. Rather, it emphasises the difficulty in particular cases of establishing what the correct judgement is. As this position illustrates, it would be wrong to link the claim to correctness with the idea that the correct judgements on moral action can be encapsulated in a relatively short set of general principles. Conversely, a stress on the differences between apparently similar positions does not imply that moral judgements are or can be relative.

This is the most important point, but having made it, it is worth considering in slightly more detail the idea that all situations are unique. Clearly, in one sense this is trivially true, but what is someone who emphasises this idea trying to get at? If someone who was facing a moral dilemma claimed that no else could ever be in a morally similar situation, this would a rather unclear claim. Would she be saying that the sort of considerations which weighed with her ought not to weigh with others? Or would she be claiming that there are additional considerations which only apply to her? The difficulty here is that in specifying what makes her situation special, the individual defines what would count as a morally similar situation. The moment she seeks to justify the claim to uniqueness, that uniqueness vanishes. The emphasis on every situation being different is thus either empty or exaggerated. As we suggested earlier, what the stress on uniqueness really expresses is a rejection, or wariness, of moral generalisations.

This substantive position is not uncommon, for the modern tendency is to reject moral systems which treat ethics as a set of relatively simple rules in favour of others which stress the complexities of acting morally. As we have seen, however, it would be wrong to see this as the emergence of relative moral judgements. To return to our example, denying that a child always has a duty personally to look after her parents in old age does not involve abandoning absolute moral judgements; rather, it involves moving from a very general absolute judgement to one which is more nuanced. At the limit it would be possible to hold that there are few or no general rules and that the right thing to do can only be determined on a case-by-case basis. Such a position would still involve holding that there are correct judgements on human action, but it would include a denial that these judgements could be determined by the mechanical applications of general rules.

In contrast to our claim that moral judgements are absolute in the sense that they are judgements it is claimed everyone should make, most contemporary moral philosophers argue that ethics is a more personal and (by implication) more relative matter. In this section we shall briefly consider two arguments of this kind before moving on to examine explicit forms of relativism. One way in which philosophers try to personalise ethics is by focusing on situations where the individual feels a strong sense of obligation. Emphasising cases where the individual's moral judgement takes the form 'This is what I must do', they argue that ethics is linked to questions of self-identity. As we have seen, both Williams and MacIntyre advance this sort of argument. For them it has two advantages. First, it seems to explain why ethics is relevant to everyone—the individual's interest in her identity seems the strongest possible basis for moral reasoning. Second, it supports a liberal position and seems to explain why different and apparently conflicting moral codes may each have their own validity; if ethics is a matter of self-identity, it is understandable that different individuals may end up making sense of their lives in different terms. This approach, however, is misguided, for it is wrong to seek a motivation for ethics outside ethics itself. The moral claim is that we should act in certain ways because they are the correct ways to act. Any attempt to justify this claim in other terms changes the nature of the claim. For example, even if it could be shown that people who acted in certain ways were less prone to depression than those who did not, this would not show that these ways of acting were correct; although it would give a reason for action, it would not show that everyone ought to act in these ways, only that those whose top priority (strongest preference) was to avoid depression ought to do so.

This point may seem less clear in relation to the argument in terms of self-identity, but this is only because it is often unclear within that argument how the reference to self-identity is supposed to be understood. Suppose, for example, that an official refuses to accept a bribe because she believes that taking it would be wrong. One way of describing this situation would be to say that her belief in honesty defines the sort of person she is and that she would not have been able to respect herself if she had taken the bribe. Emphasising this way of putting it, however, is dangerous, for either it is an indirect way of reiterating the fact that she believes taking the bribe would be wrong or it presents her action in a very different light, for example, it suggests that the offer of a bigger bribe might have convinced her that the damage to her self-respect was worth putting up with. The point is that while an individual's moral beliefs may be said to define her identity, the movement as it were is from the former to the latter and not vice versa. If the official rejects the bribe on moral grounds, it is because she believes taking it would be wrong and not because she likes to think of herself as an honest official or because she has decided that honesty is the best concept with which to define her self-identity.

The tendency of many contemporary philosophers to emphasise cases where the individual's moral belief takes the form 'This is what I must do', reflects the doubts and uncertainties that surround ethics in our society. As the notion of moral modesty illustrates, many of us are more hesitant in our claims about how it is correct to act than people have been in the past. The woman in the situation we described earlier may conclude that it is her duty to take her mother into her house whatever the strains this may place on her marriage, but she may add that she is only certain that this is right for *her* to do. This position is very similar to moral modesty and involves the same reluctance to judge others and therefore the same refusal to generalise. However, it still involves claiming that there are correct ways of acting and correct ways of judging human action. The individual who recognises that she ought to act in a certain way is prepared at least in this one case to say what the correct judgement is. She may be unsure in general about what is right and wrong and she may therefore hesitate to judge others, but she rejects the idea that all judgements of human action simply reflect the preferences or dispositions of the person who makes them. She believes that there are correct ways of acting even if she does not claim to be able systematically to say what these are.

A final argument that may be used in an attempt to personalise and/or relativise moral judgements is the claim that no individual has the right to impose her views on what is correct on other people. Ironically, this claim itself contains an absolute moral judgement.[1] What it reflects, however, is an important idea, viz. the liberal notion of respect for the autonomy of others. In the sort of dilemma we described above we may feel that it is important for the individual to make her own decision, even if we are clear about what we believe she should do. Indeed, we may believe that any attempt by us to make her decision for her would itself be wrong. Many people today see this sort of moral claim as very important, particularly in the political sphere but also to some extent outside it. However, it should be clear that it does not involve abandoning the idea that there are standards of correct behaviour that apply to everyone. In particular, it does not imply that conflicting moral judgements are equally valid. We may believe that it is important that other people make their own moral decisions, but if we value their opportunity freely to choose the Good, we must recognise that they may also opt for the Bad. To respect the autonomy of other people is not to claim that all outcomes are the same. On the contrary, the ability to choose is usually valued because some choices are held to be right and others wrong.[2]

Thus respect for others does not involves dropping the idea of correctness. We may be against imposing our values on others and still hold that our values are correct and ought to be held by everyone. Unfortunately, this is an issue where there is a lot of confusion. For example, it is fashionable to suggest that the aim of moral education should be to enable a child to choose her own values rather than to encourage her to adopt the values of those bringing her up. This sounds edifying but can easily reflect or embody confusion. In reaction to some traditional styles of upbringing which sought (often fruitlessly) to impose certain values on children, the modern style is to stress the development of the child's personality and her ability to choose. It would be paradoxical, however, to suggest that a parent should not want her child to share her moral views, for the essence of those views is the belief that they should be held by everyone. What people who make this sort of claim are really trying to emphasise is that morality is more than an ability to parrot rules. What matters, however, is not the individual's ability to choose her own values but her ability to recognise that certain values are correct. Rather than simply learning that murder, dishonesty, etc., are wrong, the child needs to develop to a point where she understands why they are wrong. What the parents are trying to do is to develop the child's understanding and hence her ability to distinguish correctly between right and wrong, and this is rather different from forcing her to learn by heart a set of easy-to-apply rules.

One other factor which can confusedly lead people to reject the idea of absolute moral standards is hostility to certain types of traditional moral codes. As we have already mentioned, there is a tendency nowadays to reject the idea that acting correctly can be reduced to a set of relatively simple rules. There have also been changes in what people hold to be morally important. In particular, many people now believe that various traditional sexual prohibitions are misguided and that these questions do not raise any moral issues, or if they do, that these are not of the sort encapsulated in traditional notions of purity or chastity. These two factors can reinforce each other. On the one hand, in certain areas of personal behaviour people are less inclined to advance general rules; for example, rather than believing that adultery is always wrong, many would hold that such questions need to be examined in the context of the particular relationships concerned. On the other hand, many people see actions that were previously regarded as wrong as morally unproblematic, for example sex between consenting adults before marriage. These changes, however, affect the content of people's moral beliefs, not their logic; the rejection of simple moral rules or of specific sexual prohibitions does not involve a rejection of right and wrong in general. In the latter case, those who hold these views are not rejecting the idea that there is a correct way of acting, but claiming that most sexual behaviour falls into the domain of the permissible. It is not that they reject the idea of standards that apply to everyone; rather, that they reject a certain set of judgements which have traditionally been made.

So far we have discussed various attempts to avoid the absolutism implicit in the claim that there are correct ways of acting, and have argued that they either do not succeed or that they involve abandoning the idea of right and wrong altogether. The latter is, of course, a logically possible position, for relativism poses a real challenge to ethics. This challenge is not new. It has always been possible to hold that the idea of right and wrong is a delusion and that moral judgements are simply disguised expressions of preference. What is new is the extent of our familiarity with other value systems and the tools we have developed to explain human beliefs and behaviour. It is not just that we are aware of numerous conflicting value systems, with many of which we may have some degree of sympathy, but we also have explanations of the social and psychological role moral beliefs can play in human life. The recognition that it is in society's interest for us to believe such-and-such or that holding a certain belief plays a vital role in holding together our personality calls into question our commitment to that belief.[3] We are confronted with the idea that we hold it not because it is correct but because we have been conditioned to hold it or because holding it contributes to our sense of self. If we accept this idea, it is possible that we will continue to act in the same way (because otherwise we feel bad etc.) but we will no longer be doing so because we believe that this is the correct way for everyone to act.

There is no general way of responding to the challenge explanations pose to our beliefs. All we can do is reflect in the face of the challenge on whether we are still committed to the belief. And, of course, different people may come to different conclusions. We *may* conclude that our moral reactions simply are reactions *or* we may persist in claiming that there are correct judgements on human action. Here, it is also worth noting that relativism (and the offering of external explanations of our reactions) is not just a general challenge to ethics but also a challenge to particular moral beliefs. Even if we maintain our belief in right and wrong, we may still need to consider particular moral judgements in the light of the claim that they are simply prejudices of one kind or another. For example, is our horror at incest simply the product of age-long social conditioning or is incest morally wrong? As with the general challenge of relativism, there are only substantive answers to such questions. There is no independent test we can apply, no expert opinion that can decide the issue for us. As with any moral judgement, it is a matter of reflecting on the issue and reaching a conclusion about what we believe to be correct.

Most contemporary moral philosophers approach these issues in a rather different way and we shall argue that their views are much more relativist than they realise. This partly reflects confusions about the claim that there are correct ways of acting and partly a substantive rejection of this claim. Again, Bernard Williams is a good example, since his views on relativism are both typical and clearly expressed. Interestingly, he argues that relativism is not a threat to our moral beliefs but can in certain contexts actually complement them. His position rests on a distinction between real and notional confrontations.

93

A real confrontation between two divergent outlooks occurs at a given time if there is a group of people for whom each of the outlooks is a real option. A notional confrontation, by contrast, occurs when some people know about two divergent outlooks, but at least one of those outlooks does not present a real option.

(*Ethics and the Limits of Philosophy*, p. 160)

Williams argues that where a confrontation is notional, i.e. where a set of values is not a real option for us, it is not appropriate to ask whether those values are good or bad. He calls this relativism of distance and argues that any other views rest on an incoherent notion of objectivity in ethics.

Williams' account of relativism underlines the points we made in Chapter 1, for it supports the idea that for him ethics is simply an agreed code by which a particular group of people live. If his position is interpreted in this way, it becomes understandable why he does not see relativism as a challenge. If different groups have different codes of social practice, either these codes will be rivals and there will be a clash (and potentially one code will overthrow the other by convincing enough members of the other group of its attractions) or they will not be rivals, in which case the clash is purely notional and there is no question of advancing one code against the other. What is lacking in this account is the notion of correctness. For Williams, no ethical system can be correct, so the real question is which one 'works' best for a particular group. If one code triumphs over another, it has proved its superiority only in the sense in which soccer has proved its superiority to rugby by being more widely played.

This criticism of Williams suggests he has embraced a broader relativism than simply what he calls relativism of distance. However, this is something he explicitly denies. As a prelude to the remarks quoted above, he considers relativism in the traditional sense and rejects it. His starting point is the idea that our moral beliefs are the expression of deeply internalised reactions and that these reactions of their nature incline us to reject the beliefs of other groups. The traditional grounds for doing this is that our beliefs are correct, but in Williams' view this idea is confused. Nonetheless, he denies that we are obliged to suppress our desire to impose our moral beliefs on other groups, for this would involve taking relativism 'to issue in a non-relative morality of universal toleration' (*ELP*, p. 159). Instead he argues that holding deeply internalised values will incline us to impose them on others and that there is no reason for us not to do so, since it makes no sense to claim that doing this is objectively wrong. As this suggests, what Williams rejects is not relativism but inconsistent relativism. He accepts that our values are essentially preferences, but argues that this is no reason not to impose them on others.

This position is confused, for although Williams' avowed aim is to encourage us to maintain our faith in our moral beliefs, his treatment of our moral beliefs as deeply-held preferences involves abandoning the claim that marks them out as moral. The form of our judgements on human actions is no longer 'this is how people ought to act' but rather 'this is how we as a group want people to act'. If we encounter a different ethical system, the only question on Williams' account is 'Should we attack it or adopt it?'; the question 'Is their system correct and ours wrong?' has already been dismissed as meaningless. Rather than facing up to these points, Williams avoids them through ambiguity. In particular, he does not make clear what would be involved in reflecting on a value system that was a 'real option' for us. If this is equivalent to asking ourselves whether they or we are right about how people should live, the notion of correctness is central and relativism in all its forms is rejected. On the other hand, if it involves an assessment of which value system best promotes some end we as a group happen to have, the reflection is practical, not ethical. On Williams' approach, if we ban ritual sacrifice, this is because we prefer to live in a society where such practices do not occur. A tribe which allows ritual sacrifice has different preferences, and if our society interacts with them, either this will change our preferences or we will seek to impose our preferences on them.

The final irony of Williams' position is that his relativism sometimes pushes him towards a non-relativist principle of tolerance in precisely the way he himself criticises. Consider his argument on our relation to future generations.

> To be confident in trying to make sure that future generations shared our values, we would need, it seems to me, not only to be confident in those values—which, if we can achieve it, is a good thing to be—but also convinced that they were objective, which is a misguided thing to be. If we do not have this conviction, then we have reason to stand back from affecting the future, as we have to stand back from judging the past. We should not try to seal determinate values into future society.
>
> (*ELP,* p. 173)

On one level it is hard to believe Williams means this, since from his non-philosophical writings it is clear that he is in favour of us doing everything we can to ensure that future societies are not, for example, sexist and racist. Leaving that to one side, however, his argument seems to be that, since there is no question of our values being correct, we should leave future societies to make their own decisions about what values to embrace. In itself this may seem a reasonable proposal, but it reverses his previous argument; given what he has earlier said, it would be more consistent to argue that, since values cannot be correct, there is no reason why we should not seal our values into the future if we are inclined to do so. The only reason for not doing so would be the non-relative belief that, since our values are not

95

correct, it would not be unjust or unfair to impose them on others purely for our own satisfaction. Williams thus make precisely the mistake he warns against. Furthermore, he ends up with the worst of both worlds, for the only non-relative principle he advances is one almost no one would be willing to accept. Since most people believe that their views on human action are correct, they will reject the claim that the one moral truth is that each generation should be allowed to decide these issues for themselves. Most people believe that if future generations hold different moral views from us, their views will be not just different but wrong. Few would accept that it is just the depth of an internalised reaction which holds them back from taking a neutral stance on the possible return of ritual killing.

In defence of Williams it might be argued that his relativism of distance is plausible at least with regard to the past. It would seem strange, for example, to criticise William the Conqueror for not being a democrat or Julius Caesar for not supporting women's rights. Here, the claim that these men did wrong may seem undermined by our sense that it would be almost inconceivable for them to have done otherwise. The social system and the culture in which they lived were so different from our own that, like Williams, we may feel that acting in ways we consider right was not really an option for them. Here, understanding does seem to displace judgement: the more we know about a society, the more we are likely to recognise that its members could not have acted otherwise than they did. Even Williams, however, does not adopt this view across the board, for he excepts the concept of justice from his relativism of distance. Since this concept applies to the structure of society and does not raise the question of blame, it is a special case and can be 'applied to past societies as a whole, even when we understand a great deal about them' (*ELP*, p. 165).

The reference to blame here is important, for if we separate the question of whether someone is to blame from that of whether she did wrong, relativism of distance looks a lot less plausible. We may hold that Agamemnon did wrong in having his innocent daughter put to death, but accept that, given his cultural background, it would be wrong to blame him for this (or at least wrong to blame him to the same extent that we would blame someone who acted in this way today). Similarly, if we do not blame Plato for not campaigning for an end to slavery, this does not mean we believe he was right to accept it. Williams has a point when he argues that we cannot treat people of the past as our contemporaries and that what would be blamable in us may not be blamable (or as blamable) in them, but this does not imply that we must accept any form of relativism. If slavery is wrong now, it was wrong then and it will still be wrong if at some time in the future everyone comes to agree that it is an appropriate and acceptable feature of society.[4]

So far we have argued both that Williams' comments on relativism are typical of modern moral philosophy and that they demonstrate his underlying rejection of ethics. There is one part of his account, however, that seems far removed from relativism, and that is his defence of 'thick' moral concepts as examples of ethical knowledge. His argument here, however, underlines his confusions about the nature of moral claims. The sort of concepts he is talking about are those such as cowardice, bravery and gratitude, which mark out certain actions as belonging to a certain type and simultaneously enjoin (or condemn) them. Williams argues that a purely descriptive equivalent of such concepts may not exist, for we can only know how to apply them by adopting the evaluative viewpoint which gives them their point. He then argues that we should recognise that statements applying these concepts can be true and that the people who use them can have ethical knowledge even if we ourselves reject the concepts and so cannot.

Williams recognises that this seems to contravene the 'disquotation principle', which holds that if a statement is true, an outside observer must be able to make it in her own person; he rebuts this objection, however, by offering the counter-example of a school slang where certain expressions were only applicable when used by a member of the school. Here, the disquotation principle would not apply, and he argues the same is true with respect to ethical concepts. 'In both cases, there is a condition satisfied by the locals and not by the observer, and in both cases it is a matter of belonging to a certain culture' (*ELP*, p. 144). This argument is misleading, for the two cases are not comparable. The key point is that the slang statements which we recognise as true can be translated into true statements in our own language. With statements employing thick concepts, however, it is not clear what it means to accept they are true if we reject the value judgements embodied in them. Recognition of a statement's truth seems to amount to nothing more than accepting that those who use these concepts would in fact make that judgement. The claim by a Macedonian of the time that Alexander the Great's wars of conquest were noble is true if and only if other contemporary Macedonians would have concurred in making it. This is a highly misleading position to take, for what matters about the statement that an action was, for example, noble is not whether a certain group would have made it but whether we accept that everyone should indeed seek to emulate actions of this type.

Williams' confused approach is also apparent in his claim that we can only know how to apply a thick concept by adopting the evaluative viewpoint of which it is a part, for we can certainly distinguish between the claim that a certain group would call a particular type of action 'noble' and the claim that it merits endorsement. In fact, this issue arises within as well as between societies and is typical of moral argument. If a racist describes those who work for white superiority as 'right-thinking individuals', her concept provides a basis for picking out a particular group of individuals and there may be no independently-definable equivalent to it. It would be strange, however, to claim that we must therefore see the racist as possessing a certain type of ethical knowledge inaccessible to everyone else. The fact that her concepts serve to pick out objects in the world in a consistent manner does not insulate it from our disapproval. Her judgements may not be capricious, but that does not mean we cannot condemn them as wrong. This argument can be extended, for the distinction between thick and thin concepts has no real basis. The racist's concept of what is right also picks out a particular set of events on a non-capricious basis, so that, if Williams' argument was sound, these claims too should be recognised as true and as expressions of knowledge. In fact, his argument amounts to treating all moral concepts as right in their own terms and this simply underlines the relativist nature of his position. Having rejected the idea of correctness, he believes that moral judgements can never be more than what a particular group of people are inclined to say.

Williams' account of thick concepts leads on to his claim that reflection can destroy knowledge. This would occur if a homogeneous ('hypertraditional') society abandoned its thick concepts when confronted with alternatives to them. Reflection will have destroyed their knowledge not because their beliefs turned out to be false, but because after reflection they can no longer use the concepts essential to those beliefs.

> A certain kind of knowledge with regard to particular situations, which used to guide them round their social world and helped to form it, is no longer available to them. Knowledge is destroyed; moreover, if they think about their earlier beliefs, they will now see them as the observer saw them, as knowledge they do not share.
>
> (*ELP,* p. 167)

This is a paradoxical claim and reflects Williams' belief that reflection undermines traditional ethics by showing that moral judgements cannot be objectively correct. As we have argued, however, this is mistaken. Reflection certainly indicates that moral judgements cannot be true in the sense that empirical judgements are true, but this does not undermine the claim that there are correct and incorrect ways of acting. Confronted with rival views on what is right and wrong, the hypertraditional society may do any of three things: it may continue with its beliefs (i.e. stick with its thick and its thin concepts), change them (i.e. adopt other thick or thin concepts) or, à la Williams abandon a belief in right and wrong altogether. In the latter two cases it would have no reason to regard its previous beliefs as constituting knowledge—either it will believe that its previous concepts and beliefs were mistaken or it will believe that all such concepts and beliefs are misguided.

One important point this brings out is that in ethics the concepts we use reflect and in a sense help constitute our substantive position. This is because our concepts express what we believe to be the correct way of understanding the world and show how we think everyone ought to act. Rejecting a moral concept amounts to rejecting a particular moral view. For example, if we reject the concept of nobility according to which Alexander's wars of conquest were noble, we do so because we do not believe that these concepts provide the correct terms for understanding the world and, more specifically, because we do not believe that everyone ought to seek to emulate such actions. Similarly, we may reject the claim that there is a natural order in the world (or human rights or a divine law etc.) that everyone ought to respect. Here, we reject both certain ways of acting and the concepts which are used to frame the claim that these ways of acting are incumbent on everyone. This point applies to all moral concepts including what Williams calls 'thin' concepts, for we may reject a conception of what is right just as we can reject a 'thick' concept relating to a virtue. In fact, the connection between substantive beliefs and the use of particular concepts exists in relation to the fundamental moral concept of right and wrong. The anti-moralist's substantive view is that there are no standards everyone ought to follow; she therefore rejects the concept (and related ones) that embody this idea.

Returning to Williams, we can see that his claim that reflection destroys moral belief arises from his underlying failure to understand what objectivity means in ethics. He believes that reflection must (or should) lead the hypertraditionalist society to abandon its thick concepts and argues that it is the objectivist (rather than the non-objectivist) model of this change that has to deny that these people had ethical knowledge. The reason for this is that he sees the objectivist model as claiming that there is a set of concepts the holding of which can be shown by science (psychology or sociology) to be appropriate for human beings. Since the hypertraditional society has never confronted this question, it can hardly claim to have the answer to it. Furthermore, since there is no answer to it, any knowledge claims would be wrong. This version of the objectivist model, however, misses the point. In a different sense to that suggested by Williams, the hypertraditionalists can and do claim to be right to have the concepts they have, for these concepts define how they believe human beings ought to live. They may, for example, believe that living correctly involves a respect for the natural order and a recognition of humanity's limited place in it. Anyone who rejects this idea or applies it incorrectly fails to live in the way everyone ought to live.

As we have emphasised, the objectivist or moralist who makes this sort of claim does not hold that moral judgements are true in the sense that empirical judgements are true or that they are provable. Rather, she believes that they are correct, i.e. that they do not simply express preferences but reflect a view or a set of standards that should be adopted by everyone. Moral knowledge (if we want to use this term) means knowing what is right and what is wrong, and in that case assessing whether someone possesses moral knowledge involves assessing whether she makes what we believe are the correct moral judgements. On Williams' approach, everything looks different, for he treats the claim that ethics is objective either as the claim that moral judgements are true in the same sense as empirical judgements or as the claim that everyone has a demonstrable reason to make these judgements. His mistake lies in failing to recognise the nature of the claim that there is a correct perspective on human action. Instead, he looks to sociology and psychology, rightly suspects that no proof will be forthcoming from them and concludes that ethics is a matter of a particular group deciding how it wants to live together. On the non-objectivist model which he supports, a group's ethical beliefs are 'a part of their way of living, a cultural artifact they have come to inhabit (although they have not consciously built it)' (*ELP*, p. 147). This leaves Williams holding a position that is relativist, but is not ethical. By his own account, in condemning something he is not claiming that it is objectively wrong but is simply expressing a reaction which he recognises is a product of the way he was brought up and which, for the moment, he has no reason for wanting to change.

The Canadian philosopher Charles Taylor takes a very different approach to ethics than Williams and, like us, argues that naturalism fails to do justice to the nature of moral claims. In fact, he goes further than we do, for while we have argued that believing in objective right and wrong is possible, he claims it is unavoidable. *Mirabile dictu* it is not accepting ethics that is impossible, but rejecting it. This conflicts with our account, for if the notion of correctness embodies a substantive claim, it must be logically possible both to affirm it and to deny it. In this respect, therefore, Taylor's defence of ethics is too ambitious. In other respects it is too modest, since rather surprisingly it too contains significant relativist elements. Indeed, we shall argue that Taylor is almost as confused about objectivity in ethics as his opponents and that their relativism ends up influencing his approach with the result that in his case too it is unclear whether his position should indeed be seen as involving a belief in right and wrong.

The starting point of Taylor's book, *Sources of the Self*, is an attack on projectionism, and central to that attack is the claim that moral frameworks are inescapable. Taylor defines these frameworks in terms of what he calls 'strong evaluation', that is evaluation which involves 'discriminations of right or wrong, better or worse, higher or lower, which are not rendered valid by our own desires, inclinations, or choices, but rather stand independently of these and offers standards by which these can be judged' (*SS*, p. 4). According to Taylor, evaluations of this kind are a crucial part of human life. For example, he claims that as conscious beings we cannot avoid the issue of how we should understand our lives and that this will involve judgements about what we consider better or worse, higher or lower, etc. Furthermore, he argues that the use of strong evaluation is not just a personal necessity but is integral to an individual's self-identity and to her recognition as a self by others. In short, his claim is that 'living within such strongly qualified horizons is constitutive of human agency, that stepping outside these limits would be tantamount to stepping outside what we would recognize as integral, that is, undamaged human personhood' (*SS*, p. 27).

In examining this argument the first thing to consider is the concept of strong evaluation itself—what exactly does Taylor mean by discriminations that are not rendered valid by our own desires but stand independently of them and offer standards by which they can be judged? The notion of validity here is not immediately clear, while the alternatives posed are not necessarily exclusive. For example, if an individual wants to become famous, this goal is not independent of her desires but does provide a standard by which other desires can be assessed, i.e. as promoting or obstructing this goal. Similarly, someone who reacts negatively to certain desires in others and in herself thereby discriminates between her desires, but she need not hold that the basis on which she does this is independent of her, for she may see this as simply the expression of dispositions that happened to have been inculcated into her. Thus the question of whether we discriminate between our desires (have standards against which we assess them) is quite separate from the question of whether there are standards that are independent of the individual in the sense that everyone should recognise them. Furthermore, only those who make the second type of claim are involved in what Taylor calls strong evaluation.

Taylor, however, blurs the distinction between evaluation and strong evaluation and this enables him to argue that anyone who evaluates must believe in ethics. One of the reasons this claim is plausible is that most people want to make moral judgements and agree with Taylor that there are correct and incorrect ways of acting, better and worse outcomes, etc. As we have emphasised, however, it is quite possible to deny that there is a correct way of assessing actions and events. Instead, the individual may hold that all evaluations are relative to a goal and that commitment to any goal is simply an expression of an individual's preferences or dispositions. On this view, all evaluations are on a par or, rather, different sets of evaluations have their supporters, but this reflects how those people are disposed rather than some intrinsic merit of the evaluations themselves. For someone who holds this view the claim 'X is better than Y' boils down to 'I prefer X to Y' or 'Given that I am disposed in such-and-such a way, I would choose X over Y'. This approach reduces moral claims to the status of preferences. For example, the claim that helping people is better than harming them is reduced to one individual's claim that she happens to prefer (or is currently disposed to favour) actions of the former type.

This sort of position may seem unattractive, but this is the position most contemporary philosophers hold to be obviously correct and, *pace* Taylor, it is a logically possible position. Strong evaluation is avoidable and anyone who rejects the idea that there are correct judgments on human action is committed to avoiding it. Such people may continue to say that democracy is better than tyranny etc., but in their mouths all this means is that because of the way they happen to be disposed, they favour one and condemn the other. Although they reject the idea that one is objectively superior to the other, they prefer one to the other and there is no reason for them not to advance this preference. On their approach it may be quite appropriate to summarise the situation by saying that their upbringing has disposed them to favour democracy and so far nothing has caused them to try to alter their pro-democracy inclinations.

Taylor has several arguments against this type of position; the first is that strong evaluation is a prerequisite for ascribing intentionality to someone. This claim, however, is only plausible if we fail to distinguish between evaluation and strong evaluation. Someone who rejects ethics still has preferences and so can have intentions and make choices. She may find the life of an artist more satisfying than that of a business person and get more pleasure (or a pleasure she values more highly) from listening to Beethoven than to Bob Dylan. The actions (and reactions) of such a person may even be similar to that of someone who believes in right and wrong. She may be appalled by violence and may feel good when she acts in a generous way. The only difference between her and the moralist is her belief that all judgements of action (and all actions) are rooted in preferences and that no set of preferences is correct.

Taylor rejects such an account, arguing that the choices we have been discussing are 'issues of strong evaluation because the people who ask these questions have no doubt that one can, following one's wishes and desires, take a wrong turn and so fail to live a full life' (*SS*, p. 14). This is ambiguous, for even if there is nothing more to human action than preferences, these may be complicated and the individual may be mistaken about what would bring her satisfaction. She may regret acting on an impulse or her preferences may change. For example, she may bemoan the fact that as a student she was more interested in having fun than in preparing for a successful career. Looking back she may see the decisions she made then as mistakes—maybe when as a student she chose not to become an accountant, she thought she wouldn't mind living on a low income but now she does. Of course, this is not the kind of mistake Taylor has in mind. He is talking about situations where people believe they have not lived as they ought to have lived and he is right that many people do assess their past in moral terms. But this does not prove his point. It may be true that most people believe there are better and worse ways of living life, but this shows that most people want to make moral claims, not that doing so is unavoidable.

At this stage Taylor might reply that the non-moral approach misses out on something and that when the individual seeks to make sense of her life, as every individual must do, she will inevitably be involved in strong evaluation. Again, however, this is not quite correct, for it confuses our need to make sense of the world with the possibility of making sense of it in moral terms. It is true that we would expect most people to have something to say in response to the question 'Why are we here?', but one possible answer is that our existence has no particular purpose. This is one conclusion about how the world should be understood and it may be combined with the rejection of ethics and the belief that there are no standards of behaviour which everyone ought to follow. Someone who holds this view need not lapse into a lethargic stupor nor spend all her time bemoaning the senselessness of life. On the contrary, this far-from-notional figure may have all sorts of interests and ambitions; indeed, she may love life and enjoy it to the full. Of course, she knows that it is all transient and that the goals she pursues are simply a reflection of her preferences/dispositions, but this recognition need not stop her having those goals. Just because the desire to eat is a biological impulse does not mean the individual cannot get pleasure from food and more sophisticated satisfaction from fine cuisine.

This point can be taken further, for, as we noted earlier, the anti-moralist's range of possible goals can have much the same complexity as that of any other individual. She may form attachments and favour the interests of others over herself or she may have preferences about preferences and be displeased with herself when she acts on some desires rather than others. It is true that some of these more complex preferences may have an element of fragility, for when she reprimands herself for a moment of greed, she may reflect that what causes her to act in this way is simply another type of desire, for example the desire to admire her own self-discipline. This thought *may* make her less inclined to curb her greedy impulses, but it is also possible that it will not affect the extent to which she finds these impulses distasteful. In a similar way it is possible that the belief that objectively nothing matters will depress an individual and inhibit her actions; it is also possible, however, that this belief will exhilarate her and stimulate her to new activities. There are certainly no grounds for suggesting that anyone who has this belief must choose coarse pleasures over those that are more refined. She may opt for sensual pleasure or self-discipline, the joys of taking or the joys of giving, but whatever she calls 'good', the point is that she believes that it is her being disposed in a particular way that makes it so.

Against this it might still be argued that someone who sees her life in these terms is missing something. One way of putting this would be to say that such a life is not distinctively human in the sense that it is not essentially different from that of an animal; the desires are multi-levelled and so more complex, but that is all. This argument, however, begs the question. It is no objection to the anti-moralist's view to point out that her position treats human and animal behaviour as essentially the same, for in a sense this is precisely what she believes to be the case. She may accept that recognition of this often provokes a crisis in the adolescent, but this is no argument against her belief that the idea of objective meaning is misguided.[5] She may see difficulty in facing up to this truth as a sign of immaturity or she may agree that this idea is hard to live with but still claim that it is true. Of course, Taylor's position is very different. He believes that 'not to have a [moral] framework is to fall into a life which is spiritually senseless' (*SS*, p. 18), but this is simply his substantive view. If he believes the life of the anti-moralist is impoverished, it is because he believes in objective right and wrong. Like Kierkegaard who claimed that the godless are in despair, either consciously or unconsciously, Taylor believes the anti-moralist is in spiritual crisis either implicitly and so complacently or explicitly and so agonisingly.

One way Taylor seeks to buttress his argument is by relating it to the issue of self-identity. He claims that knowing who we are involves knowing what we stand for and therefore strong evaluation is crucial to self-identity. Anyone who lacked any form of moral framework would be in the grip of an appalling identity crisis:

> Such a person wouldn't know where he stood on issues of fundamental importance, would have no orientation in these issues whatever, wouldn't be able to answer for himself on them. If one wants to add to the portrait by saying that the other person doesn't suffer from this absence of frameworks as a lack, isn't in other words in a crisis at all, then one rather has a picture of frightening dissociation. In practice, we would see such a person as deeply disturbed.
>
> (*SS*, p. 31)

But the anti-moralist does know where she stands: she is someone who believes that there are no objective values. If we ask her questions which seem to involve strong evaluation ('Which do you think better, the scholar's life or that of the pleasure-seeker?', 'Is democracy superior to dictatorship?'), she does not have to say that she does not know. On the contrary, in each case she rejects the question or at least recasts it. She may answer that she prefers the scholar's life to that of the pleasure-seeker or that she prefers people who have that preference. Or she may explain that having been brought up the way she has, she loves democracy and would rather die than live under a dictatorship. In each case she has a view but would accept that if she was disposed differently, she would have a different view and that independently of this there is no question of whether the view is correct. It is certainly an uncomfortable aspect of her position that she must see her clash with the Nazi as simply the clash of people with different preferences, but insofar as we see this as uncomfortable this simply underlines our belief that there are correct ways of acting. Most of us do want to say that Nazism was objectively wrong. We may also agree with Taylor that someone who rejects ethics is cutting herself off from the spiritual side of human life. If we make these judgements, however, this is simply an expression of our own belief in right and wrong.

Having made these points, it is worth considering some other aspects of Taylor's account, in particular those which suggest that moral judgements are relative not absolute. Ironically, the concepts in terms of which Taylor tries to show that ethics is inescapable both point towards subjectivism as much as objectivism. If ethics is a question of making sense of our lives, there would seem to be no possible objection to different people making sense of their lives in quite different ways. Similarly, if ethics is a matter of forging a self-identity, it seems natural to leave it up to the individual to decide which concepts in her case best fulfil this role. These points might be seen as a positive feature of Taylor's account, since they seem to justify tolerance and a respect for others. Unfortunately, they do so at the cost of undermining the distinctive notion of correctness. They guard against the possibility of someone imposing her views of right and wrong on others by undermining the notion of right and wrong altogether.

The important point is that ethics is not about the individual finding a way of understanding the world with which she can live; rather, it is about trying to understand the world correctly. Similarly, it is not about finding the most appropriate terms to define one's self-identity, but about reaching a conclusion on what is right and wrong. The source of Taylor's confusion is that he sometimes treats these pairs of claims as paraphrases and sometimes not. If they are treated as paraphrases, however, the notion of correctness cannot be avoided. Holding moral views involves claiming that anyone who understands the world correctly will accept that cetain standards of behaviour are correct and should be followed by everyone. These standards provide the individual with the concepts by which she should live her life (and in that sense define herself). For example, if she believes that everyone should be honest, she herself will try to be an honest person and act honestly. However, this does not mean an individual with moral beliefs must seek to *force* other people to act in accordance with her beliefs. Although ethics involves making claims about how other people should act, this is quite compatible with a respect for the right of others to make their own moral choices. The point is that this respect does not involve believing that whatever choice they make will be correct. Taylor may not disagree with this conclusion, but as we shall see in his efforts to make his account plausible to his naturalist opponents, he himself is drawn towards their relativism to such an extent that the nature of his own position becomes fundamentally unclear.

The ambiguity of Taylor's position is already evident at the start of his argument, for he begins by noting that our moral reactions have two facets: on one hand, they are like instincts, on the other, they seem to involve certain claims. Taylor points out that the latter facet is nowadays often seen as misguided or dispensable; the attempt to articulate these claims is treated as 'so much froth, nonsense from a bygone age' (*SS*, p. 5). But he rejects this approach and argues that our moral reactions cannot be treated like any other reaction, for they have special properties as is shown by the possibility of criticising them in terms of consistency. By contrast, it would make no sense to accuse someone of being inconsistently nauseated. 'The issue of inconsistency can only arise when the reaction is related to some independent property as its fit object' (*SS*, p. 7). Taylor claims that this shows that we must take into account both features of our moral reactions; they are not only gut feelings, but also implicit acknowledgements of claims concerning their objects. There is no path from a scientific description of the world to ethics. 'But it doesn't follow from this that moral ontology is pure fiction, as naturalists assume. Rather we should treat our deepest instincts, our ineradicable sense that human life is to be respected as our mode of access to a world in which ontological claims are discernible and can be rationally argued about and shifted' (*SS*, p. 8).

This approach glosses over the choice which these two ways of looking at our moral reactions offer us. Either we stand by the claims we are inclined to make and maintain that there are correct ways of acting or we see the tendency to make these claims as a natural human instinct which reflection shows to be misguided. We have argued that there is no independent way of resolving this issue and that different people may come to irresolubly conflicting conclusions on which is the correct position to take. Taylor's rationalism, however, makes acceptance of this impossible and, so while his opponents argue that belief in objective right and wrong is misguided, he is forced to argue that it is unavoidable. He then has to present ethics in such a way that this is plausible. He does this by blurring the distinction between having an understanding of the world and having an ethical understanding of the world (i.e. one which involves the claim that there are correct ways of acting).

Taylor also confuses the real issues by trying to assimilate moral judgements and empirical claims. For example, he suggests that, like sense experience, ethics is a 'mode of access to the world', and argues that, as in physics, we should adopt the Best Account, i.e. the account which currently has the most evidence in its favour. While his opponents relegate moral terms to the realm of mere appearances, he claims that they are

> part of the story that makes best sense of us, unless and until we can replace them with more clairvoyant terms. The result of this search for clairvoyance yields the best account we can give at any given time, and no epistemological or metaphysical considerations of a more general kind about science or nature can justify setting this aside. The best account in the above sense is trumps.
>
> (*SS*, p. 58)

106

Taylor is right that claims from science cannot disprove ethics, but the way he presents his argument leaves empirical and moral claims looking misleadingly similar. Ethics is not a mode of access to anything nor is there evidence for moral claims. Nor can we adjudicate between moral codes in terms of which is the best-supported theory. Rather, moral claims are concerned with how we should act and form part of different ways of understanding the world, each of which holds that there are standards of behaviour that everyone should respect. There are no independent ways of adjudicating between these rival accounts of how the world should be understood. We may try to persuade other people that understanding the world in a particular way is correct, but it is misleading to suggest that we can do so on the basis of some independent assessment that it is the best account currently available. There is no sense in which we can test moral claims to determine which offers the best explanation of the facts.

Taylor's rationalism and his assimilation of empirical and moral statements are also evident in his approach to moral argument. Although he rightly rejects the idea that there can be independent proof of a moral position, he presents the attempt to defend moral claims as similar to trying to establish a scientific theory. According to Taylor, the aim of moral argument is not to establish 'that some position is correct absolutely, but rather that some position is superior to some other' (*SS*, p. 72). This provides the cue for the return of something that looks rather like moral proof, for he suggests that reasoning in transitions can be proof-like. 'We can show one of these comparative claims to be well-founded when we can show that the *move* from A to B constitutes an epistemic gain' (ibid.). This is at best misleading, for while we can try to persuade someone of the correctness of a moral claim, we cannot 'show that it is well-founded'. Talk of epistemic gain masks the issue in grand language. If we believe that B is the correct moral claim and that A is not, the move from A to B is an epistemic gain, and conversely if we believe that A is correct, the opposite move is an epistemic gain. Taylor also talks of error-reduction in ethics, but to say that a moral argument is error-reducing is simply to say that the claim it advances is correct.[6] There is no escape from the substantive nature of moral debate and, while we may be convinced that something is right and may try to convince others, it will always be logically possible for them to deny that adopting our position would be an epistemic gain.

One factor which may have led Taylor to overlook this is that in philosophy substantive positions are often mixed in with conceptual confusions. He is right, for example, to note that utilitarians often equivocate about strong evaluation, and since they sometimes affirm it and sometimes deny it, pointing this out to them takes the debate forward. However, this advance involves the elimination of confusion rather than error; no substantive position has been shown to be wrong, rather the utilitarian has been asked to clarify exactly what her position is. Similarly, it is a confusion to claim that projectionism is compatible with ethics, and one of the aims of this book is to show that this is so. However, clarifying this point does not involve taking a substantive stance in relation either to projectionism or to ethics. Both these positions are open to the individual; all this book seeks to do is to show that someone who tries to combine them does not make clear what she really believes. The claim is not that a particular position is wrong, but that no clear position has been defined.

So far these criticisms of Taylor relate to his attempt to show that belief in objective ethics is unavoidable; however, the confusions embodied in this part of his argument reflect his lack of clarity about the nature of the claim to objectivity in ethics, and in view of this it is not surprising that he often gets pulled towards relativism. In fact, he often seems to suggest that moral concepts are objective only in the sense that they are not defined by the individual but are the products of social interaction. His point seems to be that the individual's struggle to understand the world takes place in a cultural space which is not of her own making and is in that sense objective. This sort of claim can be accepted by Taylor's opponents and fits very well with their position, since by suggesting that this is the only notion of objectivity relevant to ethics, it tacitly accepts that in themselves moral claims are empty or misguided. By the same token, however, this sort of claim conflicts with Taylor's wish to defend ethics. Accepting that an individual's values are independent in the sense just defined does not involve accepting that there are correct ways of acting. On the contrary, it implicitly involves rejecting the idea of right and wrong.

To illustrate this point, let us consider a specific example, viz. the claim that all human beings should be treated as equals. What is important about this idea is not that it has a history and pre-dates the individual who advances it, but that it is advanced as a claim that everyone ought to acknowledge regardless of their preferences, dispositions or background. Seeing this claim as the product of cultural history does not reinforce the claim to correctness but introduces a totally different notion of objectivity and one which involves moving away from the idea that the moral claim itself is either right or wrong. If an individual comes to see her commitment to equality merely or essentially as the product of a particular cultural history, she abandons the claim that inequality is wrong. She no longer treats her opposition to inequality as the recognition of a truth; instead she sees it as a reflection of how she happens to disposed. She may still feel bad about inequality because that is the way she was brought up and she may therefore seek to minimise it (or her awareness of it). However, she no longer makes the moral claim that it is something that ought to be opposed by everyone regardless of their preferences or of their personal history.

Within the context of objectivity as cultural determinism, Taylor seeks to reintroduce the notion of correctness via what he calls 'hyper-goods', for these are goods which embody claims that purport to apply universally. They are 'goods which not only are incomparably more important than others but provide the standpoint from which these must be weighed, judged, decided about' (*SS*, p. 63). The first point to note here is that, by implication, not all moral goods are hyper-goods. This is a further illustration of Taylor's tendency to blur the distinction between evaluation and strong evaluation. His 'moral' goods which do not involve universal claims are precisely what the anti-moralist believes all goods are, viz. goods whose goodness simply reflects the dispositions or preferences of the person who want them. If there is to be any scope for distinctively moral claims within Taylor's approach, this must therefore be in relation to hyper-goods. As we shall see shortly, however, these goods too he interprets in a relativistic way.

To appreciate this point, we need to consider the distinction Taylor draws between two possible ways of reacting to a clash of goods. The first possibility, which he calls 'the comprehending strategy' and sees as Aristotlean, is to affirm the value of all goods and seek to maximise them to the greatest extent possible. This strategy is seen as based on a recognition that the goods are bound up with a particular mode of social interchange and does not particularly relate to hyper-goods. The second strategy, which he calls 'revisionist', involves rejecting the validity of any goods that stand in way of our chosen hyper-good and does seem to involve making claims about what is correct. For example, Taylor notes that 'when we stand within the moral outlook of universal and equal respect, we don't consider its condemnation of slavery, widow-burning, human sacrifice or female circumcision only as an expression of our way of being' (*SS*, p. 68), and since within our culture we may feel committed to this outlook, he argues that we should embrace its universal claims.

The first strategy clearly involves relativism, but surprisingly so does the second, at least as presented by Taylor. The point is that making universal claims (or strong evaluations) involves rejecting the idea that they only hold if we recognise them (choose to 'stand within' that particular moral outlook). Take the moral outlook of universal and equal respect that Taylor mentions. If we accept this view and reject the comprehending strategy that would accept the validity of other approaches, we cannot treat our stance as a matter of historical or cultural necessity. We cannot, like Taylor, say that adopting the comprehending strategy would be attractive in principle but that 'if we could ever have done this, we are plainly too far gone in our recognition of hyper-goods to go the whole comprehending route' (*SS*, p. 66). This kind of statement suggests that a commitment to hyper-goods is part of our culture and so something we cannot get away from. The point, however, is that we believe it would be wrong to get away from it. It is our moral beliefs, not some cultural necessity, that prevent us from seeing our rejection of human sacrifice as the product of a particular cultural history. It is not a question of alternative self-understandings not being open to us, but of our rejecting alternative views as wrong. If we treat this rejection as determined (culturally, psychologically or however), we no longer affirm the moral claim as correct, but treat it as a reaction we have and with which we must reckon. The claim that something is wrong is transformed into the claim that we personally are disposed to react against it.

Taylor's uncertainties about correctness are also apparent in the contrasts he draws between modernity and the past. For example, he suggests that nowadays every moral vision is indexed to a personal vision in a way that was not true previously. It is easy to see why he makes this claim, since there is much wider and more obvious moral disagreement in our society than in times gone by. But this does not alter the nature of the claims people make. A moral claim is substantive whether it is made by one person or by a whole society, and this is as true of the past as of the present. Today's claims about how the world should be understood are no more personal in terms of their content than earlier claims. In both cases what is at issue is the correct way of understanding the world, not the way that happens to appeal to a particular individual. Taylor makes a similar error when he suggests that in the past empirical and moral concepts were on the same footing in that what explained the basic structure of the world also defined the Good—his favoured example are Plato's Ideas. By contrast, he suggests that the modern is characterised by a radical split between the two—any modern moral vision is 'inseparable from a certain subjectivism' (*SS*, p. 428). This is confused. Neither the logic nor the status of moral claims has changed; if anything is different, it is only that modern society is more fragmented and more ambiguous in its relation to ethics. Our ancestors may have been as certain that murder was wrong as they were that grass was green, but this does not put their moral claims into a different category from moral claims that can be made today. On the one hand, their equal certainty in both cases does not eliminate the differences between the two types of claim, and on the other hand, there is no logical barrier to our having the same certainty about moral claims that they allegedly had.

A final example of this sort of confusion occurs when Taylor contrasts the situation of a contemporary individual with that of Luther, for he writes as if the latter grappled with the problem of what is right, whereas our problem is to define our identity and give our lives a meaning. However, if the latter problem really does relate to whether we want to make distinctively ethical claims, it is simply a misleading way of formulating the first problem. The contrast between the modern question 'what is the right framework for me?' and Luther's question 'what is the right framework?' is mistaken, for accepting this difference involves rejecting the idea that there is a correct framework. Taylor, however, does not recognise this and is left in an ambiguous position. Although he seeks to encourage people to make moral judgements, he seems to want to relativise these judgements by introducing a reference to the person who makes them. He writes 'for most of us, certain fundamental moral questions are still put in universal terms; those, for instance . . . dealing with people's rights to life and integrity' (*SS*, p. 28), but he makes this sound as if it were a contingent fact about us, about the self-identity we have come to have. However, for those who hold moral beliefs, the matter is not optional. They believe these issues ought to be approached in universal terms and that someone who defines herself in terms of different moral concepts, or who finds a different sense in life, is wrong.

Like other contemporary philosophers, therefore, Taylor is ambiguous on the crucial issue of whether there are correct ways of acting. His account suggests that the pretension of moral claims to objective correctness is unfounded. He seems to hold that when an individual claims an action is wrong, she is claiming that the understanding of the world that makes sense to her, with her particular cultural background, involves condemning this type of action. However, the reference to cultural background is at odds with the type of claim being made. Either the individual believes that a particular understanding of the world is correct or she believes that her tendency to hold these views about the world is culturally determined.[7] His stress on the individual developing an understanding of the world that makes sense to her is also misguided, for what matters is that she believes that it is correct. Otherwise understanding the world becomes a purely personal issue, a matter of the individual finding a moral vision that suits her. Although this may sound vaguely like ethics, it makes nonsense of all the ideas that are distinctively ethical. Imagine someone saying 'No one should commit this sort of action because the understanding of the world that my cultural background leaves me feeling happiest with rules it out'. If the individual wants to make claims about the correct way for her and others to act, the only basis for doing so is the claim that a certain way of understanding the world is correct, not that it makes sense to her personally nor that it best fits with other views her culture has led her to hold.

The payoff of Taylor's argument is his suggestion that there is only one adequate moral view available to the modern individual. Here, Taylor's challenge to modern philosophy reaches heroic proportions, for belief in God, which is generally dismissed as obsolete, turns out to be the only view open to contemporary individuals. He claims that atheist moral sources are inadequate in the sense that they generate moral claims that they do not have the resources to satisfy. The only way of bringing together the moral claims we want to make and our recognition of human weakness and evil (including in ourselves) is to embrace a belief in God and reply on grace to bridge the gap between what should be the case and what is realistically likely to be the case. Otherwise we are condemned to make moral claims that do not hold together, both in the sense that we cannot live up to them and in the sense that they combine a respect for the human with the recognition that human beings are in many ways worse than other animals rather than better.

This argument is interesting but confused; what does it mean, for example, to suggest that alternative moral sources are inadequate? Is this a comment about the power of humanism to motivate? Is the point that if we don't believe in God it is unlikely that we will act as we believe we should? Even if this were true, however, it would not show that our moral views were wrong only that many of us cannot live up to them. What is strange about this argument is the suggestion that we can choose our moral beliefs according to their motivational efficacy. In fact, Taylor's attempt to show that everyone should believe in God takes us straight back to the confused, subjectivist elements in his account, for someone who does not believe in God cannot take her difficulties in living up to her moral principles as proof that God exists. Nor can she as it were lapse into a belief in God on the grounds that this is the only way to motivate herself. Tautologically, the only grounds for belief in God is the belief that He does exist. We cannot decide which way of understanding the world we believe to be correct on the basis of which would be the least difficult to live with. Conversely, if someone believes that treating other people with respect is the correct way to act, she is thereby committed to seeking to act in this way. If she fails to live up to this belief, this is a reflection on her, not on the correctness of her principle.

5

OBJECTIVITY AND THE
METAPHYSICS OF ETHICS

Take any action allowed to be vicious: Wilful murder, for
instance ... The vice entirely escapes you, as long as you
consider the object. You never find it, til you turn reflexion into
your own breast and find a sentiment of disapprobation, which
arises in you, towards the object. Here is a matter of fact; but
tis the object of feeling, not of reason. It lies in yourself, not in
the object. So that when you pronounce any action or
character to be vicious, you mean nothing, but that from the
constitution of your nature you have a feeling or sentiment of
blame from the contemplation of it. Vice and virtue therefore
may be compared to sounds, colours, heat and cold, which,
according to modern philosophy, are not qualities in objects
but perceptions in the mind.

(David Hume, *A Treatise on Human Nature*, pp. 468–9)

The question of whether value judgements are objective is often seen as the
central issue of moral philosophy, but it can easily be a source of confusion,
since the objective/subjective dichotomy does not provide the most useful
way of approaching the questions raised by ethics. One risk with these terms
is that objectivity is identified with provability so that the issue becomes
whether moral claims are provable with the implication that if they are not,
they should be treated as subjective and as merely expressing what one
individual happens to feel. A related risk is that the objective/subjective
dichotomy encourages us to think that the key issue in ethics is whether
moral claims are based in reality or merely reflect our reaction to it. Seeing
the issue in these terms is misguided, for it fails to recognise the nature of the
claim to correctness in ethics. The real issue is not whether moral claims
reflect some strange, action-guiding feature of reality, but whether there are
judgements on human action which everyone should accept (and act on)
regardless of their own preferences or dispositions. Do we believe there are
conclusions about how to act that anyone who is capable of thinking about
the world ought to draw? To put it another way, does the correct way of

understanding the world involves recognising certain judgements of human action as correct or does it involve accepting that all such judgements simply reflect the reaction of the person who makes them?

Contemporary philosophers have generally taken a rather different approach to this and have continued the objectivity debate, arguing over the merits and demerits of realist and anti-realist accounts of ethics. Both approaches, however, are flawed. Although the realist approach recognises that ethics involves a claim to correctness, it seeks to interpret that claim as relating to some action-guiding feature of reality. By contrast, anti-realism is clear that statements about reality cannot have logical implications for how we should act, but it takes this to imply that ethics is a matter of our reactions. This involves rejecting the claim to correctness; and, therefore, anti-realist accounts of ethics are in an important sense not accounts of ethics at all. The flawed starting point of both approaches is the assumption that ethics is either based on some feature of reality or a matter of our reactions. The realists are forced to embrace the first view because they recognise that accepting the second view would involve rejecting ethics, while the anti-realists embrace the second view because they realise that the first view makes no sense. Our account, however, involves rejecting this dichotomy. Ethics is defined by the substantive claim that moral judgements do not simply reflect the reactions of those who make them; however, this does not involve claiming that reality (or rationality) compels us to act in certain ways. The ethical claim is that there are judgements on human action which reflection ought to (but not must) lead every thinking individual to make, regardless of how she happens to be disposed.

Our approach may seem to dismiss the objectivity question too easily, for it is tempting to assume that something must be true of reality if moral claims are to be justified. Surely there must be some empirical support for the claim to correctness otherwise the claim is unjustified? Once we take this approach, however, we are well on the way to rejecting ethics. Baffled as to what empirical evidence could support moral claims, we may easily conclude that the attempt to distinguish between moral judgements and expressions of preference is confused and that the special claims of ethics are incoherent. Alternatively, we may focus on the inability of the moralist to provide specific evidence to support her claims and infer from the centuries of failure in trying to establish them that they are wrong. But these conclusions have the wrong starting point, for it makes no sense to seek empirical support for the claim that there are correct ways of acting. What is at issue here is how the world should be understood rather than specific claims about what exists. If, for example, someone claims that there is a natural order in the world that everyone must respect, this is not something that could be researched empirically. It would be just as mistaken to hope that science might substantiate this claim as to suggest that sub-particle physics or chaos theory calls it into question. The order being asserted is a moral order, and the claim is that our relation to the world will only be correct if it is in these terms. Ethics is based on reality in the sense that it involves putting forward what is claimed to be the correct understanding of the world. If we ask 'What must be true about reality for a belief in right and wrong to be correct?', the answer is that it must be true that everyone should recognise certain judgements about human action as correct.

These points can be reinforced by considering a more specific example such as the claim that murder is wrong. As Hume notes, it is not clear what basis in reality this claim has; if we look for special facts of the matter, none is apparent. But the question itself is misguided. What is at issue is whether in considering murder the individual is simply expressing her personal distaste for murder or whether she is claiming that everyone capable of thinking about what it involves must recognise that it is wrong. Here, is worth noting that the moralist does not hold that assessing something is *never* a matter of preference; rather, she holds that while in relation to some questions nothing is at issue except a personal reaction, in relation to others there is an assessment everyone should recognise as correct. No one would suggest that there is a correct answer to the question 'Is blue a more beautiful colour than red?' or 'Is football a better game than basketball?'. The answers to these questions clearly depend on what criteria are used and beyond that, on the reactions of different individuals. If someone prefers blue to red or football to basketball, that's all there is to it. But most people distinguish this kind of case from other assessments. They claim that if someone judges that murder is an acceptable act, this reflects a failure to understand the issue correctly, a failure to judge as everyone should judge.[1] Here it is held that a proper understanding of the matter can only yield one conclusion. Furthermore, the claim is not merely that all human beings should reach this conclusion, but that any being capable of thought should do so.

As these remarks suggest, the only claim about reality that all moralists agree on is that understanding the world correctly involves recognising certain judgements about how people should act as correct. Their specific beliefs may vary enormously. They may believe that everything that happens has a purpose or is in accordance with some plan, or they may believe that everything is the product of chance. There is, therefore, no one metaphysics of ethics. Rather, there are different conceptions of the world which can be classified together in virtue of the fact that they all claim that there are correct ways of acting. One typical modern response to these different conceptions is to treat all such pictures of the world as empty, i.e. as cultural products which have a social function but no objective content. This position seems reasonable, but in some ways it is puzzling, for how can every picture of the world be wrong? Why is every attempt to make sense of the world condemned to failure? In fact, this response is misleading, for any position including this one involves claiming that the world should be understood in a particular way. In this case, for example, certain types of claim are treated as lacking objective significance, and the basis for this may be the belief that the correct view of the world is as a mass of contingent causes and that human beings like any other animals are simply the blind product of causal processes. The real claim, therefore, is not that all understandings of the world are culturally determined, but that any view other than this one is a culturally determined reaction with a social use but no objective content. This is a possible substantive view and it is not without its historical antecedents; however, it is no less substantive than any other view and it is therefore misguided to see it as unquestionably correct.

The influence of science is, of course, one of the reasons for the popularity of this kind of view. It makes no sense, however, to claim that, in contrast to the results of science, all other claims about how the world should be understood are the purely emotional response of an individual, group or species. The sort of issues that we are discussing are not capable of being resolved by scientific investigation, but they cannot be avoided and *any* response to them involves taking a substantive stance. Any way of understanding the world must deal with the question of whether there are correct ways for people to act; a negative answer to this question—just as much as a positive answer—involves making sense of the world in a particular way. The attempt to deny this can only reflect a lack of self-understanding. If, for example, we abstract from our own humanity and treat this whole area as simply the product of the psychological needs of a particular type of animal, viz. human beings, we overlook the fact that this position itself constitutes a certain way of making sense of the world. There can be no question, therefore, of sticking to science or of only accepting the verified products of empirical investigation, for these methods cannot resolve the type of issue here in question.[2] Rather, drawing on all aspects of her experience including what science can tell her, the individual has to reach a view about how she thinks the world should be understood.

This argument may look like a sleight of hand, for the moralist seems to escape by arguing that the case against her claims is as weak as the case in favour of them. Those who deny that there are correct ways of acting may claim that their difficulty is trying to prove a negative; surely the burden of proof lies with the moralist? Isn't the onus on her to show that her claims have some basis? This response is misguided, for both parties are in the same position: each defends a particular way of understanding the world and neither can prove her position. The moralist claims that thinking about the world and about human action should lead everyone to recognise that there are correct and incorrect ways of acting. Her claim is that this is the conclusion everyone should reach in making sense of the world. If someone rejects this and claims that thinking about the world reveals that we are just another species of animal and that what we call good and bad reflects biological or psychological impulses, this is an alternative picture of the world and the two individuals face a conflict at bedrock. As this example illustrates, one of the sources of philosophical difficulty in this area compared to others is that, while most of us agree on a broad range of empirical claims, we have much more diverse views on the correct way of understanding the world overall. This does not mean, however, that all these issues can simply be bracketed off as empty, for this bracketing off is itself part of a particular way of understanding the world that claims to be correct and is therefore very much a party to the disputes.

A rather different challenge to our account could come from religious believers (and possibly from a certain kind of atheist who does not believe in right and wrong), for they may claim that in order for ethics to be possible God must exist. In logical terms, however, God's existence does not provide ethics with a special foundation. Rather, religious belief is simply one kind of view that involves holding that there are correct ways of acting. Furthermore, even in relation to religious believers it would be misguided to see their moral beliefs as having empirical foundations. Although religious belief combines an existence claim with beliefs about how everyone should act, belief in God is not a normal existence claim. It is also important to note that even in this case it is possible to draw a distinction between the existence of a Supreme Being and claims about how we should act. One way of illustrating this is to note that, even if everyone accepted God's existence, it would still be possible, like Ivan in *The Brothers Karamazov*, to challenge His goodness. For the religious believer, such a challenge can only reflect a terribly distorted view of the world. In her opinion anyone who takes this position is denying something that should be recognised by everyone and in so doing is taking up the wrong relation to God. Such an individual's failure to understand the world correctly shows itself in actions that are (morally) wrong. Clearly, however, there is nothing here that could be investigated empirically. No empirical evidence could show that praise and worship is the right way to act in relation to God. The religious believer holds that recognition of God's goodness and majesty is the right way of understanding the world and that anyone who denies this is wrong. Her belief takes the form of an existence claim, but what it advances is a comprehensive picture of how we should make sense of our lives and of the world.

These arguments are intended to show that the real objectivity question in ethics is whether we accept the claim that there are ways of acting that everyone should recognise as correct. Holding this belief, however, does not involve any specific claims about the nature of what exists. Rather, it reflects what the individual believes to be the correct way of understanding the world. Accounts of how the world should be understood can be divided into two broad categories—those that involve claiming that there are correct ways of acting and those that involve claiming that an individual's views on how people should act simply express her preferences or the way she happens to be disposed. The conflict at bedrock between these different views cannot be resolved by any discoveries about what exists, but this does not mean that

117

the dispute is empty. On the contrary, each party believes the other's position is fundamentally wrong. Both see the other's lives as based on an error. In line with their different views, however, there are differences in the significance of this error. From the anti-moralist's perspective, the moralist is mistaken and risks acting foolishly, for she may feel obliged to do what the anti-moralist believes she has no reason to do. From the moralist's perspective, the anti-moralist is mistaken and risks acting badly, for she may do what the moralist believes no one ought to do.

As we noted earlier, our approach to the question of objectivity is at odds with that of most contemporary moral philosophers and involves a different interpretation of the claim that there are correct ways of acting. A more typical approach is adopted by John Mackie in his book, *Ethics: Inventing Right and Wrong*, which, as the title suggests, attacks the claim that value judgements can be objective. Mackie accepts that this claim is integral to our moral judgements (*E*, p. 35) but he argues that it is false and that our inclination to make it must be explained by an error theory. Many of his remarks, however, show that he sees belief in objective right and wrong as involving some sort of empirical claim. For example, he argues that 'if there were something in the fabric of the world that validated certain kinds of concern, then it would be possible to acquire these merely by finding out, by letting one's thinking be controlled by how things are' (*E*, p. 22). This suggests that objective values are entities we might come across in our exploration of the world—as if physics might discover that there is indeed something in the fabric of the world that validated our moral concerns. On this basis it is not surprising that one of his main arguments against ethical objectivism is what he calls the argument from queerness—the claim that 'if there were objective values, then they would be entities or qualities or relations of a very strange sort, utterly different from anything else in the universe' (*E*, p. 38).

Mackie supports this metaphysical version of the argument with an epistemological version. He asks how we could be aware of this authoritative prescription and attacks the notion of intuition as an empty answer to this question. Like the other version, however, this form of his argument depends on treating the ethical as quasi-empirical: it is only because ethics is treated in covertly physical terms that the demand for a special sense seems appropriate. But this is misguided. To see what is wrong with murder does not require a third eye, and recognition that the correct view of rape is that it is wrong does not need a special faculty. What is at issue is not the perception of a quality which somehow escapes the microscope, but an acceptance of the claim that not all judgements about human action are on a par.

The other plank of Mackie's attack on objective values is the argument from relativity, but rather than recognising this as a challenge to the substantive claim that there is a correct perspective on human action, he dwells on the quite separate issue of how best to explain variations in belief. His

118

argument is that 'the actual variation in the moral codes is more readily explained by the hypothesis that they reflect ways of life than by the hypothesis that they express perceptions, most of them seriously inadequate and badly distorted, of objective values' (*E*, p. 37). This misses the point. Someone who believes in right and wrong does not do so because examination of the variety of moral codes has convinced her that this is the best explanation of the views people hold. Rather, she makes the substantive claim that there are correct ways of acting and, while rival claims of what is right and wrong may lead her to question either her particular moral views or the idea of right and wrong in general, this will not be because they are evidence against a hypothesis over-hastily adopted. Here, uniformity and variation are equally irrelevant. If almost everyone held the same views on human action, this would not prove that there was a correct view, and if everyone held different views, this would not prove the opposite.

Mackie's stress on explanation again treats moral judgements as if they were empirical claims, for it suggests that the key issue is whether these judgements are illusory or veridical. But this is not what is at issue in ethics. The correctness of a moral judgement does not lie in its being an accurate description of the world but in its being the judgement that everyone should indeed make. If we reject the claim to correctness, all moral beliefs are misguided rather than illusory, while if we accept this claim but disagree with someone's view as to what is the correct way to act, her judgement is not illusory but wrong—in our opinion it is not the judgement of that action everyone ought to make. Mackie ignores these points. He assumes that objective values would have to be entities which somehow caused people to believe and act in certain ways, for only in this way could they fill the explanatory role he wants for them. In fact, the correctness or otherwise of the claim that everyone ought to recognise a certain type of action as wrong can make no contribution to an explanation of the prevalence (or lack of it) of this moral belief.

All of Mackie's arguments purport to show the falsity of the claim that moral values are objective; however, as his descriptions of these values suggest, his real problem is making sense of the notion of objective values. He mentions Plato's Forms as one possible picture of such values, but his explanation of this picture brings out his uncertainty about what it means.

> An objective good would be sought by anyone who was acquainted with it, not because of any contingent fact that this person, or every person, is so constituted that he desires this end, but just because it has to-be-pursuedness somehow built into it.
>
> (*E*, p. 40)

The phrase 'somehow built into it' underlines Mackie's well-founded suspicion of the idea that any object might enjoin or compel action; while the talk of being 'acquainted with it' indicates that values are again being seen as some kind of object or at least something we might physically come across. A much clearer account of the objectivity claim in ethics is given in his discussion of categorical imperatives where he makes clear that what he is rejecting is the claim that there are reasons for acting which are 'unconditional in the sense of not being contingent on any present desire of the agent to whose satisfaction the recommended action would contribute as a means' (*E*, p. 29). This definition comes closer to the ethical idea that there are things we ought to do independently of our desires; Mackie, however, offers no arguments against it. All he does is assert that any claim that someone ought to do something will rest on an input that cannot be objectively validated or is not capable of being simply true or valid as a matter of general logic (*E*, p. 30). Insofar as this is a recognition of the substantive nature of moral judgements this is true, but Mackie is wrong to infer from this that the validity of this input is therefore 'constituted by our choosing or deciding to think in a certain way' (ibid.). This is precisely the substantive issue on which Mackie and the moralist disagree: while she believes that there are judgements about human action which everyone ought to make, he suggests that it is up to the individual to choose what she accepts as right and wrong.[3]

Mackie sums up his argument against objectivity in ethics by listing five considerations which favour moral scepticism:

> First, the relativity or variability of some important starting points of moral thinking and their apparent dependence on actual ways of life; secondly, the metaphysical peculiarity of the supposed objective values, in that they would have to be intrinsically action-guiding and motivating; thirdly, the problem of how such values could be consequential or supervenient upon natural features; fourthly, the corresponding epistemological difficulty of accounting for our knowledge of value entities or features and of their links with the feature on which they would be consequential; fifthly, the possibility of explaining, in terms of several different patterns of objectification, traces of which remain in moral language and moral concepts, how even if there were no such objective values people not only might have come to suppose that there are but also might persist firmly in that belief.
>
> (*E*, p. 49)

Of these points, the second, third and fourth all involve failing to recognise the specific nature of the claim to objectivity in ethics, while the first and the fifth reflect the relativist challenge to ethical belief and Mackie's substantive conclusion that a belief in objective right and wrong should therefore be rejected as a self-delusion. He believes that our moral judgements are essentially a reflection of our dispositions and that the rise of the particular beliefs traditionally seen as moral is the product of the process of evolution. This is a logically possible view but, while it offers an alternative to the ethical view, it does not refute it.

The weakness of Mackie's attack on objectivism and the confusions of his own position can be underlined by considering his account of ethics without objectivity. He begins by claiming one possible task of moral philosophy is to offer a systematic description of our moral consciousness or part of this, and he suggests that this is what Rawls does in *A Theory of Justice*. He adds, however, that it would be a mistake to see this as defining an objectively valid science of conduct; we must remember that the description of a sense of justice 'whether it is just yours and mine, or that of some much larger group, has no authority over those who dissent from its recommendations or even over us if we are inclined to change our minds' (*E*, p. 106). This claim follows logically from Mackie's subjectivism but brings out the difficulties of erecting an ethical system on this basis. If our moral impulses are just impulses and cannot bind others, why should they bind us? If we really believe that our inclination not to commit, say, tax evasion is simply a cultural prejudice, why should we heed the voice of conscience rather than stifle it? Here, it is no use saying that it is unfair to urge others to pay taxes, while not doing so ourselves, for on Mackie's view the idea of fairness is itself nothing more than an evolutionarily successful instinct. While we may in general welcome the consequences of this instinct, we have no reason to encourage it in ourselves.

Mackie seems to accept the above conclusion when he provocatively suggests that 'the truest teachers of moral philosophy are the outlaws and thieves who, as Locke says, keep faith and rules of justice with one another, but practise these as rules of convenience without which they cannot hold together, with no pretence of receiving them as innate laws of nature' (*E*, p. 10–11). However, this is not just provocative but downright misleading. The 'honesty' of thieves is more apparent than real; what lies behind it is not a belief in honest conduct, but a calculation of the risks involved and, where it is safe to do so, the thief may well decide to betray the trust of her fellow. Co-operation is possible even under the law of the jungle but only if both parties have something to offer each other and if both are strong enough to maintain their bargaining position. From this perspective, it is not surprising that it is a problem for Mackie as to why or how morality can extend to the mentally and physically handicapped. As he puts it, these people 'are never in a position where we should need to bargain with them. Consequently a moral system which ignored their well-being could still achieve what I have said to be the object of morality' (*E*, p. 194).

Mackie does, of course, want to go beyond the law of the jungle and he seeks to do this by stressing the disadvantages of a society based on the war of all against all. However, this appeal to the interests of the individual is an argument against anarchy rather than in favour of ethics. All it justifies is an agreed set of rules for social conduct with a policing authority to ensure they are obeyed. The individual would accept that it was in her interests that certain rules applied to everyone and it would be up to the policing authority to ensure that it was never in her interests to risk breaking them herself. Mackie, however, wants an internal as well as an external policing agency. His point seems to be that, if we want people to act decently towards each other, it is best if in addition to fearing being caught, they also have an in-built tendency to comply with the rules. It is worth noting that this need for an additional mechanism only arises because Mackie rejects the validity of moral claims as such. He wants the individual to be disposed to obey the rules even when this is not in her interest and yet he rejects the idea that obeying them is objectively the right thing for the individual to do. His solution is to argue that even if it is not always in the individual's interests to act decently, it is in her interest that all members of society (herself included) are disposed to act decently. Therefore she has reason to be disposed to be moral.

Mackie's argument is by now a familiar one. It is the equivalent of solving the Prisoner's Dilemma by both parties agreeing to have a mental implant which prevents them from adopting non-cooperative strategies. However, in practice, and particularly in relation to ethics, there are two problems with this 'solution': first, both parties have an interest in only pretending to have the implant and, second, there is no guarantee the implant will work. Having agreed that it would be best for everyone to be disposed to act morally, every individual will favour propaganda for ethics while secretly hoping that it will have no effect on herself. Furthermore, the attempt to instil ethical dis-positions will be undermined by books like Mackie's, for if someone is held back from breaking the rules by a sense that doing so would be wrong, she need only recognise that this is simply a socially-induced disposition and she will realise that her sense of right and wrong only applies if she wants it to. The only way Mackie can avoid this dilemma is by noting that, as it happens, many of us are already disposed to value moral action and so feel bad when we do not do so.[4] Unfortunately, this position suffers from exactly the same fragility as the previous one, for a conversion to moral subjectivism may undermine our pangs of conscience either instantly or progressively. It is also important to recognise that this position does not add up to a return to moral belief. On this approach, if someone discovered that deception caused her less heartache than she imagined, she would no longer have any reason to avoid it.

The fundamental problem Mackie faces is that he wants to put forward an account of how people ought to act and yet at the same time he is committed to rejecting the claim that there are correct ways of acting. His subjectivist account of ethics seems weak precisely because it lacks the notion of objective right and wrong that most people (and even Mackie himself) are strongly attracted to. Certainly his positive account would make better sense without the subjectivism he emphasises. If, however, he accepted that there was a right way for human beings to treat each other, he would have to recognise that it was a matter of deciding what we believe is right, not choosing what is right. On this interpretation, Mackie's subjectivism would have to be reinterpreted as an attack not on objective values in general but on a certain sort of objective value. What he is most obviously reacting against is religious ethics, and in its place he could be seen as insisting, first, that claims about the correct way of acting should connect up with human well-being in a recognisable manner and, second, that they should be realistic about the limitations of human beings and not make crazy demands that few or no one will be able to meet. On this interpretation, the essence of Mackie's position would be that, although God does not exist and although there is no order in the universe, we should still be fair to each other in our mutual dealings. If someone asked why we should be fair, all Mackie could reply would be that not doing so is wrong, that ruthless selfishness is no way to live and that someone who lives like this has failed to understand the most important aspects of human life. This interpretation leaves Mackie making substantive claims about how it is correct for people to treat each other and, like any other moral position, these claims can be disputed. His position, however, would not based be on any hypothesis about metaphysical entities—it would involve a belief in objective right and wrong, but it would not imply that reality somehow compels us to act in a certain way.

As this last interpretation shows, Mackie's position is confused: his lack of clarity about the notion of objectivity in ethics leads him to deny that there are any objective values, while his defence of fairness and decency implies on the contrary that there are correct ways of acting. Unfortunately, the situation is complicated by a further strand in Mackie's argument, for as well as rejecting ethics on confused metaphysical grounds he is also sometimes inclined to reject it on substantive grounds. In essays such as 'Morality and the Retributive Emotions' he signals his acceptance of a certain kind of scientific world-view which holds that all phenomena including human action should be understood in causal terms. On this view, a human being is an animal like any other and it makes just as little sense to say that a murderer should not kill as to say that a lion or a natural event, such as a hurricane, should not do so. As we shall see in Chapter 6, there are many problems with this approach, but it is particularly paradoxical in relation to Mackie's stress on choice, for this approach implies that all human choice is an illusion—what we do is determined by the dispositions we have been caused to have and 'deliberation' is a facade behind which the real machinery operates. On this view, it is unclear whether we should continue to talk of people acting at all and there is certainly no scope for discussing how they ought to act. To be consistent, therefore, Mackie would have to choose between his moral convictions and this substantive view—either he believes that everyone should strive to be fair or he believes that how each individual acts is simply a reflection of the dispositions the evolutionary process chanced to give her.

Mackie's attack on the objectivity of value is typically modern; a less fashionable approach is to try to defend that objectivity, and this is what Thomas Nagel seeks to do in *The View from Nowhere*. Nagel wants to get away from treating values as entities, but his account of ethics still treats moral claims in quasi-empirical terms. Furthermore, in tackling the objectivity issue he uses a host of different concepts of objectivity without recognising that this is what he is doing. He starts with a conception of objectivity that seems to undermine ethics.

> It can seem, when one looks at life from outside, that there is no room for values in the world at all. So to say: 'There are just people with various motives and inclinations, some of which they may express in evaluative language; but when we regard all this from outside, all we see are psychological facts. The ascent to an objective view, far from revealing new values that modify the subjective appearances, reveals that appearances are all there is: it enables us to observe and describe our subjective motives but does not produce any new ones. Objectivity . . . applies here with a nihilistic result: nothing is objectively right or wrong because objectively nothing matters.'
>
> (*TVFN*, p. 141)

Nagel recognises the attractions of this view. Indeed, in his discussions of life, death and meaning he seems to accept its truth; when he discusses ethics, however, he claims it is mistakenly reductive. Instead, he urges us to explore the possibility that there is a different concept of objectivity more appropriate to this area. The concept he introduces, however, leads away from the real issues, for it initiates an empty debate as to whether our reasons for action are real or illusory. He resolves this question by invoking pain as proof that reasons for action can be real and claims that our negative reaction to pain should be seen as a recognition of its objective badness. Apparently we are against pain as such, rather than each simply being against her own pain. In contrast to the conclusion contained in the above passage, Nagel now argues that some things do matter objectively. Unfortunately, this creates a new problem. Far from there being no objective reasons for action, there are so many that the individual risks being overwhelmed by them; now the problem is finding some refuge from the limitless mass of impersonal demands.

One striking feature of this argument is the change in the implications of the move to objectivity; initially it seems to rule out moral action, later it seems to make such action mandatory. This suggests that different notions of objectivity are being confused. To clarify the issue, let us first consider objectivity in its 'nihilistic' aspect. This idea seems to reflect the modern view of the world as a purposeless mass of causes and the implication that an individual's judgements and actions simply express the way she happens to be disposed. On this view, all reasons for action are reasons for a particular person; if something matters to someone, the ultimate explanation for this is that she is disposed in a particular way. Against this background, it is clear what is involved in denying that value is objective. When the anti-moralist says that nothing matters objectively, she is denying that there is anything more to action than the subjective perspective the agent happens to have; what she rejects is the idea that there are things that ought to matter to everyone.

In his defence of ethics, however, Nagel misinterprets this position. He takes the denial that there are reasons for everyone as a denial that there are any reasons for action at all. The anti-moralist who denies there are correct reasons is interpreted as making the crazy claim that all reasons for action are illusory. She is then 'refuted' by pointing to the case of pain. In reality, of course, the anti-moralist does not deny that someone in pain has a reason to act; rather, she denies that this person's pain automatically gives everyone else a reason to act. Her view is that other people's pain is only a reason for action for those who happen to be disposed not to like other people suffering. What she denies is the claim that objectively the individual ought to help regardless of how she happens to be disposed. Thus Nagel's argument rests on an ambiguity. While the anti-moralist claims that all reasons are subjective in the sense of only applying to the individual whose reason they are, Nagel attacks the crazy claim that all reasons are subjective in the sense of being illusory. The claim that there are no objective reasons for action, i.e. reasons incumbent on everyone, is construed as the 'barely conceivable' idea that the sufferer may be wrong in thinking her pain gives her a reason for action.

Having used the truism that pain is a reason for action to 'refute' his opponent, Nagel proceeds to reinterpret this claim so as to give it an ethical content. Now the ambiguity works the other way, for the claim that pain is a reason for action is re-interpreted as the claim that objectively we must take other people's pain into consideration when deciding how to act. Additional support for this move is provided by a type of thought experiment.

> The pain, though it comes attached to a person and his individual perspective, is just as clearly hateful to the objective self as to the subjective individual. I know what it's like even when I contemplate myself from outside, as one person among countless others. And the

same applies when I think about anyone else in this way. The pain can be detached in thought from the fact that it is mine without losing any of its dreadfulness. It has, so to speak, a life of its own. That is why it is natural to ascribe to it a value of its own.

(*TVFN*, p. 160)

This meditation on the dreadfulness of pain rests on the ambiguities we noted earlier. The non-issue of whether the badness of pain is a subjective illusion is conflated with the moral question of whether other people's pain gives us a reason to act. The limp conclusion is that it seems 'natural' to assume that they do.

One way Nagel supports this claim is by arguing that the objective view cannot overrule our subjective aversion to pain because 'we regard ourselves as too close to those things to be mistaken in our immediate, non-ideological evaluative impressions' (*TVFN*, p. 158). This is confused on various levels. As Wittgenstein argued in his remarks on the privacy of sensations, it makes no sense to see the individual as closer to her pain than anyone else. She is not the privileged spectator of her sensations, but the person who expresses them. One consequence of this is that it makes no sense to suggest that she might be mistaken about the unpleasantness of pain. Error is not over-whelmingly unlikely, it is impossible. Furthermore, these points about the concept of pain do not have any substantive, let alone ethical, implications. 'Pain is unpleasant' is a tautology, not a value judgement. A selfish individual will dislike being in pain, but this does not compel her to seek to minimise the pain of other people. Her hostility to pain cannot be seen as a tacit admission that there is indeed a correct evaluative point of view.[5] Similarly, she can admit the reality of other people's pain without agreeing that her actions should attach equal weight to her pain and to that of other people.

The claim that Nagel fails to recognise the nature of the objectivity claim in ethics may seem surprising, for this is precisely the criticism he makes of Mackie. When the latter argues that values are not 'part of the fabric of the world', Nagel notes that this argument fails to recognise the specific nature of the ethical.

The objective badness of pain, for example, is not some mysterious further property that all pains have, but just the fact that there is reason for anyone capable of viewing the world objectively to want it to stop. The view that values are real is not the view that they are real occult entities or properties, but that they are real values: that our claims about value and about what people have reason to do may be true or false independently of our beliefs and inclinations.

(*TVFN*, p. 144)

These points are well made, but they do not prevent Nagel from falling into confusion. His emphasis on the issue of whether objective reasons are real or illusory is as confused as Mackie's insistence that objective values would have to be some sort of entity. Instead of focusing on the question of whether there are correct ways of acting and what these are, Nagel sees the key question as whether postulating the existence of certain types of reason is a good hypothesis. Despite emphasising that values are not features of empirical reality, he sees the search for moral truth as similar to the search for factual knowledge.

> If the possibility of real values is admitted, specific values become susceptible to a kind of observational testing, but it operates through the kind of explanation appropriate to the subject: normative explanation. In physics, one infers from factual appearances to their most plausible explanation in a theory of how the world is. In ethics, one infers from appearances of value to their most plausible explanation in a theory of what there is a reason to do or want.
>
> (*TVFN*, p. 146)

This comparison is misleading and the reference to 'observational testing' obscure. In fact, the notion of plausibility is a substitute for moral judgement; asking whether it is plausible to claim that there are objective reasons against committing murder amounts to asking whether we believe that murder is wrong.

The confused assimilation of moral and empirical claims is also evident in Nagel's expression of hope that utilitarianism is false (*TVFN*, p. 205). This is a puzzling remark, for what are we supposed to make of such a hope? If we believe that utilitarianism correctly tells us how we should act, how can we hope that it might be wrong? What is strange here is the idea that ethics can progress in the way science progresses. And what is even more strange is the idea of making moral claims the object of hopes—presumably the lustful hope that adultery will turn out to be permissible! The error lies in the suggestion that we are not yet in a position to judge, that we must as it were wait on the evidence. This is confused. If Nagel believes utilitarianism does not offer a correct account of what we ought to do, this itself is a sufficient (indeed, the only possible) basis for rejecting it. There is no scope for either hope or fear; if we believe that an action is wrong, there is no danger that new discoveries or some theoretical breakthrough will suddenly prove that it is right.

The ambiguities in Nagel's account become even more apparent when he considers the question of how we should act, for it turns out that what we have objective reason to do is not necessarily what we ought to do. This claim underlines how confused Nagel's position on objectivity in ethics is.

Having moved from the truism that everyone who is in pain has a reason for acting to the substantive claim that each individual's pain should be a reason for everyone, he now seeks to protect the individual from the flood of objective reasons. One way he does this is by splitting the individual into an objective and a subjective self, so that although there are objective reasons why we should give some of our goods to the poor, there are subjective reasons why we do not do so. Nagel sees his task as adjudicating between these positions and determining what, all things considered, is a reasonable way to act. In the end, however, he accepts that there is no perfect solution. The objective position is just too demanding, 'it gives us more than we can take on in real life' (*TVFN*, p. 231); all we can do is recognise the problem and try to minimise the tension between the two parts of the self.

This tragic conclusion is a product of Nagel's confusions. His treatment of reasons as quasi-physical entities whose existence needs to be tested for creates a nonsensical gap between claims about which objective reasons exist and the question of how we should act. One consequence of this is that it becomes unclear what his moral position actually is. For example, he suggests that objectively people in rich countries ought to sacrifice some of their comforts for those in poorer lands. He then accepts that there are reasons why people do not do this and seems to endorse those reasons. This would seem to indicate that he does not believe that people have a duty to abandon their comforts. In that case, however, the claim objectively people ought to do this turns out to mean nothing. This confusion arises from trying to treat objectivity in ethics as a question of whether certain types of reason exist. The real issue is whether we believe that certain ways of acting are correct, i.e. incumbent on everyone regardless of their desires or dispositions. The claim that objectively the individual should help her neighbour even if she has no subjective reasons for doing so is more clearly expressed as the claim that she should help her neighbour even if she does not want to.

Another way Nagel seeks to protect the individual from the flood of impersonal reasons is by asking whether in addition to agent-neutral reasons (reasons that apply to everyone) there might also be agent-relative reasons (reasons that apply to a particular agent). The form of this question ('Do agent-relative reasons exist?', 'Are they real or illusory?') is again confused, while the discussion brings out the shortcomings of Nagel's realism. The two types of reasons he considers are what he calls 'reasons of autonomy' and deontological reasons. The first type of reason arise from the desires, projects and commitments of the individual and, since they reflect a choice or preference on her part, Nagel claims they do not have a validity for everyone. 'Their value is not impersonally detachable because it is too bound up with the idiosyncratic attitudes and aims of the subject' (*TVFN*, p. 168). This distinction, however, is arbitrary, for, if objectively we should help others avoid pain, why don't we have to help them avoid disappointment?

What Nagel is groping for is a more refined account of our duty to others, but his approach makes achieving this difficult. Modifying his earlier argument, he suggests that 'the impersonal authority of the individual's values diminishes with distance from his inner condition' (*TVFN,* p. 169). This claim is obscure as well as dubious, for what does it mean to say that pain is nearer to the individual's inner condition than disappointment? All this *ad hoc* metaphysics does is hide the real issues. What matters is not how far the individual's impersonal authority extends but how we believe one person should act in relation to another. Nagel's hypotheses about which reasons are real and which illusory are simply an indirect and unnecessary way of presenting his answer to this question. Where his 'hypotheses' are plausible it is because they agree with our moral beliefs about what is right.

Earlier we saw that Nagel argues that it is sometimes reasonable not to do what objectively we ought to do; in his discussion of agent-relative reasons, he has to make the opposite move and argue that reasons can be real and not objective. Ironically, he supports this claim by invoking the nihilist picture he rejected at the start of his discussion. For example, he claims that it would be dotty to think it mattered impersonally whether or not some individual fulfilled her ambition of climbing Kilimanjaro (*TVFN,* p. 170). But this seems inconsistent—if it matters objectively every time someone has a headache, why shouldn't this matter too? In fact, Nagel's statement is much more obscure than it seems—the claim that one person's disappointment does not matter impersonally may seem plausible, but what does matter impersonally? A major earthquake? The collapse of a solar system? Having started on this line of thought, it is tempting to claim that 'impersonally' it would not matter if the whole universe ceased to exist. This reflects the special concept of impersonality that is being invoked here, for built into this concept is the idea that objectively nothing matters. Use of the concept may, for example, reflect a vision of the world as a network of causes with no purpose or meaning. This is a particular substantive view; it is one way of understanding the world, but it is not necessarily the correct way.

Nagel's reaction to this conception of the world is ambivalent. He accepts that our wishes do not objectively matter but holds that our pains do. More generally, he seems to want to reject the implications of the claim that objectively nothing matters, while accepting that the claim itself is true. If he really does believe that objectively our most compelling personal concerns are insignificant (*TVFN,* p. 9), he should recognise that our pains are as insignificant as our concerns. The moralist, however, does not believe that our concerns are objectively insignificant; in her opinion human happiness and suffering do matter as do the individual's decisions about how to act. The essence of her position is that there is a real difference between doing good and doing evil and she certainly believes that this difference is objective in the sense that it ought to be recognised by everyone. What Nagel calls the objective viewpoint—the view from nowhere—is not the indisputably correct perspective on human action; it is simply a modern expression of moral scepticism. The picture of the world as valueless makes sense, but it is a picture which a belief in ethics explicitly excludes.

While Nagel allows that reasons of autonomy have a certain validity, he is less certain of the status of deontological reasons; although he offers a partial defence of them, he admits that he himself is only half-convinced by it. In his view, our reluctance to use evil means reflects an understandable revulsion at having to will evil even in the short term. Rightly repelled by what is bad, we hesitate to embrace it even when, all things considered, it will produce good. This account explains our deontological impulses, but, as Nagel recognises, it does not justify them. Once again we face a clash between the objective and the subjective views.

> When I view my act from outside and think of it as resulting from a choice of the impersonally considered state of the world in which it occurs, [overriding my revulsion at the means] seems rational. In thinking of the matter this way, I abstract my will and its choices from my person, as it were, and even from my actions, and decide directly among states of the world, as if I were taking a multiple choice test. If the choice is determined by what on balance is impersonally best, then I am guided by good and not by evil.
>
> (*TVFN*, p. 183)

Despite this, the individual may still be unwilling to commit the deed if the force of her subjective reasons overwhelms her.

This is a strange defence of deontological reasons, since upholding the subjective view seems to involve seeing the error of our ways and yet sticking to them for old times sake. Although Nagel sympathises with our deonto-logical concerns, he is forced to conclude that objectively they are misguided. The confusions in this argument become clear when Nagel considers a specific example, viz. the case of someone who by killing one innocent person would save the lives of five others (*TVFN*, p. 184). He believes it is clear that from an objective (impersonal) point of view the one should be killed; however, he argues that the victim's appeal to her killer may work on the subjective level. If we choose not to save the five, they can rightly protest that, impersonally, they should have been saved, but the one can make a direct appeal ('*You* are killing me') and subjectively this may be effective.

Even in its own terms, this argument proves little, since the effectiveness of the latter appeal does not show it is right. If Nagel really believes that the one should die for the five, the relative strengths of their rhetoric is irrelevant. It is clear, however, that he has doubts about this position and it is certainly the case that what he claims to be the objectively right thing to do differs markedly from what most people believe to be the correct way of acting. The point is that most people do not believe that such situations should be seen in terms of calculation; rather, they believe that we have no right to kill another person no matter how many others this might save. Here it is ironic that Nagel builds into his concept of objectivity a substantive moral claim that he himself is not fully happy with. He is confused, however, if he believes that he (or anyone else) is logically compelled to adopt it. Furthermore, if he is uncertain whether or not he believes that the means justifies the end, he cannot avoid the issue by splitting himself into an objective and a subjective self and having one part of himself affirm each view. Ultimately his practice will indicate what he really believes to be the correct thing to do.[6]

Nagel's final strategy for dealing with the conflicting demands of the impersonal and the personal is to hope that it will diminish with time. Trusting in moral progress, he pushes his problems into the future, suggesting, for example, that many of our deontological restrictions are likely to be modified under pressure from the impersonal standpoint. This hope of progress may seem edifying, but Nagel does not simply believe that we will come to act more morally; rather, for him moral progress consists in our finally beginning to understand what acting morally really involves. In his view,

> it is evident that we are at a primitive stage of moral development. Even the most civilised human beings have only a haphazard understanding of how to live, how to treat others, how to organise societies. The idea that the basic principles of morality are known, and that the problems come in their interpretation and application, is one of the most fantastic conceits to which our conceited species has been drawn.
>
> (*TVFN*, p. 186)

This is a strange passage and underlines Nagel's tendency to assimilate ethics and science as if we must wait to discover the truth about ethics just as we must wait to find out the truth about the Big Bang. This is misguided, for in the case of ethics we already possess all the evidence we need; if we believe a certain type of action is wrong, there is no danger that new data will confirm the speculative hypothesis that it is not. The belief that something is wrong is as it were self-contained. Precisely because it is not an empirical hypothesis, it is not something that awaits confirmation. If Nagel is unhappy with the whole range of existing views on how we should treat each other, he has only to specify exactly what aspects of these beliefs he finds inadequate and a moral breakthrough will instantly occur.

As these points suggest, Nagel is confused. The central flaw in his account is his failure to recognise the nature of the objectivity claim in ethics. His general strategy of defending the subjective perspective as disclosing a reality not available to the objective view simply underlines his inability to see ethics in any but quasi-empirical terms. Furthermore, he ends up agreeing with his opponents on the most significant point, for like them, he rejects the idea that there are correct ways of acting. One consequence of this is that he embraces relativism, accepting, for example, that there may be forms of morality incommensurable with our own that would be appropriate for Martians (*TVFN,* p. 186). Here, the idea seems to be that, since we would have no access to their subjective perspective, we would have no means of saying what it is right for them to do. This is misguided. The moralist need not hesitate to condemn a Martian for murder, deception or whatever; the subjective Martian perspective on these acts has no implications for any judgement about whether they are right or wrong.[7] Nagel, however, reduces the ethical claim that there are correct ways to act to the idea that our way of thinking makes us find certain actions attractive. As this final example illustrates, it is not just that Nagel is confused about ethics; rather, he has serious doubts about its central claim. In fact, his doubts and his confusions interact, so that although he sets out to offer a defence of ethics, it is impossible to be sure what he believes. As with many other contemporary philosophers, it is hard to determine whether or not he believes that there are correct ways for people to act.

Having criticised Nagel's attempted realism, it seems appropriate to consider the merits of anti-realism, a prominent exponent of which is Simon Blackburn whose attack on realism has taken many forms. In a 1973 essay he argues that realism cannot reconcile two claims which are essential to it, viz. the claim that moral qualities are supervenient on natural qualities and the claim that no moral property is entailed by any property ascribing naturalistic properties to its subject. The realist faces the impossible task of simultaneously claiming that 'the truth of a moral proposition consists in the existence of a state of affairs, which it reports; that the existence of this state of affairs is not entailed by the existence of other, naturalistic facts, yet that continuation of these facts entails that the moral state of affairs continues' (*Essays in Quasi-Realism,* p. 111). In later essays, Blackburn focuses less on the obscurity of realism and more on the way it conceals what ethics is really about. In particular, he criticises the attempt to give ethics a spurious authority by casting it in a pseudo-scientific form. Realism reduces to the pretense that 'just as the analytic chemist breaks open the hidden nature of water, so too the philosopher as scientist breaks open the hidden nature of the good' (*EQR,* p. 208). In his view the attempt to treat moral philosophy as a form of quasi-scientific theory-building disguises the fact that what is being put forward are substantive moral views.

> By all means we may urge and argue that all and only societies that embody the difference principle are just, or that all and only actions that promote happiness are good. But we should remember that only a loss of understanding about what we are doing comes from

thinking of ourselves as thereby identifying in a scientific spirit, the property that is justice or goodness, as opposed to deciding, from a moral perspective, the properties of just and good institutions or actions.

(*EQR*, pp. 208–9)

These criticisms are well made; treating ethics as a window onto a non-empirical reality can only conceal its true nature and render its claims philosophically dubious. The attempt to treat moral statements as similar to empirical statements leaves the former even more obscure and questionable than they initially appeared. To avoid this danger Blackburn offers an anti-realist interpretation of moral claims which he believes makes their coherence clear. He calls this approach 'quasi-realism', since he believes that the anti-realist can make the same statements as the realist, differing with her only on their philosophical interpretation. His position, however, rests on the mistaken idea that moral judgements must either describe the world or simply express our attitudes/dispositions. This fails to recognise the distinctive moral claim that there is a correct perspective on human action which everyone should adopt. It is this idea rather than the claim that values are in the world (or that moral judgements describe states of affairs) that constitutes belief in objective right and wrong; Blackburn, however, accepts the realist's account of what objectivity means and differs with her only on whether it is coherent. Unlike Mackie, he does not invoke an error theory to explain the objectivist element in our moral language and practices; rather, he sees the only errors as those of philosophical interpretation. On his account, the recognition that value is not objective leaves our moral practices untouched. In particular, he denies that anti-realism undermines traditional moral beliefs. 'To think that there are no moral truths is to think that nothing should be morally endorsed, that is, to endorse the endorsement of nothing, and this attitude is one that it would be wrong to recommend, and silly to practise' (*EQR*, p. 129).

The philosophical move which the above quotation embodies is typical of quasi-realism and constitutes Blackburn's main contribution to contemporary debate. However, it rests on an ambiguity, for rejecting the idea that anything can or should be morally endorsed is not equivalent to endorsing the endorsement of nothing. The anti-moralist rejects the idea of objective right and wrong and holds that all judgements about human actions (including her own judgements) are essentially expressions of preference; however, this does not prevent her from reacting to the behaviour of others. Her rejection of ethics does not involve indifference to everything, all it does is put on record her belief that in opposing or welcoming anything all the individual does (and can possibly do) is express the way she happens to be disposed. The peculiarity and interest of Blackburn's position is that he agrees with this view on a meta-ethical level and rejects it on the ethical level.

133

He believes that it is misguided to claim that there is an objectively correct position but that we can still claim that certain things intrinsically deserve to be condemned and therefore that certain judgements should be made by everyone.

For Blackburn what distinguishes moral judgements from expressions of preference is that they express not just an attitude, but an attitude towards attitudes. To explore this idea, let us consider Bertrand Russell's condemnation of bull-fighting, which is discussed by both Blackburn and Mackie. Having argued that moral judgements are essentially subjective, Russell recognises how hard this is to accept:

> Certainly there *seems* to be more. Suppose, for example, that some-one were to advocate the introduction of bull-fighting in this country. In opposing the proposal, I should *feel*, not only that I was expressing my desires, but that my desires in the matter are *right*, whatever that might mean. As a matter of argument, I can, I think, show that I am not guilty of any logical inconsistency in holding to the above interpretation of ethics and at the same time expressing strong ethical preferences. But in feeling I am not satisfied.
>
> (quoted in Mackie, *Ethics,* p. 34)

Mackie uses this passage to illustrate his claim that ordinary judgements contain a claim to objectivity which must be repudiated; in his view the idea that our desires might be right is an error, but an error which is built into our moral vocabulary. As Blackburn points out, however, Mackie ignores the implications of his own 'error' theory; avoiding the issue of what a corrected moral vocabulary would look like, he proceeds in the later stages of his book to outline an ethical theory which employs the very concepts he earlier claimed were flawed. Blackburn himself seeks to resolve this problem by arguing that the claim to objectivity is not part of our moral concepts but a mistaken theory about them. Thus, while Mackie concludes that Russell is wrong to think his desires might be right, Blackburn believes that there is nothing wrong with this idea if it is interpreted correctly. According to Blackburn, Russell's claim does not imply that his condemnation of bull-fighting somehow describes or corresponds to reality, rather it expresses a condemnation of those who do not condemn bull-fighting. It is 'a proper, necessary expression of an attitude towards attitudes. It is not something to be wrenched out of our moral psychology; it is something we need to cultivate to the right degree and in the right places to avoid the (moral) defect of indifference to things that merit passion' (*EQR,* p. 153).

But does Blackburn's quasi-realist interpretation of moral concepts work? On his account, Russell's sense that he is right to oppose bull-fighting reflects the fact that he does not just condemn bull-fighting but also condemns those who do not condemn it. The pressure towards this position is understandable, since if he did not condemn bull-fighting enthusiasts, Russell would seem to be undermining his own position—he would seem to be accepting that there is nothing wrong with bull-fighting after all. As Russell seems to recognise, however, and Blackburn does not, pursuing this line is an attempt to have it both ways. If Russell sees his judgement as simply the expression of an attitude he happens to have, he may still seek to prevent the occurrence of what he dislikes, but he cannot claim that his attitude is 'right', that intrinsically bull-fighting merits everyone's condemnation. This is where Blackburn thinks quasi-realism can square the circle. The trick, however, lies in a lack of clarity about what a quasi-realist Russell would be doing in condemning those who support bull-fighting. On the moralist's account, this condemnation is a direct reflection of the claim that there is a correct view on bull-fighting, viz. that it is wrong. On Blackburn's account, it is the expression of a complex attitude, but what lies behind this complication? If Russell does not accept that there are correct and incorrect ways of acting, in what sense can he condemn anything? He can react against bull-fighting enthusiasts, and since they promote what he dislikes, he has every reason to be hostile to them, but he cannot condemn them (or indeed, bull-fighting itself), for he does not believe that there are correct or incorrect ways of acting. In the absence of the moral claim that bull-fighting is wrong, there is no basis for his having an 'attitude to attitudes'. As a quasi-realist, Russell can object to bull-fighting enthusiasts only in the sense that he can object to people who wear loud clothes. He does not like what they like, but he recognises that there is no question of right and wrong and that it is simply a matter of different preferences/dispositions.

Another way of seeing what is wrong with quasi-realism is to note that it involves an infinite regress. The notion of an attitude to an attitude is intended to capture the idea of something being wrong in itself, but even from Blackburn's perspective this notion has to be taken further. Suppose someone condemns murder. According to Blackburn, in doing this the individual expresses an attitude to murder and an attitude to attitudes to murder. If we reject the idea of objective right and wrong and so the notion of a correct reaction, the only plausible way of interpreting this is that the individual reacts negatively to such actions and reacts negatively to those who condone murder (do not react negatively to it). On its own, however, this does not amount to the moral condemnation of murder, for the individual must also react negatively to those who do not react negatively to those who condone murder. Similarly, she must react negatively to those who do not react negatively to those who do not react negatively to those who condone murder. This endless regress of attitudes to attitudes and attitudes to attitudes to attitudes may appear to capture the moral claim but only because it indefinitely defers the issue of the type of claim the individual is making. She appears to claim that her attitude is correct but then explains that this simply means that her attitude is buttressed by an attitude to those who do not share her attitude. When asked whether this second attitude is correct, she says 'yes', but again explains that this only means that she condemns those who do not condemn those who do not condemn what she condemns. The aim of this endless process of interpretation and reinterpretation is to bury the question of whether the individual believes that her position is correct or holds that it is simply a (complex) reaction she happens to have. The only reason Blackburn is able to combine a rejection of objective ethics with a commitment to ethical judgements is because he hides this contradiction in the ambiguity of an infinite regress.

The importance of this point means that it is worth illustrating with a further example, so let us consider the case of cruelty which Blackburn discusses in 'How to be an Ethical Realist'. He argues that the question 'What makes cruelty wrong?' is an ethical rather than a meta-ethical question: since it does not make sense to suggest that there might be some state of affairs which makes cruelty wrong, this question can only be seen as asking us to indicate what it is about cruelty that we do not like. Similarly, the suggestion that it is our attitudes that make cruelty wrong should be interpreted not as a meta-ethical claim, but as a highly implausible moral view. Certainly, it is not Blackburn's view, for he recognises that 'what makes cruelty abhorrent is not that it offends us, but all those hideous things that make it do so' (*EQR,* p. 172).

This response is disingenuous, for it avoids the issue of whether cruelty is objectively wrong or simply something to which some individuals react negatively. Defining cruelty—specifying what is being reacted against—does not clarify the key issue of the status being claiming for this reaction.[8] If the individual accepts that it is simply a matter of her having a dis-preference for cruelty, then it is hard to see why she should object to cruelty occurring when she is unaware of it. Furthermore, her negative reaction does not amount to believing that cruelty as such is wrong. Even if she dislikes the idea of cruelty taking place anywhere, on her own account all that is at stake is her reaction, and her discomfort is minimised when she believes that no cruelty is taking place, not when no cruelty is actually taking place. Although she herself cannot say this because the admission may be counter-productive, what she does not know about cannot cause her any unpleasant reactions.

Thus Blackburn's account does not correspond to moral belief. It is also implausible, for once the notion of objective right and wrong is rejected, the kind of reaction he emphasises looks very odd. He can postulate such complex dispreferences, but interpreted in the way he suggests, they can only look like strange hang-ups. It would be like someone who disliked ice cream objecting to other people eating ice cream even if she never even knew they did so. Blackwell may reply that most people would condemn the attitude 'I don't mind cruelty as long as I do not know about', but this is beside the point, for all it does is remind us that most people are not quasi-realists. The reason they condemn this sort of attitude is because they believe that cruelty is wrong rather than simply something to which they have a negative reaction. By contrast, Blackburn's attitude-to-attitudes account can only be plausible by constantly shifting its ground. He claims that we have a negative reaction to cruelty but that it is not just a negative reaction, since it is supplemented by a negative reaction to those who condone cruelty. To stop there, however, would suggest that there is nothing wrong with not having a negative reaction to those who condone cruelty; so it turns out that the attitude to attitudes must be supplemented by an attitude to attitudes to attitudes. Here, the infinite regress is obvious. The point is that, if we ever stop and admit that our position is just an attitude we happen to have, we fall short of the moral claim, whereas if we stop paraphrasing the claim to correctness we have abandoned quasi-moralism for a belief in objective right and wrong.

So far we have concentrated on Blackburn's claim that the quasi-realist can make the same statements as someone who believes in objective right and wrong. Here, the ambiguity lies in his treatment of the first-order claim that it is correct, for example, to condemn bull-fighting. The quasi-realist seems to make this claim, explains it in a way that undermines it and when pressed, reintroduces the notion of correctness only to explain it away again. This ambiguity is matched at the meta-ethical level, for Blackburn rejects the distinctive moral claim that there is a correct perspective on human action and yet still claims to believe in ethics. Here, the ambiguity lies in his interpretation of what is involved in rejecting ethics. Blackburn's position is based on the assumption that judgements on human action are essentially the expression of dispositions. This excludes the idea that there are correct judgements or judgements that everyone should make, and so involves a rejection of ethics. Blackburn, however, claims that rejecting ethics would involve not having any preferences about how other people act, and on the basis of this definition he claims not to reject ethics.

This argument is as misleading as the earlier one. As well as making the rejection of ethics almost inconceivable, it conceals the real issue raises by the notion of objective right and wrong. The key question is whether we believe that there is a correct perspective on human action, and, *pace* Blackburn, denying this is quite compatible with having preferences about how people act. Indeed, someone who takes this view may act in a way that is similar to the moralist—if she has been brought up in a particular way, her preferences may to a large extent correspond to the moralist's judgements. The difference between the two parties is the status they claim for judgements on human action; the anti-moralist treats an individual's views, including her own, as a reflection of the way that individual happens to be disposed, while the moralist holds that there is a correct set of judgements that should be recognised as such by everyone. This is the real issue and the one Blackburn needs to take a stand on. However, if he sticks with quasi-realism, the clearest way of describing his position is to say that he rejects the idea of objective right and wrong.

To underline these points let us consider quasi-realism from a different angle, for if his project is to succeed, Blackburn must show that quasi-realism is compatible with our current moral practices, for example he needs to show it can account for obligation. The problem he faces here is combining the constraint of obligation with a recognition of its self-created nature. As he himself puts it, 'the chains and shackles of obligation must come from outside us. Can anything both be felt to have this power and be explained as a projection of our own sentiments?' (*EQR*, p. 153). To examine this issue Blackburn considers the case of a couple who want to marry, but one of whom (Fred) believes that he has a duty to do otherwise. Blackburn does not say why Fred believes this, but he does argue that Fred can make sense of his moral scruples from a quasi-realist perspective.

> Fred has been brought up in a certain way, and a consequence of this upbringing is that he looks on certain courses of action with horror. He will keep his respect, be able to live with himself, only if he conducts his life in a particular way, and this prompts a range of feeling that is sufficiently strong to oppose immediate desire and that gains expression when he describes the conduct as 'wrong'. Whether it was a good thing that Fred was brought up like that is a matter of judgement. But it can hardly be doubted that it is a good thing that people should sometimes feel like that, for otherwise they are more likely to do the most awful things.
>
> (*EQR*, pp. 154–5)

Here, it is typical that Blackburn should refer to 'awful things' and so invoke the objectivist framework that he rejects on the meta-ethical level. If he is being consistent 'awful things' can only mean things he personally happens to disapprove of and disapprove of people not disapproving of, etc. As we have seen, however, this does not add up to the claim that it is correct to see these things as awful or that they are awful in themselves.

Leaving this point to one side, the key issue is whether Fred believes that he ought not to marry Mabel. By not specifying what holds Fred back from marriage, Blackburn obscures this question, and it is vital to his argument that he does so, for if we press Fred on whether he thinks it is right for him to marry Mabel, he will either have to adopt an objectivist position or admit that it is just a question of him overall not being inclined to marry her. Blackburn seeks a third option by arguing that Fred can endorse the upbringing which has given him this negative reaction and that this is what being morally opposed to the marriage amounts to. This argument does not work—all it does is defer the issue. The key question now is the basis on which Fred endorses this type of upbringing. Either he claims that this is simply a preference he happens to have or he endorses the upbringing on the basis that the reaction it inculcates is right. In the first case there is no question of right and wrong and Fred simply finds himself in a complicated position (he wants society to instil these reactions in people, but finds that in his case these reactions interfere with other wants he has). In the second case the reference to social policy is unnecessary, since Fred's endorsement of the policy of encouraging this reaction is a consequence of his belief that it is right. He believes it is wrong to marry in this sort of situation and therefore believes society should encourage people to believe this.

To illustrate these points, let us fill out Blackburn's example. Suppose the obligation which stands in the way of Fred marrying Mabel is that he has promised to marry someone else. If Fred felt no compunction about breaking promises, there would be no problem, so we must assume that he has been brought up to feel reluctant to break them and guilty when he does so. The key question is how Fred understands the pricking of his conscience. Suppose he rejects the idea that certain types of action are correct and sees his reactions simply as a set of dispositions he has come to have. Even in this case he may still have reason to hesitate before marrying Mabel, for he must decide whether his feelings of guilt are likely to outweigh the hoped-for pleasures of married life. But this situation clearly does not involve Fred's believing that marrying Mabel is wrong, so let us incorporate the further twist that Fred endorses the policy that has created his feelings of guilt, i.e. he endorses the policy of instilling reactions in people so that they feel bad if they renege on promises of marriage. If he endorses this policy because he believes it is wrong to break a marriage promise, he is making a straight-forward objectivist moral claim. By contrast, if he treats his support for this policy simply as a reflection of how he happens to be disposed (i.e. as the expression of a personal preference), he is left in the slightly uncomfortable position of wanting others to be given an upbringing that, as it happens, he himself regrets having received.[9]

The same points apply in relation to any feelings of hypocrisy Fred might have if he goes ahead with his marriage to Mabel. If he sticks with quasi-realism, he will see these feelings, too, as simply a reaction he has come to have. As with broken marriage promises, he may prefer that people feel bad about being hypocritical, but if rejects the notion of objective right and wrong, the only barrier to acting hypocritically in his own case (as in that of others) is a calculation of whether the bad feelings will outweigh the benefits. Thus Blackburn's twist does not alter the basic story; once we drop the idea that his reactions may be right, all we can say of Fred's situation is that because of a certain upbringing (that he may or may not want others to be given) he has acquired an aversion to marrying Mabel who he otherwise very much wants to marry.

What prevents Blackburn from recognising these points is his assumption that the claim to correctness cannot be understood in its own terms. He believes that 'the quasi-realist affirms all that could ever be properly meant by saying there are real obligations' (*EQR*, p. 157). But this assertion is misleading for it rests on the belief that traditional claims about obligation do not really make sense. The situation is similar as far as Blackburn's relation to ethics in general is concerned. He believes that all prescriptions are simply the expression of dispositions and that there is no basis for claiming that some prescriptions (and dispositions) are objectively superior to others. This is a perfectly coherent position, but it involves rejecting the fundamental moral claim that certain prescriptions are correct and should be followed by everyone. Identifying this claim with the nonsensical idea that states of affairs might be prescriptive (that reality might somehow tell us what to do), Blackburn takes it for granted that any reasonable individual must recognise that her beliefs about how people should act simply reflect how she has come to be disposed. This undermines the very possibility of ethics before the discussion has started and is contradicted by Blackburn's own readiness to claim that certain judgements may be correct. The attempt to explain this idea in terms of moral judgements being judgements about the judgements other people make confuses the issue but does not change it. Ultimately, Blackburn has to say whether his views on human action simply reflect how he happens to be disposed or whether they are views he believes are correct and should be adopted by everyone. Either it is a matter of reactions and we simply react negatively to people who make different judgements from us. Or we believe in right and wrong and condemn people for acting and judging in ways which we believe are incorrect.

6

ETHICS AND MODERN
PHILOSOPHY

At the end of my lecture on ethics, I spoke in the first person. I
believe that is quite essential. Here nothing can be established.
I can only appear as a person speaking for myself.'

(Wittgenstein, *Wittgenstein and the Vienna Circle*, p. 117)

One of the main contentions of this book has been that modern philosophy's position on ethics is confused; in particular, we have argued that
many contemporary philosophers reject the distinctive moral claim that
there are correct judgements of human action without recognising that this
involves rejecting ethics. In this chapter we shall explore the reasons for this
confusion in more detail. As we have seen, one of the main sources of
confusion is a reluctance to accept that reasons come to an end. Wittgenstein
showed that the denial of bedrock lies behind philosophical problems in
many areas, and this is particularly true of ethics. Our beliefs about right and
wrong are among our most important convictions, and the suggestion that
their correctness cannot be proved is unsettling. This disquiet may be
increased by the assumption that the claim to correctness fails unless it can
be given unimpeachable support. We tend to assume that if we cannot prove
that our moral judgements are correct, this shows that they are simply
disguised preferences. Faced with rival claims to correctness, we think that
unless we can show that other people are wrong, we cannot claim to be right.
But this is misguided. The claim that there are actions which everyone
should recognise as right or wrong is a substantive claim which can be
supported with reasons but which cannot be proved. Of course, the impossibility of proof is a feature of any substantive claim, but this general point
creates a special difficulty in the field of ethics, for here we face not just
possible disagreement at bedrock but actual disagreement. It is a confusion,
however, to take this to show that the claims of one party to the dispute (the
moralist) are wrong.[1]

The demand for proof is a feature of both modern and past moral philosophy, and this is not at all surprising. Ethics is concerned with fundamental

questions about how we should understand the world and about how we should live, and it has always been one of philosophy's main aims to provide definitive answers to these questions. But this goal is impossible, for while we can reach conclusions that we are certain are correct, we cannot prove their correctness in ways everyone must accept. The search for proof also brings risks, for it can distort our account of the nature of moral claims. For example, the substantive account of how every individual should act may be confused with an account of what it is in every individual's (uncontroversial) interests to do. A good contemporary illustration of this process is the claim by Bernard Williams that if ethics could be given an objective foundation, this would have to consist in a deduction from the findings of psychology. This is confused. Even if we could show that acting in certain ways was beneficial to anyone who had goals which most people have, this would not establish that those ways of acting were correct and incumbent on everyone. On the contrary, someone who claims that the individual should tell the truth because this is in her interests thereby avoids rather than endorses the claim that the individual should tell the truth because this is the correct thing to do. Far from providing ethics with some kind of foundation, therefore, this line of argument leads away from ethics and suggests that it is wrong to claim that something should be done purely and simply because it is the right thing to do.

Modern and past philosophy may share a desire for proof, but they differ significantly in their relation to ethics. Modern philosophy at least in the Anglo-Saxon world has moved away from metaphysics and sought to ally itself more closely to science. This shift has changed both its aims and its content. In particular, philosophy has become less concerned with seeking answers to what might be called the great questions of life. This is a major break with previous philosophy, for the metaphysical systems of the past do seek to answer these questions. Each articulates what is claimed to be the correct way of understanding the world, and even if the search for proof can distort or confuse the vision put forward, each also incorporates a substantive and specific moral vision. By contrast, modern philosophy, particularly in its analytic form, is not explicitly concerned with articulating an understanding of the world and our place in it. One consequence of this is that nowadays ethics can often seem a philosophical backwater. Accepting some form of the fact/value distinction, modern philosophers seem to believe that it is science that will tell us the correct way to understand the world. Values are therefore treated either as a matter of personal choice or as a question of social organisation. The key ethical claim that understanding the world correctly involves recognising certain ways of acting as correct is tacitly rejected.

The prevalence of this type of view among modern philosophers is no doubt the product of many factors, but in part it reflects the loss of moral certainty in our society and an increase in moral scepticism. All the contemporary philosophers we have discussed are wary of the claim that there is a correct perspective on human action; indeed, most reject this idea and hold that the correct way of understanding the world involves recognising that all value judgements are subjective, i.e. expressions of the preferences or dispositions of those who make them. According to this view, the world has no meaning, and any claims about its meaning (apart, of course, from this one) are the projection of human needs and desires. In itself, of course, there is nothing new about this view. There have always been people who were suspicious about the absolute nature of moral claims and who rejected ethics; the change, however, is that what was once a dissenting opinion is now close to a consensus view, at least on a theoretical level. To modern ears, talk of the correct perspective on human action (and of what it is correct for individuals to do) is deeply suspect and, rather than entering into debate on what that perspective is, many philosophers (and many non-philosophers) are inclined to deny that there is such a perspective at all.

The inclination to reject the claim to correctness may be reinforced by the modern familiarity with a wide variety of cultures both across different places and across different times. In the face of this diversity many people are inclined to draw the substantive conclusion that an individual's perspective on human action is determined by the culture in which she happens to live. This sort of position rejects the claim that certain types of action are incumbent on everyone and implies that all judgements on human action should essentially be seen as ways in which the individual happens to react. According to this view, different groups of people favour different types of act because of their upbringing and that is all there is to it. There is no scope for the claim that one group is right and another wrong. Similarly, on this view there is no objective basis for a third party telling the individual how to act. If someone says 'You should not do X', this person is expressing her preference for people not doing X (or is simply reacting in a way she has come to be disposed to react) and there is no reason why anyone else should see this as binding on her. As Williams puts it, moral judgements are not overriding.

The relativism which this rejection of ethics involves does not imply that the individual will always act selfishly in a narrow sense. If an individual develops affections for others (as most do), she will have a reason to take their preferences into account; other things being equal, she will prefer not to do what displeases them. Similarly, some moral reactions may have been inculcated into her as a child (on the mistaken basis that they were correct) so that she may prefer not to lie, cheat, steal or whatever. Indeed, these preferences may be so ingrained in her that she is inclined to pass them on to her own children. Although she believes that there is nothing objectively wrong with lying, it would painful for her to think of her child as a liar and so she tries to inculcate into her an inclination to tell the truth. For these reasons, even after rejecting ethics the individual may act in ways similar to

143

the moralist. The basis of her actions, however, will be quite different. Furthermore, if she happens to have little affection for others or if 'moral' reactions were never inculcated into her (or have become weakened), she will have no reason to act in ways that would traditionally be called moral. With Mackie, she should recognise that there are no constraints on her action except those she herself imposes. If she wants to act in a certain way, she has no reason to let herself be held back by the misguided claim that there are certain ways in which no one should act.

This modern version of moral scepticism is one way of understanding the world and it is a possible substantive view. In part, however, it may arise from confusion about the notion of objectivity in the context of ethics. For example, it may reflect the belief that if their claim to correctness is to be justified, values must either be shown to be part of the furniture of the universe or be derivable from rationality. When these ideas are rightly rejected, the conclusion is often drawn that values are subjective. Against this, we have argued that belief in right and wrong does not involve claiming that special entities exist or that there are certain beliefs that all rational beings must hold qua rational beings. Rather, it involves claiming that making certain judgements about action is part of understanding the world correctly. According to the moralist, someone who rejects these judgements has a distorted view of the world and has failed to recognise what really matters in life. However, these statements do not take us any further. They simply paraphrase the claim that the correct way of understanding the world involves recognising that there are correct ways of acting. The philosophical difficulty lies in accepting that there is nothing further to be explained. The substantive claim made by the moralist is that anyone who understands the world correctly will recognise that there are ways she should and should not act. This is a position which can be rejected but which the moralist claims ought not to be.

As we have seen, the philosophical temptation in the face of this position is to demand proof (or at least some form of further support) rather than accepting that reasons come to an end. However, while past philosophers tried to provide proofs, most modern philosophers recognise that proof is impossible and conclude from this that the notion of objective values is wrong. In this way their reluctance to accept that reasons come to an end leads them to reject a particular type of view, despite the fact that the alternative is just as unprovable. The modern consensus is encapsulated in the idea that while factual statements are objective (i.e. can be correct/incorrect), value statements are not (and therefore cannot be). This position is somewhat paradoxical, for while facts are not supposed to generate values, it is held to be a matter of fact that all value claims are fundamentally flawed and that the claim to correctness they embody is misguided. What is apparently a logical distinction seems to justify one approach to understanding the world. Anyone who claims that the world should be understood in moral terms is simply wrong. The correct position (the 'objective' view) is that the world is a mass of causes with no purpose and meaning. As for judgements of human action, these are all on a par as the expression of different dispositions or preferences. This view is factually correct; as Williams might put, if we know anything about the world, we know this.

It is no coincidence that this argument ends in bare assertion. Ultimately, all the individual can do is advance the view she believes is correct. This brings us back to the issue of bedrock and illustrates what is wrong with the above approach, for it seeks to use the fact/value distinction to legislate in favour of a certain view (or type of view). The possibility of drawing a distinction between statements about what exists and claims about how people should act does not show that the latter cannot be correct. While it is certainly possible to hold that all judgements of human action simply express the preferences/dispositions of a particular group/individual, this claim is not something that has been (or could be) demonstrated by scientific investigation nor can it be established by a process of conceptual analysis. On the contrary, the claim is itself part of a particular substantive position and, like any such position, the reasons that can be offered for it come to an end. Those who hold it can seek to persuade other people that it is correct, but the logical possibility of disagreement cannot be excluded. One way of bringing out what is wrong with this approach is to note that it makes nonsensical demands of science, for it suggests that the only open questions about how we should understand the world are scientific questions. However, the idea that science must be accepted as the ultimate arbiter on all questions of existence (including that of God) is itself confused, and even if it was not, there are a host of issues about how we should make sense of the world that science cannot pronounce on. In particular, science cannot tell us whether everyone should recognise certain actions as correct and therefore it cannot pronounce on the issue of whether moral claims are 'objective' or 'subjective'.

Making these points does not involve denying that science can play an important role in an individual's reflection on the correct way to understand the world. Reaching conclusions about what significance to attach to the work of Einstein, Freud and Darwin, etc. is part of what is involved today in reflecting on the human situation. Certainly, some take the successes of modern science to show that the world has no purpose or meaning and this conclusion may lead them to adopt a position of moral scepticism. But other conclusions are also possible. On the one hand, it is possible to have an understanding of the world that is heavily influenced by science and still believe that there are correct ways of acting. Someone may, for example, believe that the existence of conscious beings is a chance phenomenon but still hold that anyone capable of thought should recognise that causing suffering is wrong. In her opinion any conscious being who rejects this claim goes wrong, i.e. fails to recognise what should be recognised by everyone. On the other hand, it is possible to hold that science provides an incomplete or, in some (or many) respects, inadequate basis for understanding the world. Here, belief in science may be measured against other beliefs (and not just religious beliefs), and it is misguided to think that philosophy can endorse science (or a particular version of it) as correct. No one would deny that the scientific way of investigating the world has been colossally successful, but once we start talking about fundamental issues of how we should understand the world, there is scope for irresolvable disagreements both on the limits of science and on how the conclusions of science should be understood.

So far the points we have made relate directly to ethics; however, if we really want to understand modern philosophy's difficulties with moral claims, we need to discuss some issues that may seem more philosophy of mind than moral philosophy. What we need to consider are certain fundamental issues connected with human action, for modern philosophy's approach to this subject is another reason why it finds ethics so hard to understand. The difficulty again relates to bedrock, but in this case what is at stake is the language-game of agency or intentionality. Unable to accept that reasons come to an end, the tendency among modern philosophers is to treat our language-game as unacceptable and to seek either to replace reasons with causes or to treat the former as a variant of the latter. This has important consequences for ethics, for the causal approach to human action involves treating people's actions as caused by their dispositions and seeing their judgements on human action, too, as caused reactions. This conflicts with the position of the moralist who holds that people can choose how they act and that there are correct ways of acting. She believes that there are correct judgements on human action and that everyone should act in accordance with them regardless of how they are disposed.

The moralist's approach involves treating human[2] action as different from other types of event, particularly processes involving inanimate objects but also the behaviour of animals. Such an approach may seem uncontroversial, but it is implicitly rejected by many contemporary philosophers who hold that human behaviour, like any other phenomenon, is the product of causal forces. On the causal view, the individual's judgements on human action are reactions she has been caused to acquire, while her intentions (her account of the choices she thinks she makes) are at best an imperfect reflection of the real factors that determine her behaviour. Not only is it misguided to talk of the individual recognising good and evil, but even if it was not, this would be irrelevant, since the real explanation of her behaviour is to be found in the history of causes which has made her the person she is.

The way the causal approach affects modern philosophers' accounts of ethics can be illustrated by considering Thomas Nagel's discussion of human action in *The View from Nowhere*. Nagel recognises that what he calls the objective view calls into question our notion of agency, but he puts this issue to one side as a matter for the philosophy of mind and concentrates on the issues of autonomy and responsibility. The difficulty he sees in relation to these issues is that from the objective standpoint 'actions seem no longer assignable to individual agents as sources, but become instead components of the flux of events in the world of which the agent is a part' (*TVN*, p. 110). This creates a clash between the subjective and the objective views. From the inside a number of possibilities seem open to us and we seem to choose between them; from the outside, however, this appears to be an illusion, for if a complete specification of the condition of the agent and the circumstances of actions is given, there seems to be nothing further for the individual to contribute (ibid., p. 113).

These claims reflects Nagel's belief that only causal explanations really explain; he holds that 'there is no room in an objective picture of the world for a type of explanation of action that is not causal' (ibid., p. 115). The individual's account of her intentions may make her actions intelligible, but it does not explain them because it does not explain why she acted on the reasons she did.

> If autonomy requires that the central element of choice be ex-plained in a way that does not take us outside the point of view of the agent . . . then intentional explanations must simply come to an end when all available reasons have been given, and nothing else can take over when they leave off. But this seems to mean that autonomous intentional explanation cannot explain precisely what it is supposed to explain, namely *why I did what I did rather than alternatives that were causally open to me*. It says I did it for certain reasons, but does not explain why I didn't decide not to do it for other reasons. It may render the action subjectively intelligible, but it does not explain why this rather than another equally possible and comparably intelligible action was done.
>
> (ibid., p. 116, author's italics)

Nagel's conclusion is that the autonomy we experience from the inside is an illusion; the reality is that our behaviour, like everything else in the world, can only really be understood in causal terms.

This conclusion has obvious implications for the issue of responsibility, for if autonomy is an illusion, there would seem to be no basis for holding people responsible for their actions. According to Nagel, holding someone responsible involves assessing the courses of action that were open to the individual from her perspective. In his view, 'when we hold [someone] responsible, the result is not merely a description of his character, but a vicarious occupation of his point of view and evaluation of his action from within it' (ibid., p. 121). Noting that we do not usually condemn cats and rattlesnakes, he suggests that this is because 'our understanding of their actions and even of their point of view puts us too far outside them to permit any judgements about what they should have done' (ibid., p. 121). This is an eccentric claim and gives an indication of how confused about these issues Nagel is. This detour, however, does not affect the fundamental point already made in his discussion of autonomy, viz. that the individual's sense that alternatives were open to her is an illusion.

> Either something other than the agent's reasons explains why he acted for the reasons he did, or nothing does. In either case the external standpoint sees the alternatives not as alternatives for the agent, but as alternatives for the *world*, which involve the *agent*. And the world, of course, is not an agent and cannot be held responsible.
>
> (ibid., p. 123)

The inescapable conclusion is that our judgements of responsibility are misguided—they depend on forgetting that we are just part of the world and that our lives are just part of the caused progression of events.

Nagel sees these conclusions as disquieting but correct; he does, however, seek to mitigate their impact. For example, he suggests that 'we might try, first, to develop as complete an objective view of ourselves as we can, and [then] include it in the basis of our actions wherever it is relevant' (ibid., p. 127). This suggestion cuts across his earlier arguments, for if we cannot act, how can we try to act in a particular way? If our behaviour depends on the causal factors that precede it, what scope is there for the intervention of the will? Nonetheless, Nagel thinks his strategy can offer various kinds of protection from the disquiet generated by the objective view. His first idea is that we can protect some judgements by explicitly recognising their subjective character. For example, he argues that in a restaurant we choose by opening ourselves up to the play of inclinations and appetites, and he claims we can do so 'without fear that from a more detached perspective it might appear that one of the weaker [appetites] should really have been preferred' (ibid., p. 131). According to Nagel, what this example shows is that at least in some cases the objective view does not undermine action based on our subjective perception.

Typically, however, this quotation introduces a completely different notion of objectivity and so switches the debate to a different issue. The objective view now relates to questions about how it is correct to act (what 'should really have been preferred'). It is no longer a matter of whether our actions are caused, but whether there are cases where it would be misguided to criticise our actions for not taking into account the wishes of others. As well as presupposing that we act (as opposed to being caused to behave in certain ways), this move introduces unannounced a substantive (if conventional) view of when it is permissible for the individual to consult only her own wishes in deciding how she to act. The switch to a different notion of objectivity is even clearer in Nagel's second suggestion, which is that morality is a kind of freedom. The idea here is that by seeing ourselves as one individual among many we protect ourselves from the claim that our actions are simply the expression of our own selfish desires. This suggestion embodies a further substantive claim about how it is correct for people to act, but it has nothing to do with what Nagel earlier called the objective standpoint. Furthermore, if the view he first describes is correct, there is no scope for trying to act less selfishly; the individual will act as the causal factors dispose her to act and that is all there is to it. From the 'objective' standpoint, selfish and altruistic actions are at best different types of causal patterns, while the confusions of ethics (and of trying to act altruistically) are simply an extension of the illusion of autonomy.

Nagel is led into these contradictions by his belief that only causal explanations really explain. This is confused and reflects a failure to understand the language-game of intentions. More generally, it reflects a failure to recognise the special nature of the concepts that are involved in our relation to human beings. One way this relation is expressed is in terms of the Inner/Outer picture, for we treat the behaviour of human beings as the expression of an inner world of thoughts, feelings, intentions, etc. This is essential to our treatment of someone as a conscious agent. Although we do sometimes ask 'What caused you to do that?', what we want to know is the intention behind the individual's action; we are interested in her account of how this action fits in with the rest of her behaviour. This account is not based on observation and does not involve hypotheses about causes. On the contrary, the individual simply says what her intention was and her sincere statements are definitive. They tell us what we want to know when trying to understand her behaviour as the action of a conscious being. Of course, if what she says is incoherent or if her sincere statements do not tie in with her behaviour, we will not be able to treat her as an agent. But that is not the normal situation. Our normal relation to a human being involves treating her behaviour as the actions of an agent with an inner world of thoughts, feelings, intentions, etc. The Inner/Outer picture is thus crucial to our relation with human beings, and it lies at the heart of all our psychological language-games, for within these the individual is assigned a privileged position in relation to her own Inner—her sincere utterances tell us what her thoughts, feelings, intentions, etc. are. Rather than treating the individual's behaviour as caused by factors yet to be discovered, we treat her as an agent and are interested in her (sincere) account of why she acted as she did.[3]

Understanding human action is therefore not like understanding an inanimate process, and the approach we adopt is a very different approach to that we adopt when we are seeking to explain something in causal terms. Although it is possible to apply a causal approach to aspects of human action, it is a mistake to think that this is what our normal language-games already do. In particular, it is wrong to claim that reasons are causes seen from the inside. In giving her reasons, the individual does not see or describe anything, she simply speaks and, insofar as we treat her as an agent, her sincere statement has a special authority—it tells us what she was trying to do or why she acted as she did. By contrast, if we wanted to explain her behaviour in causal terms, we would have to find ways of testing our causal hypotheses. Claims by the subject—no matter how sincere—would be beside the point or rather would simply furnish further data to be explained. The two language-games are fundamentally different. The individual's account of her reasons (her past intentions) is no more an account of causal processes seen from the inside than her expressions of intention are an account of causal processes seen before they have even occurred.

Recognising these points, we can see that the confusions of Nagel's account arise from his treatment of reasons as flawed causal explanations. His objection to intentional explanations is that they that do not explain why the individual chose to act on one set of reasons rather than another, but this is confused. The reasons the individual gives do explain her choice—they are precisely what we are interested in when we ask someone why she acted as she did. By citing certain reasons rather than others, she tells us what she was trying to do and so enables us to understand her action. This is very different from her showing that the causal factors were such that only one result was possible; indeed, this idea is excluded, for insofar as we treat the individual as an agent it is assumed that she could have acted on different reasons or in a different way entirely. Nagel, however, insists that intentional explanations ought to be causal explanations. After the individual has given her reasons for acting, he seeks further explanations and thereby rejects as inadequate what for most of us is precisely the explanation we are interested in. Misunderstanding the language-game, he rejects the individual's account of why she acted as she did and holds that the real explanation must consist in an account of the causal factors which lay behind her illusion of choice.

Nagel's misconceptions about the Inner are evident in his suggestion that we choose from a menu in a restaurant by opening ourselves up to the play of inclinations and appetites. This suggests that choosing involves observing the play of forces within some inner forum, when in fact what happens is that the individual simply says what she wants. The notion of a desire does not relate to a physical force or an entity, for desires are not identifiable independently of the person to whom they are ascribed. We say the individual has a certain desire on the basis of her sincerely saying that she wants something or because she acts in a way for which we think her sincere explanation would be that she wanted that thing. If we were trying to explain the individual's behaviour in causal terms, our approach would have to be very different. The elements in a genuinely causal account would have to be identifiable independently of the agent and, although the individual's words and deeds might suggest that a particular causal factor was operating, there would have to be some other way of confirming this. As it is, talk of an individual's desires has a place within our treatment of the individual's behaviour as the actions of an agent. In Nagel's example, saying the individual had a desire for pecan pie indicates that she chose this dish because she wanted it rather than because she wanted to impress the waiter or was trying to spin out the length of the meal. Similarly, the claim that she had a greater desire for pecan pie than for ice cream tells us how we should understand her action rather than giving information on the relative strength of forces within her. For example, it rules out the idea that she chose the former because it was cheaper than the latter, and this is confirmed by what the individual says when we ask her (if her answer is sincere). The key point is that, although a causal approach to human action is theoretically possible, it cannot include any of our psychological concepts in its causal explanations, for these concepts are all characterised by the privileged position assigned to the speaker/agent.

Nagel, however, does not accept these points. Instead he insists on treating everything in causal terms and this creates problems when he tries to understand ethics. Since he implicitly rejects the idea that human beings act, it is not surprising that he finds it hard to understand the claim that there are ways people ought to act. Since he does not believe that people are responsible for their actions, it is hard for him to see them as doing right or wrong. His tragic vision of the world (what he calls the 'objective view') is that we are insignificant cogs in the vast causal mechanism which is the universe. But he does not stick to this view consistently. If he did, he would treat people's views on human action as something to be explained in causal terms and hold that people's reaction to their own actions and to those of others were simply further caused phenomena. Inconsistently, he rejects these conclusions. Although it cuts across everything else he says, he suggests that people do act and that the correct way to act is on the basis of an impartial assessment of everyone's concerns. This is a possible (and fairly traditional) moral position, but it is out of place in the wider context of his account. Nagel then caps this contradiction with a further confusion, for, having advanced a view on the correct way for people to act, he recognises that this sets a rather demanding standard and accepts that it is reasonable for the individual not to adhere to it or not to adhere to it all the time. In short, his position is that it may be correct not to act in the way that is the correct way to act, and that anyway, objectively, the idea that we act is an illusion.

Nagel's book shows how a causal approach to human action can stand in the way of understanding ethics. Furthermore, his account is confused insofar as it seeks to combine a causal approach to human action with a commitment to ethics. But what if someone recognised the clash with ethics but still maintained that the causal approach was correct? What if someone claimed that, despite our language-game, it just is the case that human action is caused? This seems a reasonable position and is worth considering in more detail, since otherwise there may be a temptation to think that, if scientific progress has not absolutely disproved moral claims, it has at least made then extremely implausible. As we have noted, most contemporary moral philosophers do tend to see traditional moral claims as having been undermined by science, and many of their difficulties arise from the attempt to eliminate from ethics assumptions they believe have been shown to be false. Part of the argument here is substantive, but there is also a significant element of confusion and that is what is of interest to us. Our aim in the discussion that follows is not to advance a particular substantive position but to show that we do not have to take a causal approach to human action. In fact, rather than being self-evidently correct, this approach is somewhat obscure and it is not all clear what it really involves.

One way to approach this issue is to ask why, despite our normal language-games, people are still inclined to claim that human behaviour must be caused. As the word 'must' indicates, this is not an empirical claim; rather, it is an application to human behaviour of the principle that every event has a cause. So what is the basis of this principle? This may seem a strange question, and the temptation is to claim that it is a manifest truth which has been confirmed on innumerable occasions by scientific investigation. It would be more accurate, however, to put things the other way round and say that this principle partly defines scientific investigation. It forms the basis of a hugely successful approach to explaining (and manipulating) the world and, given the success of this approach, it is not surprising that we are inclined to claim that there are no limits to its applicability. It is wrong, however, to treat the claim that every event has a cause as some sort of a priori truth. Rather, it is equivalent to the injunction 'If you have not found a causal explanation, keep looking'. The point is not that every event we have ever investigated turned out to have a cause, but rather that as far as we are concerned, no investigation is complete until a cause has been found.

This approach has, of course, been phenomenally successful and it is not surprising that we tend to assume that it can be applied everywhere. In a sense, however, the idea that everything has a causal explanation is an astonishing, almost mystical idea. Do we really believe that in some far distant future there will be a causal explanation of every last detail of every occurrence? Do we also believe that everything that has ever happened was as it were causally implicit in the original state of the universe? These questions suggest that it is at least possible that the causal approach is not universally applicable. Wittgenstein certainly believed that we might one day recognise limits to what can be explained in causal terms. He suggested that the belief that everything could be explained in causal terms reflected the way that certain types of example dominated our thinking, e.g. the case of one billiard ball hitting another.

Had the case always been that of the apple tree with the leaves dancing about, don't you think we would have had a different idea?—As things are now, you might say: 'if only we knew the velocity of the wind, the elasticity of the leaves, etc. then we could forecast the movements of the leaves.' But we would never dream of saying this if we hadn't already been successful, and collossally so'

(*Philosophical Occasions 1912–1951*, p. 431)

The success of science encourages us to assume that the world is a vast network of causes, all of which we shall one day track down, but why must this be true? In fact, talk of necessity is misplaced, for there is no guarantee that we will one day discover a causal explanation in every case where we currently do not possess one.

These general points apply with added force in relation to human action, for the regularities we have detected in the behaviour of living entities, let alone conscious beings, are extremely limited. The gap here is between an almost total inability to explain the specific actions of animals and human beings and the claim that all such behaviour is causally explicable. On the evidence of the causal explanations we have so far developed, how likely is it that we will one day be able to predict the behaviour of a specific animal over, say, a 24-hour period? And if this is less than certain, how plausible is it to claim that we will ever be able to predict the successive individual thoughts that make up a human being's waking life? It may, of course, be argued that these questions underestimate what has already been achieved or that they underline the amount of work that lies ahead of us. They should, however, at least encourage us to recognise the possibility, first, that there are limits to the applicability of causal concepts and, second, that human action might be one area where we encounter these limits. Wittgenstein certainly seems to have thought that this was the case.

No supposition seems to me more natural than that there is no process in the brain correlated with associating or with thinking; so that it would be impossible to read off thought-processes from brain-processes. I mean this: if I talk or write there is, I assume, a system of impulses going out from my brain and correlated with my spoken or written thoughts. But why should the *system* continue further in the direction of the centre? Why should this order not proceed, so to speak, out of chaos? The case would be like the following—certain kinds of plants multiply by seed, so that a seed always produces a plant of the same kind as that from which it was produced—but *nothing* in the seed corresponds to the plant which comes from it; so that it is impossible to infer the properties or structure of the plant from those of the seed. So an organism might come into being even out of something quite amorphous, as it were

153

causelessly; and there is no reason why this should not really hold
for our thoughts, and hence for our talking and writing.

(*RPP1*, para. 903)

As the reference to the example of the seeds suggests, Wittgenstein's point
is a general one; it applies, however, with particular strength to the case of
thoughts both because the regularities we have so far detected in this area
are relatively insignificant and because it is not clear what a causal account
of thinking would look like. This second point is crucial, for thinking is
unlike any kind of physical process. Not only do thoughts not come in
discrete units, but their content is given by the subsequent (sincere) utterances of the thinker. If someone thinks (or says) 'I must go to the bank', we
may ask 'Did you mean a river bank or a money bank?' or we may ask 'Did
you mean the Midland bank in Oxford, or any Oxford bank or any Midland
bank?' Similarly, we may ask 'When you thought (said) "must", did you
mean you would go even if your partner asked you not to or did you mean
unless something comes up, and, in the latter case, what sort of circumstances did your "must" exclude?' The answers to these questions (and an
indefinite list of others) give the content of the individual's thought, and it is,
to say the least, unclear how any of this might be correlated with an account
in terms of brain-states.

Leaving these points to one side, there are other fundamental difficulties
with the claim that human action is caused. These arise from the clash
between a causal approach to human action and our normal language-game,
for treating human action as caused implies abandoning the concepts
involved in relating to someone as a conscious being or person. The idea that
the individual thinks and acts is replaced by the idea that changes in her
brain-states result in particular experiences and particular behaviour. This
new approach involves using the same concepts in relation to animate and
inanimate objects; in a significant sense, therefore, it involves relating to
them in the same way. This is a radical suggestion, to say the least, and,
while it is possible to imagine what would be involved in treating other
people as machines, it is harder to imagine what would be involved in taking
up the same relationship to oneself. What would it mean for the individual to
treat her own actions as caused? More specifically, what would it mean for
her to believe that all her thoughts were caused, including this one? Once
again, these questions underline the obscurity of the claim that everything is
caused. Certainly in relation to human action it is not at all clear what
holding this belief would really involve.

To underline these points, let us consider the example of belief. A belief is
characterised by the fact that it has grounds, not causes. If someone says 'I
believe the earth is round because I have been caused to believe this', it
would be unclear whether or not we should see her as really holding this
belief. Insofar as she treats her view as having a causal explanation, she

ceases to treat it as a belief and so calls into question her commitment to its correctness. If someone adopted this approach generally and treated all her beliefs as caused, the result would be not just confusion but contradiction, for the individual would be claiming both that causal factors explained why she held her 'beliefs' and that these beliefs were based on a rational assessment of the issue concerned. The confusion would become manifest if we asked her: 'Do you really believe that all your beliefs are caused or have you simply been caused to believe this?' If she replies that careful consideration of the issue caused her to reach this conclusion, she is mixing up the two language-games in a confused and misleading way. In effect, she is accepting that her beliefs are not caused but is disguising this by the purely verbal manoeuvre of treating reflection as a form of causation. Of course, another possible response to this question would be for the individual to persist with the causal approach and maintain that her belief that all beliefs are caused was itself caused. If someone took this line, we would be left in the strange situation of having a discussion with someone who claimed not to be able to participate in discussions.

The only other way the individual could seek to dodge the above question would be by stressing different aspects of her claim at different times. Having claimed that it was true that all her beliefs were caused, she would accept that she was caused to hold this belief too. Then she would have to claim that it was true that she was caused to believe that all beliefs were caused. Having made this claim, she would accept that she was caused to believe that she was caused to believe, and so on. In this way she seems to be able to express normal beliefs *and* to explain those beliefs in causal terms. This argument, however, does not work. It conceals the contradiction but does not resolve it.[4] Every belief the individual says she holds is undermined by the subsequent claim that its basis is causal not rational, i.e. that the explanation for her holding it is not that it is correct but that she was caused to hold it. Here, two explanations are offered and ultimately one or other must be treated as empty;[5] either the individual affirms the belief (and hence her capacity to respond to the merits of the issue) or she drops any claim to truth and accepts that what she is disposed to say (and take as a basis of action) is something to be explained in causal terms.

These points bring out some of the difficulties with the claim that all aspects of human life must be explained in causal terms. In particular, they highlight the fact that this claim has implications for our relation to others and to ourselves. If we believe human behaviour is caused, we will presumably cease to treat individuals as agents. We will also have to stop regarding ourselves as agents and see our deliberations and choices as illusions hiding the real causes of our behaviour. Similarly, we would have to treat the idea that our thoughts are guided by a rational process of reflection as a further illusion. This is a paradoxical claim and leaves anyone who claims that human action and thought are caused in a difficult position, since if she claims her statement is based on a rational assessment of the facts, she ceases to treat it as causally determined, and if she claims her statement is caused, she ceases to treat it as an evidence-based claim about reality. This suggests that at least some aspects of thought cannot be explained in causal terms. If this is accepted, however, the motivation for this whole approach is weakened, for the starting point was the belief that every phenomenon must be explained in causal terms. Once we accept that thinking is not caused, we have less reason to claim that human action must be caused; indeed, since thinking can itself be described as a kind of action, we have accepted that people can act.

Against this, it may be objected that we have been using a simplistic and out-of-date notion of causation and that modern physics has shown that causation need not be deterministic. This response, however, misses the point. Modern physics has not shown that causation is more complicated than we thought; rather, it has lead us in particular fields to modify our concept of causal explanation. In these fields we have given up the search for causes in the traditional sense and have accepted a different but related type of explanation. To a large extent this development underlines the points we have been making, for it indicates that the notion of causation is a tool for investigating reality and that this tool can have limits and can require modification. In itself, however, this development has no direct relevance to human action, for even if quantum mechanics involves significantly modifying traditional notions of causation, it does not involve introducing notions of agency, rationality or choice. The clash between the concept of causation and that of agency cannot be resolved by pointing out that the former faces a different sort of problem in a totally different area of its application. It is also no use arguing that, if we can modify the concept of causation in the area of quantum mechanics, we can also modify it in the area of human action, for the fundamental opposition which we have been emphasising makes any attempt at modification pointless. Any concept related to that of causation would be in conflict with the concept of agency. There are only two options: either we abandon the idea that we are thinking agents or we place limits on the application of causal concepts.

These issues are important for ethics because most modern philosophers assume that all aspects of human action must be explained in causal terms and this assumption colours their approach to moral claims. Their accounts of human action tend not to explore the issues we have discussed, but it is clear that their position on this issue conflicts with the moralist's key claim that the wrongness of certain actions is in itself a sufficient reason for people not to commit them. Modern philosophers also assume that judgements on human action must essentially be seen as the caused product of dispositions. Accordingly, the claim that everyone ought to act in a certain way is treated not as a claim that is correct or incorrect, but as the product of a certain upbringing. This is another assumption that rules out ethical views. Although the claims of the moralist take the form of judgements about how everyone should act, these claims are seen as expressing the reaction of one individual and 'objectively' all such reactions are held to be on a par. Thus the idea that certain ways of reacting are correct is rejected. Furthermore, it would in any event be seen as irrelevant, since there is no scope for a belief about what is right to override the dispositions that are seen as determining an individual's actions. Against the background of this kind of approach, it is not surprising that moral philosophers find ethics hard to understand.

Thus there are two main reasons why modern philosophy has difficulty understanding ethics: one is a reluctance to recognise that reasons come to an end, the other is the assumption that both human actions and judgements on human action must be seen as caused. Over and above these reasons, there is a methodological factor that adds to the confusion of contemporary philosophers' accounts and that is the failure to separate comments that are intended to clarify ethics from those that advance particular substantive claims. Most philosophical accounts seek to throw light on the nature of ethics and to indicate what types of moral claim, if any, are valid. But this is misguided insofar as it suggests that conceptual analysis can provide a basis for substantive claims. As we have seen, there is no independent way of resolving the issues at the heart of ethics (or for that matter, specific moral questions). Rather, the starting point for any understanding of ethics must be a recognition that the claim that there are correct ways of acting and its denial are both logically possible views. Even if this point is accepted, it is still ill-advised to mix up conceptual and substantive claims, for the project of clarification is almost inevitably overshadowed and distorted by the attempt to justify a particular view. If we really want to achieve clarity, then it is vital to separate conceptual points about the nature of ethics from substantive claims about which substantive views are correct.

The failure to separate conceptual from substantive points is a particularly significant weakness in modern moral philosophy because of its ambivalence to ethics. In fact, its confusions about moral claims and its ambivalence interact. On the one hand, philosophers' difficulty in understanding the claim to correctness prevents them from recognising the issue on which they need to take a stand. On the other, their wish to combine contradictory views encourages them to misconstrue the nature of moral claims. Keen to demonstrate their modern scientific outlook, contemporary philosophers are quick to conclude that from an objective point of view moral claims are either not justified or at least seriously flawed. They then seek ways of reconciling this recognition with most people's and their own commitment to moral judgements. This combination makes it difficult to determine what their real views are. It is not clear whether their rejection of ethics is mainly a result of confusion or whether being less confused about

157

ethics would simply enable them to reject it more consistently. Certainly the philosophers whose substantive position it is hardest to be certain about are those who follow their colleagues in brushing aside the claim to correctness but then put themselves forward as defenders of ethics. In such cases it is genuinely impossible to reach any conclusion on whether or not they believe in right and wrong.

As a final way of illustrating these points, let us consider James Wilson's book *The Moral Sense,* which is a typically modern attempt to take a scientific approach to ethics. This book is intended as a defence of ethics but is based on the assumption that judgements of human action cannot be correct. It therefore seeks to defend moral reactions on the grounds that they are useful. This is a typically modern approach, but it suffers from a fundamental flaw. Even if it could be shown that it was advantageous to believe that murder was wrong, this would not provide the individual with a basis for holding this belief. On the contrary, insofar as the individual holds that this belief is misguided, holding it is no longer an option for her. Thus the basic structure of Wilson's argument is flawed.[6] However, an examination of its specific features is a good way of underlining many of the points this book has been trying to make.

Wilson begins by noting modern society's contradictory attitude to ethics. Like us, he claims that a theoretical suspicion of moral beliefs goes hand in hand with the use of moral concepts in everyday life. The aim of his book, however, is to resolve this contradiction by restoring people's confidence in ethics. Dismissing claims that morality is outmoded, he wants to show 'that mankind has a moral nature to which we commonly and inevitably appeal when trying to defend our moral arguments' (*TMS,* p. vii). Placing himself in the tradition of eighteenth-century thinkers such as Joseph Butler, Francis Hutcheson, David Hume and Adam Smith, Wilson does not seek a rational foundation for ethics but tries to clarify ethics by exploring the origin of our moral feelings. He claims that moral values are neither arbitrary nor specific to a particular time, place or culture but reflect fundamental and universal human traits, the universality of which science can testify to and explain. Invoking a wealth of scientific evidence, he hopes to show that relativism is misguided and that moral values are an essential part of human nature. The final words of his book sum up his vision of ethics:

> Mankind's moral sense is not a strong beacon light, radiating outward to illuminate in sharp outline all that it touches. It is, rather, a small candle flame, casting vague and multiple shadows, flickering and spluttering in the strong winds of power and passion, greed and ideology. But brought close to the heart and cupped to one's hands, it dispels the darkness and warms the soul.
>
> (*TMS,* p. 251)

Wilson's argument is, as it were, a last ditch attempt to defend ethics. Traditional attempts to prove the rationality of ethics are replaced by an attempt to justify it by reference to science. Rather than seeking to prove the validity of moral judgements, he claims that acting and judging morally is natural for human beings. The essence of his position is that moral values are to some important degree innate and 'appear spontaneously amid the routine intimacies of family life' (*TMS*, p. 229). He supplements this claim by arguing that moral values have advantages both for the species and for the individual and that these (particularly the former) explain why through the process of evolution we have come to react in this way. This argument sounds plausibly scientific, but it avoids the key issue of ethics which is whether it is correct to claim that there are correct ways of acting. Confused about what this claim involves but (rightly) convinced that attempts to prove ethics fail, Wilson treats ethics simply as a way we react. The problem with this approach is that it implies that moral judgements cannot be valid in themselves and so involves abandoning the claim that there are correct ways of acting. If Wilson's arguments worked, they might convince us to act as if we believed in right and wrong, but this would not amount to regaining our moral beliefs. We might agree that it was in our interest to react negatively to certain actions, but we would have abandoned the idea that these actions were wrong.

To underline these points, let us consider Wilson's claim that judging and acting morally is natural for human beings. This claim raises many questions, but the real issue from our point of view is what is supposed to follow from it. The fact that most people spontaneously act (and judge) in a certain way does not show that this is the right way to act (and judge). Even if everyone held the same moral values (which is not the case), this would not establish that those moral values were correct. To take an example from a different context, it may be 'natural' to believe that the sun goes round the earth, but this does not mean that it is true. Against this, it may be argued that the case of human action is different and that, since there is no question of truth, showing that ethics is natural is a valid way of defending it. The thrust of this argument would be that ethics is not an error (a collective self-delusion) but a spontaneous and useful reaction, the occurrence of which science can explain. But ethics cannot be defended in this way, for the essence of moral belief is that assessing human action is not a matter of reactions, but that there are judgements everyone should make. By contrast, if we accept the claim that judgements on human action simply reflect the way we happen to react, there is no scope for claiming that one reaction is right and another wrong. We may be happy we react in a particular way and dislike the way other people react, but by our own account we would have to recognise that our clash with them was just a matter of them reacting one way and us another.

As these points suggest, the scientific evidence Wilson marshals and the explanations he offers have no place in an account of ethics, for claims about how most people react (or how most people spontaneously react) are irrelevant to the issue of how it is correct to act. Furthermore, insofar as scientific explanations are seen as relevant, they have precisely the opposite impact to that Wilson imagines, for the only relevance they can have is to persuade us *not* to take our moral reactions at face value. Suppose, for example, a woman is attracted to her brother but feels horrified at her own desires. One way she can understand this reaction is as a recognition that sexual relations between family members are morally wrong. If she holds this belief, she will see it as her moral duty to avoid such relations and will be glad that one part of her instinctively recoils from them. A very different way of understanding her reaction would be to see it as something that has been caused by the evolutionary process. Someone who sees this explanation as the key to understanding her negative reaction ceases to treat her reaction as the recognition of a truth everyone should accept. In other words, she abandons the claim that incest is wrong. She may agree that the reaction she experiences has been (and possibly still is) useful from the point of view of the species, but from her own point of view it is simply an obstacle to her desires. Understood in this way the reaction may still affect her actions but it does so in a different way. If she does not act on her desires, it will not be because she holds that a particular view is correct but because a reaction she happens to have undermines the attraction of what she would otherwise be inclined to do.

These points can be further illustrated with examples from Wilson's book, for the explanations he offers are often overtly reductive. Take the notion of conscience itself. Wilson suggests that a sense of duty tends to arise from a close, happy relationship between child and parents. What happens is that

> we acquire the disposition to judge our own behaviour through the eyes of a disinterested spectator, what Adam Smith called 'the man within the breast'. We acquire this internal spectator from others; eager to earn praise and avoid blame, we adjust our actions accordingly. To a degree that varies among individuals, but to some degree in all of us, we acquire a visceral reaction to the actions that we contemplate, experiencing internally and automatically the prospect of praise of blame, whether or not it will actually occur.
>
> (*TMS*, p. 108)

Here, conscience is presented not as a recognition of what is right but as a psychological mechanism with a specific explanation. The fact that this explanation has a nicer ring to it than Freud's claim that conscience is the product of repressed feelings of lust and rage makes no difference to the explanation's reductive impact. If someone who believes it is her duty to act altruistically reads Wilson's book and is convinced by it, she will recognise that her 'noble' impulse actually arises out of a child's desire for the approval of others, particularly her parents. Although she may still decide that she will get more satisfaction from fulfilling that impulse than from not doing so, she will have lost the illusion that she should act in this way because it is the correct way to act. By contrast, anyone who has no conscience (or a weak one) can read Wilson's book and reflect that, while she is excluded from the pleasures of self-righteousness, at least her approach to action is not fettered by an irrational desire for the approval of those who may already be dead.

It is important to note that these points do not imply that the notion of conscience would be undermined if a correlation could be established between the strength of an individual's conscience and some feature of her past, e.g. the warmth of her relationship with her parents. Someone who believed in right and wrong could interpret this evidence as showing that a happy childhood helps the individual come to understand the world in the correct way or, conversely, that an unhappy childhood tends to distort the individual's understanding of the world. The point is that in itself the correlation neither supports nor undermines the substantive claim that recognising a duty to others is part of the correct way of understanding the world. What does undermine this claim is Wilson's suggestion that the appropriate way to understand our moral beliefs is as the product of a psychological mechanism whose causes we can understand.

To take another example, consider Wilson's account of fairness and how this notion arises. He suggests that where children are competing for toys, they recognise that a policy of winner-takes-all is unlikely to be accepted by the adults supervising them. This leads them to the idea of fairness as a way of solving their disputes which will be accepted by the adults and is therefore in the interests of each individual child. The children enter into a tacit agreement, the nature of which is governed by two conditions.

> If both parties are to abide by it, there must be something in it for each. That something must be valuable enough to one child that he will accept the agreement but not so much that the other child will protest. Equal shares is the only rule that satisfies both conditions for children of roughly similar strength and determination. Following the rule of fairness, defined as equal shares, minimizes conflict to the advantage of both parties.
>
> (*TMS*, p. 56)

In itself this explanation is not very convincing, but even if it was correct, the only implication it would have for ethics (if seen as relevant) would be to undermine the idea that people should act fairly. Suppose an individual was contemplating acting unfairly but felt reluctant to act in this way because she believed doing so was wrong. Wilson's explanation would encourage her to see her scruples as the ingrained consequences of a policy adopted in childhood for self-interested reasons. If she accepted this, she would recognise that it would be misguided to let the idea of fairness draw her away from pursuing her self-interest, since the former is actually based in the latter. Instead, what she needs to do is to be rigorous in assessing her self-interest and recognise that acting in a 'fair' manner may sometimes be in her interests. Abandoning the moral claim that she has a duty to respect the rights of others, her criterion for responding to the claims of others is no longer fairness but an assessment of her own interests. Once again, Wilson's explanations have the effect (if accepted as correct and as relevant)[7] of debunking our moral claims.

Wilson puts forward a further argument in relation to fairness; however, this suffers from the same fundamental flaw, for rather than arguing that acting fairly is the correct way to act, he defends fairness on the grounds that it is in the individual's long-term interests. He claims that

> part of the reason why sharing persists despite increasing differences in child size and reductions in adult supervision is that as children grow older they acquire a longer time horizon . . . A child acquires, and is aware of the value having, an investment in his reputation for fair play, much as a business firm begins to see the value over the long term of having a reputation for honest dealing and quality products.
>
> (*TMS*, p. 57)

Again this claim is not very plausible. Looked at in self-interested terms, acting fairly will not necessarily be the best policy for everyone. For some people, acting unfairly may be the best way of maximising their life-chances. Furthermore, the benefits Wilson emphasises are the benefits of having a reputation for fairness and this is very different from believing in fairness, for in the latter case the individual will seek to be fair quite independently of whether and to what extent other people will find out about this. In fact, Wilson's claims boil down to the suggestion that, generally speaking, it is worth maintaining a reputation for being at least an averagely fair person. His argument suggests that in considering any particular act of unfairness we should weigh the gains from this act against the potential cost to our reputation, so that if the act of unfairness is not very profitable and there is a high risk that it would be discovered and have serious consequences for our reputation, we should not commit the act but seek to use the occasion to maximise our reputation for fair dealing. As advice on how to pursue our self-interest this argument may be correct, if obvious; what is clear, however, is that it has nothing to do with believing that everyone should act fairly.

Wilson's arguments are similar in this respect to MacIntyre's, for although they invoke various virtues, their status as arguments for ethics is undermined by the fact that they do not involve the exercise of the virtues for their own sake. The individual would not act in a certain way because she believed that it was the correct way to act; rather, she would adopt a certain policy because she saw advantages in so doing. In principle, therefore, there would always be situations where the potential gain and the risks of discovery were such as to give the individual a reason to override her general policy of acting as if she believed that acting fairly was the correct way to act. Wilson might reply that no gain could justify the risk of social opprobrium, but at best this claim would express his own personal assessment of how best to maximise his happiness. Furthermore, while this response offers a heroic but implausible challenge to the truism that pursuit of her own interests may lead the individual to act immorally, it does not address the real point which is that at best self-interest can only lead the individual to act *as if* she had moral beliefs. In fact, what is confused here is the attempt to give ethics an external justification. By definition the reason for acting morally is because it is the correct way to act.[8] The 'benefit' to the individual of acting morally is that she acts as she ought to act. Whether that makes her life pleasant or unpleasant is a separate and contingent matter. Similarly, if the immoral individual is delighted with the consequences of her actions, this does not count against the claim that she acted wrongly. Indeed, from the moralist's point of view this may simply be a further indication of her distorted understanding of the world.

These points bring out the paradoxical nature of Wilson's project, for he rejects the moral notion of correctness and then seeks reasons for continuing to act morally. This is the contradiction that lies at the heart of modern moral philosophy and, as we have seen, philosophers as different as Mackie and Blackburn or Williams and Nagel all have difficulty facing up to the implications of their rejection of the claim that there is a correct perspective on human action. Wilson is typical both in assuming that moral claims cannot be correct in their own terms and in not drawing the logical conclusion that we should stop making these claims. Instead, he rejects moral beliefs and embarks on a search for reasons to behave *as if* he held moral beliefs. This is a peculiar project and is self-defeating insofar as acting morally involves the individual's acting in a certain way *because* she believes that this is the correct way to act. In fact, as his arguments on fairness illustrate, the search inevitably ends by advocating hypocrisy, for anyone who accepted Wilson's argument would continue to claim to believe in fairness, when in fact she would simply be pursuing her long-term self-interest by trying to maintain a reputation for fairness which was in a significant sense unjustified.[9]

Wilson tries to avoid this problem by advancing arguments on a completely different level. Recognising that for reciprocity to be a rule more is needed than mere selfish calculation (*TMS*, p. 66), he claims that society instils reciprocity in order to deal with those individuals who do not have self-interested reasons to be fair. This is a typical modern argument, but it ignores the obvious point that human beings are conscious animals, so that any potential backsliders who read Wilson's book may find that doing so undermines their 'programming'. A related problem concerns the issue of who does the programming, for it will generally be in the interests of any particular individual that reciprocity is instilled into everyone except herself. Against this, it may be argued that our having reciprocative instincts is the price we pay for everyone having them. But this still ignores the fact that we are conscious, for once we follow the argument through, our reciprocal instincts again begin to be undermined. The final move Wilson makes is to claim that evolution selects people who act reciprocally (ibid.). But this argument, too, does nothing to explain why any conscious individual should act on her reciprocal instincts. If anything, it gives us a reason for ignoring such instincts where they clash with a rigorous assessment of our self-interest. All these arguments do, therefore, is to take us away from the heart of the matter, which is the claim many human beings make (and have made) that acting fairly is the correct way to act. If Wilson's aim is to defend humanity's moral sense, this is the claim he needs to discuss. All his evidence about how most people behave and his conjectures about what evolution favours are either irrelevant to this aim or, if seen as relevant, have the opposite implication to that he supposes.

These criticisms of Wilson may seem to reflect an unduly literal understanding of his claims, for surely there is something right about his claim that the correct way for us to act is based on a proper understanding of our nature? Don't some actions strike us as wrong because they seem appallingly unnatural? More generally, isn't it true that immoral action involves acting in a less than human way? The point about these statements, however, is that they introduce a different notion of what is natural, for now this notion reflects a substantive conception of the correct way for human beings to act. The claim is not that people instinctively or spontaneously act in certain ways but that there are certain ways of acting that are properly or truly human. In terms of this substantive ethical notion only a paragon of virtue could be said to live a truly human life, whereas many common ways of acting constitute a failure to act in a properly human way. We act 'humanly' not when we act as most people act but when we act as human beings ought to. In this sort of context, therefore, the notion of what is natural (or of what is properly human) is not based on observation but expresses a particular substantive view about how people should act.

Wilson invokes this kind of conception on various occasions, for example he notes that a person who lacked any sense of fairness would 'be less than human' (*TMS,* p. 78). Similarly, he writes that in urging a drug addict to overcome her addiction we are doing more than encouraging her to a goal we happen to prefer; rather, 'the goal is of overriding, even transcendent importance; to live life on human terms—that is, to acknowledge the obligation of one's social nature by discharging duties to family, friends, and employer, duties that rest on reciprocal affection, interdependent needs, the bonds of sympathy, and the requirements of fairplay' (*TMS,* p. 96). This quotation makes clear Wilson's substantive conception of how human beings should live; such a conception, however, cannot be supported by scientific observation of which types of human behaviour are common or spontaneous. In fact, such conceptions will often involve people not doing what comes 'naturally' to them. If an individual acts selfishly, Wilson may condemn her for failing to act in a properly human way. This moral judgement, however, has nothing to do with empirical evidence on whether such behaviour is common or with scientific hypotheses as to how the commonness (or otherwise) of such behaviour might be explained.

Thus Wilson's book is deeply confused. Furthermore, it embodies the very contradiction he detects in modern society, for his theoretical framework is at odds with the judgements on human action he wants to make in practice. One significant factor behind this contradiction is Wilson's confusion about what being objective in this context involves. His intention is to take a scientific look at ethics; he wants to rise above centuries of human prejudice and cast the cold eye of the scientist on the issues in this area. He assumes, however, that this involves abstracting from his own humanity and this actually makes it harder for him to give an accurate account of the topics he is interested in. His book is intended as a defence of ethics, but like most works of contemporary moral philosophy, it avoids mentioning any of the things that might actually convince someone that there are correct ways to act. However, even as an account of human beliefs, it suffers from the fact that its author feels obliged to approach this issue as if he himself was not a human being. It is ironic, for example, that the one explanation of human action he cannot accept is that someone acted in a certain way because she believed it was the correct way to act. Rather than accept this, he prefers any external explanation no matter how implausible. Consider his comments on why people keep their commitments.

> Why do we stick with a spouse even after a more attractive mate has become available, raise children through the years when the rewards seem nonexistent, keep bargains when it would be easy to evade them, and insist on fair division when an unfair one would work to our advantage? . . .

It is in part because a person who makes and keeps commitments provides other people with a prediction of his future behaviour . . . Someone who can be counted on is more likely to attract more opportunities for profitable transactions than is someone who, by his past waffling on commitments, seems a poor risk.

(*TMS*, p. 231)

This is implausible and misses the point. The reason most people stick with their spouses (and stick to commitments in general) is because they believe they ought to do this even if this will not necessarily bring them happiness. If everyone rejected such moral ideas, there would be many cases where discreetly abandoning past commitments was more advantageous than sticking with them.

Typically, Wilson tries to avoid this point by claiming that the real explanation of why human beings act morally is that evolution selects such behaviour. What is significant about this claim, however, is that it does not constitute a reason for action. Wilson gives up trying to justify our moral beliefs and instead treats the actions that follow from them as caused natural phenomena. We have already argued that this involves an implicit rejection of the claim that certain ways of acting are correct, but it also leaves Wilson in paradoxical relation to himself. On the one hand, he presumably sees himself as a normal conscious agent choosing to act in particular ways for particular reasons. On the other hand, he believes that the real explanation of his behaviour is the set of dispositions he has been caused to have by a complicated set of circumstances within the context of the evolutionary process. The same contradiction arises in relation to his moral beliefs. As a human being, he believes that sticking to commitments is the correct thing to do; as a social scientist cum philosopher, he holds that this claim is the expression of a disposition he has been caused to have. The crunch would come if he faced a situation where he wanted to abandon a commitment he had made. Here, he would have to decide what his views really are: either he makes the moral claim that sticking to the commitment is the correct way to act or he treats his inclination to make this claim (and the accompanying emotions) as the product of the evolutionary process and therefore as something that may affect his deliberations but need not guide them.

Wilson's split relation to himself is typical of much modern moral philosophy, for most moral philosophers assume that an objective approach to ethics involves treating our moral judgements as simply what a particular type of animal is inclined to say. This is a possible substantive view, but it is confused to see it as the only possible view. Furthermore, adopting it gives rise to a position that involves an uncomfortable duality, for the individual distances herself from her own actions. She is inclined to say and do certain things, but she simultaneously stands back from her behaviour and sees it as characteristic of a certain type of animal. In the case of Wilson, this duality

166

leads to contradictions for he wants to be both the detached observer of humanity's moral sense and its advocate. On the one hand, he treats claims about how it is correct to act simply as the expression of what one particular species is disposed to say. On the other hand, he endorses the claim that there are correct ways of acting and seeks to encourage other people to be more confident about making it. This combination is contradictory. The point, however, is not that Wilson is wrong to make substantive moral claims but that he should have recognised that 'being objective' about how people should act does not involving making non-moral descriptive statements but trying to defend and articulate the moral claims he believes are correct

As it is, Wilson's efforts to achieve a different kind of objectivity lead him into confusion, and that confusion extends to the very nature of the project he is engaged upon. In his desire to treat human beings like any other species of animal, he doesn't ask himself why he wants to defend (rather than simply describe) the 'phenomenon' of humanity's moral sense. What does he mean when he claims that, brought close to the heart, the moral sense dispels the darkness and warms the soul? Does he simply mean that he, James Q. Wilson, is the sort of animal that gets a buzz out of feeling that he is promoting the set of reactions he calls the moral sense? Or is he endorsing the moral sense as the correct guide to how human beings (and, indeed, any agents) ought to act? In the latter case, rather than describing how a particular species happens to react, he is affirming both the general claim that there are correct ways of acting and specific claims about what those ways of acting are.

If, however, Wilson's real position involves discounting the claims that human beings make in favour of causal explanations, his use of the word 'good' should be in inverted commas like everyone else's. If he wants to treat human beings as members of a species of animal that is caused to behave in certain ways, he should take the same approach to himself and, rather than claiming that humanity's moral sense is a good thing and ought to be fostered, he should note that some people including himself would prefer people to continue to act and judge morally. The only difficulty this would leave is that, while he claims to want to foster the moral sense, the views he puts forward undermine it. Like Williams and most other modern philosophers, he is left in the difficult position of wanting to support ethics but rejecting its defining claim. In his view, the claim that there are correct ways of acting is misguided and, rather than being taken as correct, should be seen as the expression of a disposition which for reasons we can explain many human beings have been caused to acquire.

Thus Wilson's approach is confused and contradictions of his position leave his real views unclear. On the one hand, he sees himself as defending ethics and he endorses several specific moral judgements. On the other hand, he bases his argument on the assumption that in themselves moral judgements cannot be correct or incorrect. It is therefore not clear whether or not he should be said to believe in right and wrong. To avoid these contradictions what he—like other contemporary moral philosophers—needs to do is to recognise that the central issue in ethics is whether there are correct judgements on human action. As an individual he has to decide whether he accepts or rejects this claim. If, however, he concludes that all judgements simply reflect the dispositions/preferences of an individual, he should accept the implication of this conclusion and recognise that he is rejecting ethics.

POSTSCRIPT

In this book I have argued that contemporary moral philosophy is confused about ethics and, in particular, cannot decide whether it accepts or rejects the distinctive moral claim that there are correct ways of acting. I have also claimed that while philosophy can clarify the issues this claim raises, it has no special role to play in resolving them. It is up to the individual to reach her own conclusions on whether she believes in right and wrong and, if she takes a moral view, to decide what she believes is right and wrong. No amount of conceptual clarification or analysis can contribute to this process. Once confusions have been eliminated and it is clear what is at stake in ethics, the work of philosophy comes to an end.

For professional philosophers this conclusion may seem at once disappointing and threatening. It reflects the general Wittgensteinian point that there are no philosophical problems only philosophical confusions. However, the situation in moral philosophy is not exactly the same as the general situation. On the one hand, the philosophical difficulties of ethics arise in relation to a small number of high-level issues rather than from a vast mass of different puzzles. The need and scope for extensive and detailed conceptual clarification is therefore relatively limited. On the other hand, behind the confusions of moral philosophy lie questions of fundamental importance. While resolving confusions about the concept of, say, time helps us avoid nonsensical claims and empty speculation, resolving the confusions of ethics leaves us face to face with the most important questions in life.

Against this background many of the works of contemporary moral philosophers seem frivolous and superficial. There is little sense that they express someone's deepest beliefs about the right way of making sense of the world. But in principle this is what substantive works in this area are doing. A book entitled 'Why I believe [or do not believe] in right and wrong' ought to be the most important book an individual could write. There is, of course, an issue about the extent to which such a book should be seen as moral philosophy. In some ways it is a continuation of moral philosophy, in other ways, not. Depending on the author, such a book might be part autobiography, part 'metaphysical' speculation, part confession, part sermon. It might have a tight logical structure or it might not, but it would put forward a view on how the world should be understood and it would be up to each of

169

us to make an assessment as to whether we thought that view was correct. Furthermore, the book would constitute a claim to wisdom rather than a demonstration of professional competence. For that reason the academic track record and even the intellectual ability of the author could not guarantee the validity of her conclusions. Rather, we would each have to reflect on what she claimed and reach our own conclusion on whether she was right.

NOTES

1 THE CONTRADICTIONS OF TRADITIONAL ETHICS

1 I shall use the words 'ethics' and 'morality' interchangeably. This is not to claim that the two words are used identically, and it is no doubt possible to make interesting distinctions between them. The fundamental points I wish to make, however, do not require any such distinction.

2 Terms such as 'correct' and 'incorrect' are, of course, used in a wide variety of contexts outside ethics, for example in legal contexts. The point about ethical uses of such terms is that they aim for an apparently nonsensical absoluteness. An argument is legally correct in relation to a particular legal framework; the moralist, however, claims that certain arguments are correct as such. She claims that these arguments ought to recognised by everyone, independently of their background or preferences.

3 In recent years, some philosophers have tried to avoid this issue by concentrating on the discussion of moral issues themselves. However, ignoring the apparent incoherence of ethics does nothing to eliminate this incoherence. Furthermore, there are important questions about the status of such writings, for it is not clear what authority a philosopher has qua philosopher to advance or reject particular moral views.

4 This is the situation discussed in game theory where two individuals are offered choices which they have to resolve individually but where they would fare better if they could act in concert. For example, the prisoners have a choice of confessing or not confessing to a crime and each would be better off if she confesses and the other does not, but both would be better off if neither confessed.

5 A paedophile will know that it is not generally considered acceptable for him to justify the way he acts on the basis that it gives him pleasure. Nonetheless, he may consider this justification acceptable. He may, for example, hold that all human action is essentially pleasure-seeking and that the attempt to distinguish between good and bad pleasures is misguided. We may condemn this view as wrong, but there is no reason for claiming that the person who advances it is linguistically incompetent.

6 It might seem that the institution of promising could not survive in a world without ethics, but this is not quite true. People in such a society might still decide that it would be useful if the breaking of commitments made in a particular form was subject to greater social sanctions than the failure to act in accordance with an expressed intention. A promise would be a verbal contract and might be enforced through legal sanctions or by some other form of social disapproval.

7 *Moral Luck*, pp. XX-XX.

8 In fact, it is not clear that Williams can allow reflection even in the sense described, since his emphasis on dispositions clashes with the notion of intentionality. If the individual's judgements are determined by her dispositions,

this will presumably also be true of her 'decisions' about which dispositions to preserve and which to jettison. She may think she is standing in judgement on her dispositions, but on this approach all that is happening is that the dispositions she has been caused to acquire are interacting. For a fuller discussion of this issue, see Chapter 6.

9 The point is not that without ethics there is only selfishness, but that without the claim to correctness there are only preferences. Even if the individual opts for a life of self-sacrifice, the question is whether she does this because she believes it is the correct thing to do or because it is what she wants to do.

10 In fact, the stress on the 'objectivity' of psychology is a red herring, for this objectivity relates to means not ends. Psychology might 'objectively' tell us that people who want to minimise their risk of suicide should not seek to become top sportspeople, but it can say nothing on the relative value of a life dedicated to sporting achievement and one dedicated to longevity.

2 BELIEVING IN RIGHT AND WRONG

1 This includes the possibility of someone claiming that in some circumstances there may be several actions all of which are morally permissible or indeed that in some situations no action is right. Such views still involve the claim that there is a correct way of understanding the situation, i.e. as a situation where various actions are permissible or as one where the individual cannot avoid doing wrong.

2 See p. 6.

3 The issues of tolerance and moral modesty complicate the position, but do not change its essential features. The former raises issues about respecting the right of other people to make judgements we disagree with, while the latter concerns situations where the individual feels obliged to refrain from judgement. For a fuller discussion, see Chapter 4.

4 This is true even in relation to someone who takes a pessimistic view of the capacity of the human mind. Even someone who claims that our understanding of the world is necessarily flawed must hold that this claim at least is correct. Similarly, those who hold that an individual's world-view is simply a reflection of her culture must hold that this is not true of absolutely all claims, for example, claims such as this one itself.

5 Here it is important to note that someone who maintains that all these questions are bogus is not being silent on them but is offering a definite view. She is defending an understanding of the world she believes to be correct.

6 The notion of rejecting ethics may at first glance seem too sweeping, but, as we saw in Chapter 1, rejecting the traditional notion of objectivity/correctness amounts to rejecting ethics, since it is this idea that gives moral judgements their distinctive character.

7 In a significant sense this would not be a religious conception of the world, for while it would involve belief in a Creator it would not involve the claim that there is a Being whom everyone ought to praise and worship. On this conception the Creator would simply be a uniquely powerful Being whose preferences it would presumably be prudent to take into account.

8 Imagine if that had been Samuel's response: 'God was it You that spoke to me?' 'Yes.' 'And was it You that confirmed that You spoke to me?' 'Yes.' 'Can I take it that it was You that confirmed the confirmation?' 'Yes.' and so on.

9 But what of all science's successes? At bedrock both parties to this dispute may be tempted to claim that the evidence is overwhelmingly in their favour. One points to the phenomenal success of science, the other detects multiple signs of God's

care for the world; one lists features of the world that seem incompatible with the existence of a caring God, the other points to all that science cannot explain. Both parties can point to 'evidence'; but they go wrong if they claim their position (and the evidence for it) cannot possibly be rejected.

10 As Wittgenstein remarked to M.O'C Drury: 'If I thought of God as another being like myself, outside me, only infinitely more powerful, then I would regard it as my duty to defy him' (*Recollections of Wittgenstein*, p. 108).

11 So could there be anti-moralists in heaven, if there is one? From a logical point of view, this is not excluded. According to the religious believer, however, after death God's glory and majesty will be manifest. Although distorted understandings of the world will still be logically possible, the scales will fall from the unbeliever's eyes and the correct way of understanding the world will be recognised as such by everyone.

12 It is ironic that this Wittgensteinian point is widely believed to have been undermined by Wittgenstein; indeed, some see this as his greatest achievement. In fact, the point of his rule-following argument is that it makes no sense to talk of a rule being followed 'privately', i.e. in the absence of a practice. A practice, however, must be public only in the sense that it must be logically possible for a number of people to engage in it; from a logical point of view, it is irrelevant whether many people or just one actually do so. See Baker and Hacker, *Scepticism, Rules and Language*.

13 The situation is slightly different if what she objects to is the defence of this principle in terms of rights. If, for example, she believes that what is wrong with torture is that it is against the law of God, there will still be disagreement at bedrock but the moral positions of the two individuals will be closer in the sense that many of their particular judgements may coincide.

14 MacIntyre might argue that if such an individual were possible, she would be a lesser person for not wanting internal goods. This amounts to claiming that everyone ought to want internal goods and that the individual 'goes wrong' if she does not want them. Here correctness has re-entered by the back door: the account seems to work, but only by using a concept at odds with its specific features.

15 In this context, it is not surprising that MacIntyre has doubts about whether humility is really a virtue, for it is hard to think of any vaguely similar ability that is useful from a purely prudential perspective.

3 REASON AND MORAL ARGUMENT

1 The inconsistencies of Nazi apologists point to their embarrassment in having to defend the moral position they claim to believe in. They show not that Nazism is incoherent, but that even its advocates find it hard to defend. Here, the charge of inconsistency rests on the claim that the apologist's views contain incompatible elements. In theory, this claim would only be shown to be correct if the person concerned accepted it. In practice, she may not do this, but this does not alter the logical point about what is involved in claiming that someone's moral position is internally inconsistent.

2 So are there no limits to what is logically possible? Suppose someone claimed that murder was wrong except on Mondays when it was a moral duty. This is a logically possible position in the sense that it is clear what it enjoins and prohibits. As it stands, however, it is not a position we can make any sense of, and we might well treat someone who advanced it as mentally ill rather than morally confused. This does not, however, constitute an independent endorsement of our side of the

argument. Trying to invoke limits to the logically possible in this way is misguided, for all it does is confuse what we find unintelligible with what we believe to be wrong. The claim 'I cannot understand you' is not a superior, more independently justifiable version of the claim 'you are (morally) wrong'.

3 The possibility of the other person not admitting she was wrong does not affect the underlying point. If we convince someone that she is being inconsistent, she may not want to admit this and so may falsely claim that she still disagrees and that we have misunderstood her position. This may save her from losing face, but it does not leave her moral views unchanged. She now agrees with us that a certain logically possible position is morally wrong, but she pretends that she has not been convinced.

4 This is not to deny that there are situations where an individual agrees with our account of what her principles imply, but is not prepared to admit this publicly. This description, however, still rests on the idea that what makes our account valid is her suppressed but postulated endorsement.

5 See Mulhall and Swift, *Liberals and Communitarians*.

6 Here, it is interesting to note that, while Dworkin believes he is making a logical point, the force of his example is rhetorical. What he is really trying to do is to persuade us to accept the substantive claim that there is no moral difference between a foetus in the womb and the monster's body parts in the laboratory.

7 Dworkin's suggestion to the anti-abortionist that she imagine her reaction if the moral majority insisted that pregnancies were terminated (*LD*, p. 159) can be turned against him in the case of racism, but this only shows why this point has little force. Our horror at the thought of a racist majority writing racism into the constitution should not deter us from taking the opposite step and writing the substantive rejection of such ideas into our laws.

4 MODESTY, DOUBT AND RELATIVISM

1 To that extent the claim is contradictory if taken absolutely literally. What it is really saying is that we have the right to enforce our claim that someone is acting incorrectly if what they are doing is imposing their more specific views on correct action on other people.

2 The situation is somewhat different with regard to liberalism as a political doctrine, for where the issue is defining the relation between the individual and the state it may make sense to value autonomy above all else. The claim here is not that all value systems are equally valid, but that the state should (within certain limits) treat all value systems as equally valid.

3 It is ironic that these points which challenge moral belief are often taken by contemporary philosophers, e.g. Williams, as potential foundations for justifying it. The point is that believing there are social or psychological reasons why it would be advantageous to believe that murder is wrong is not the same as believing that murder is wrong, and to put this forward as the only ground for one's belief is to concede that the belief itself is not justified.

4 Another reason Williams' position seems plausible is the idea that our concepts were simply not available to people in the past, that they as it were lacked the conceptual space in which to think that a certain thing was wrong. Even if this was the case, however, it would only relate to the issue of blame. Furthermore, this idea itself is confused. It is always possible to explore the cultural background to an individual's beliefs and we may attribute to that background their failure to recognise what we consider to be important truths. But that background did not impose logical constraints on their thoughts. If Plato did not demand that

men and women be treated equally, this was not because entertaining such an idea was literally impossible.

5 From the anti-moralist's point of view, people who do not hold this belief lead lives that are based on a delusion. They are wrong, but the anti-moralist cannot treat this as a moral error, so although she may be disposed to think poorly of such people, she cannot chide them for believing what people 'ought' not to believe. Indeed, if believing in right and wrong was shown to promote happiness, there is no reason why the anti-moralist herself should not consider being brainwashed into accepting the delusion (assuming such brainwashing was possible).

6 Taylor adds a further potential confusion when he says that 'arguing here is contesting between interpretations of what I have been living' (*SS,* p. 72). This suggests that the agent has a privileged position, since it is her experience that is being interpreted. This is misleading, for what matters is not skill in interpretation but application of the correct standards. Furthermore, the agent has no necessary privilege. If, for example, the question is whether she has become a worse person, her 'closeness' to the process may actually undermine her position as a possible judge.

7 If she believes that all conceptions of the world are culturally determined, then she must believe that at least this idea is correct and not simply culturally determined. It would make no sense to try to apply this idea to itself, for this would involve claiming both that the idea is correct (as opposed to culturally determined) and that it is culturally determined. To put it another way, if someone puts this idea forward as part of a rational discussion, she must do so on the basis of claiming that it is correct, not on the basis that it is merely something she has been caused to believe.

5 OBJECTIVITY AND THE METAPHYSICS OF ETHICS

1 As far as aesthetic judgements are concerned, it may be held that these are matters of preference or that they are not (or that some are and others are not). To take a very crude example: someone might claim that if an individual thinks Rachmaninov is greater than Bach, this shows either that she does not understand classical music or that her approach to and understanding of the world is superficial. If she does not understand why Bach is more profound than Rachmaninov, she has not yet grasped what is really important about life and the world.

2 This argument might be said to turn the projectionist attack back on itself. That theory suggests that belief in right and wrong is mistaken insofar as it involves claiming that reality validates certain ways of acting. Our argument is that projectionism is confused insofar as it holds that empirical investigation can show that there are no correct ways of acting.

3 In fact, Mackie does not always hold to this idea and understandably so, since it makes little sense. We could conceivably choose the ground rules for our society, but we cannot choose what is right and wrong, for the essence of this idea is the claim that there are ways of acting which everyone should recognise as correct. Furthermore, even where the individual rejects this claim, it is not a matter of her choosing to reject this claim but believing that it is incorrect.

4 Furthermore, that we are disposed in this way is not a coincidence, since Mackie believes that having such dispositions is evolutionarily superior (*E,* p. 113).

5 Nagel's confusions lead him to assimilate empirical and moral judgements. As his argument from personal authority illustrates, he is driven to treating badness as a

quasi-empirical property, a feature of reality which is perceptible when one is very, very close to it.

6 The point is not that he will necessarily always do what he believes is correct but that the wider context of his actions will indicate what his moral beliefs are. For example, if he consistently acts one way and shows no signs of guilt at doing so, we are likely to conclude that he does not really think that what he is doing is wrong.

7 Of course, if the Martian literally does not understand what it is doing, it will not be committing murder, theft or deceit, but that applies to Martians and non-Martians alike.

8 Similarly, Blackburn takes the claim that bull-fighting would be wrong even if we approved of it simply to mean that 'what is wrong with bull-fighting is to be discovered by looking at bull-fighting's effects' (*EQR*, p. 153). This either presupposes the idea he has called into question (the idea of objective right and wrong) or makes the trite point that it is what bull-fighting consists in that makes us react negatively to it.

9 But what if Fred does not regret his upbringing in any sense? For that to be the case his general reason for favouring a particular type of reaction would also have to apply directly in his own case. For example, suppose that Mabel is Fred's sister and that he detests the idea of inbreeding. In this case, Fred would support a general policy of discouraging incest and would be glad that he too feels an aversion for it. Once again, however, Fred would not be morally opposed to marrying Mabel; rather, all things considered he would not want to marry her.

6 ETHICS AND MODERN PHILOSOPHY

1 It might be argued that the true Wittgensteinian position is that at bedrock there are no right answers only different ways of acting. This conclusion may be valid elsewhere, but it would make no sense here, since the debate itself concerns whether or not there are correct ways of acting. If we came across people who had a different form of mathematics from us (who had something similar in some ways to mathematics, but not in others), it would be misguided to say they had gone wrong. By contrast, if they denied that there were correct ways of acting, it would still make sense for the moralist to say that they were wrong. In this case the point about bedrock is that the dispute cannot be resolved. The claim that there are standards everyone should recognise is supported by some and rejected by others. Having noted that, nothing more can be said without taking sides.

2 This need not be seen as anthropocentric, since rather than talking of human action, we could talk of the action of any creatures which we can recognise as agents. As it happens, the only creatures we currently recognise as full agents are ourselves. Therefore 'human action' is a convenient shorthand for the action of any conscious being.

3 For a more detailed discussion, see *Wittgenstein: Re-thinking the Inner* by the author.

4 The structure of this position (and the sophistry it embodies) is very similar to Simon Blackburn's quasi-realism: a contradictory position is defended through an infinite regress in which the contradictory elements are continually reinterpreted in terms of each other.

5 As we noted in the previous paragraph, the claim that the individual's grounds for her belief are what causes it simply dresses up one language-game in the clothes of another. Our normal non-causal approach to consciousness is represented in

pseudo-causal terms in order to sustain the illusion that a causal approach is universally applicable.

6 Another weakness in the structure of this argument becomes clear if we ask how its approach fits in with Wilson's emphasis on causation. If all our reactions are caused, there seems little point in discussing the question of which reactions it would be useful to have. Presumably we will have whatever reactions we are caused to have whether we are glad to have them or not. Here, we come back to the clash between the causal approach and our normal conception of ourselves as thinking beings.

7 These are two genuinely separate issues. We might accept Wilson's hypothesis that children use (or abuse) the concept of fairness as the name for a particular type of self-interested policy, but still advance the moral claim that people should act fairly regardless of whether this is in their long or short-term interests because this is the correct way to act.

8 This does not imply that actions are only moral if performed out of a sense of duty. The point is not the motive, but the basis of the individual's approach to action: does she believe that some actions are permissible and others not or does she think that it is all a matter of different people having different preferences?

9 It is unjustified because acting fairly on the grounds that doing so is more advantageous to you than acting unfairly is not the same as being committed to being fair. Believing in fairness involves being ready to act fairly even when this is not to your advantage.

BIBLIOGRAPHY

Baker, G.P. and Hacker, P.M.S. (1984) *Scepticism, Rules and Language*, Oxford: Blackwell.

Blackburn, S. (1997) *Essays in Quasi-Realism*, New York: OUP.

Bouwsma, O.K. (1986) *Wittgenstein Conversations 1949–1951*, Indianapolis: Hackett.

Cavell, Stanley. (1979) *The Claim of Reason*, Oxford: OUP.

Dostoyevsky, F. (1972) *The Possessed*, London: Penguin.

Drury, M.O'C. (1984) 'Some Notes on Conversations with Wittgenstein', in R. Rhees (ed.) *Recollections of Wittgenstein*, Oxford: OUP.

Dworkin, R. (1995) *Life's Dominion*, London: HarperCollins.

Hare, R.M. (1952) *The Language of Morals*, Oxford: OUP.

Hare, R.M. (1963) *Freedom and Reason*, Oxford: OUP.

Hume, A. (1978) *Treatise on Human Nature*, Oxford: OUP.

Johnston, P. (1993) *Re-thinking the Inner*, London: Routledge.

MacIntyre, A. (1981) *After Virtue*, London: Duckworth.

MacIntyre, A. (1988) *Whose Justice? Whose Rationality?* London: Duckworth.

Mackie, J.L. (1977) *Ethics: Inventing Right and Wrong*, Harmondsworth: Penguin Books.

Mackie, J.L. (1985) 'Morality and the Retributive Emotions', in Joan Mackie and Penelope Mackie (eds) *Persons and Values*, Oxford: OUP.

Moore, G.E. (1903) *Principia Ethica*, Cambridge: CUP.

Mulhall, S. and Swift, A. (1992) *Liberals and Communitarians,* Oxford: Blackwell.

Murdoch, I. (1970) *The Sovereignty of Good*, London: Routledge and Kegan Paul.

Nagel, Thomas (1989) *The View from Nowhere*, New York: OUP.

Nietzsche, F. (1968) *Twilight of the Idols*, Harmondsworth: Penguin.

Rawls, J. (1973) *A Theory of Justice*, Oxford: OUP.

Taylor, C. (1992) *Sources of the Self*, Cambridge: CUP.

Waismann, F. (1967) *Wittgenstein and the Vienna Circle*, Oxford: Blackwell.

Williams, B. (1981) *Moral Luck*, Cambridge: CUP.

Williams, B.(1985) *Ethics and the Limits of Philosophy*, Fontana: London.

Wilson, James Q. (1995) *The Moral Sense*, US: Free Press.

Wittgenstein, L. (1958) *Philosophical Investigations*, Oxford: Blackwell.

Wittgenstein, L. (1961) *Tractatus Logico-Philosophicus*, London: Routledge and Kegan Paul.

Wittgenstein, L. (1967) *Zettel*, Oxford: Blackwell.

Wittgenstein, L. (1975) *On Certainty*, Oxford: Blackwell.

Wittgenstein, L. (1980a) *Culture and Value,* Oxford: Blackwell.

Wittgenstein, L. (1980b) *Remarks on the Philosophy of Psychology* Volume 1, Oxford: Blackwell.

Wittgenstein, L. (1993) *Philosophical Occasions 1912–1951*, Indianapolis: Hackett.

INDEX